Lecture Notes in Computer Science 10098

Commenced Publication in 1973
Founding and Former Series Editors:
Gerhard Goos, Juris Hartmanis, and Jan van Leeuwen

More information about this series at http://www.springer.com/series/7410

Andrey Bogdanov (Ed.)

Lightweight Cryptography for Security and Privacy

5th International Workshop, LightSec 2016
Aksaray, Turkey, September 21–22, 2016
Revised Selected Papers

 Springer

Editor
Andrey Bogdanov
Technical University of Denmark
Kongens Lyngby
Denmark

ISSN 0302-9743 ISSN 1611-3349 (electronic)
Lecture Notes in Computer Science
ISBN 978-3-319-55713-7 ISBN 978-3-319-55714-4 (eBook)
DOI 10.1007/978-3-319-55714-4

Library of Congress Control Number: 2017934459

LNCS Sublibrary: SL4 – Security and Cryptology

Printed on acid-free paper

This Springer imprint is published by Springer Nature
The registered company is Springer International Publishing AG
The registered company address is: Gewerbestrasse 11, 6330 Cham, Switzerland

Preface

This year was marked by the fifth edition of the International Workshop on Lightweight Cryptography for Security and Privacy (LightSec). With the increasing deployment of ubiquitous systems and pervasive computing, the field of low-resource cryptography is becoming more relevant and timely than ever. Following the series of four previous events held in Turkey and Germany, LightSec 2016 was organized during September 20–21, 2016, at Aksaray University in Cappadocia, Turkey. This volume contains the papers presented at the workshop.

There were 18 submissions from ten countries. Each submission was reviewed by at least three, and on average 3.5, Program Committee members in a careful double-blind review process stretched over a month. Having performed a total of 63 reviews with the help of 11 external reviewers, after an active discussion phase, the committee decided to accept nine papers. The Program Committee consisted of 20 top-notch researchers in the field of lightweight security from ten countries.

LightSec 2016 featured two invited talks. On the first day, based on her unique mix of academic and industrial backgrounds, Elif Bilge Kavun from Infineon, Germany, gave an insightful lecture on "Resource-Efficient Cryptography: Addressing the Gaps in Lightweight Solutions." On the second day, Orhun Kara from TUBITAK BILGEM, representing the government sector, gave an excellent talk on "Block Ciphers vs. Stream Ciphers on Ultra Lightweight Platforms" covering the recent trends in stream cipher design.

We would like to express our gratitude to all the Program Committee members and external reviewers for their exemplary review work that resulted in selecting the high-quality papers that constitute this volume. We thank all authors for submitting their work to LightSec 2016. We would also like to thank both invited speakers for their invaluable contributions to the workshop. Special thanks go to Atilla Elçi, who served as the general chair of the workshop and whose organization was outstanding. We are indebted to the Aksaray University, Faculty of Engineering, Department of Electrical-Electronics Engineering, for hosting the event. The workshop would have been unthinkable without the constant support and astute advice of the Steering Committee in general as well as of Orhun Kara and Ali Aydin Selcuk in particular. We are also obliged to the International Association for Cryptologic Research for deciding to grant LightSec 2016 the "In Cooperation with IACR" status.

December 2016   Andrey Bogdanov

Organization

General Chair

Atilla Elçi — Aksaray University, Turkey

Program Chair

Andrey Bogdanov — Technical University of Denmark, Denmark

Program Committee

Onur Aciicmez	Samsung, USA
Toru Akishita	Sony Corporation, Japan
Roberto Avanzi	Qualcomm, Germany
Lejla Batina	Radboud University Nijmegen, The Netherlands
Tim Güneysu	University of Bremen and DFKI, Germany
Pascal Junod	HEIG-VD, Switzerland
Orhun Kara	TUBİTAK BiLGEM UEKAE, Turkey
Elif Bilge Kavun	Infineon, Germany
Miroslav Knezevic	NXP Semiconductors, Belgium
Gregor Leander	Ruhr University Bochum, Germany
Albert Levi	Sabanci University, Turkey
Amir Moradi	Ruhr University Bochum, Germany
Shiho Moriai	NICT, Japan
María Naya-Plasencia	Inria, France
Ventzi Nikov	NXP Semiconductors, Belgium
Thomas Peyrin	Nanyang Technological University, Singapore
Francesco Regazzoni	ALaRI — USI, Switzerland
Matt Robshaw	Impinj, USA
Erkay Savas	Sabanci University, Turkey
Ali Aydin Selcuk	Bilkent University, Turkey
Kerem Varici	Université catholique de Louvain, Belgium

Additional Reviewers

Selcuk Baktir
Dusan Bozilov
Keita Emura
Oğuzhan Ersoy
Takanori Isobe
Ferhat Karakoç

Anna Krasnova
Joost Renes
Tobias Schneider
Cihangir Tezcan
Alexander Wild

Contents

Cryptanalysis

Faster Key Recovery Attack on Round-Reduced PRINCE

Shahram Rasoolzadeh and Håvard Raddum[✉]

Simula Research Laboratory, Bergen, Norway
{shahram,haavardr}@simula.no

Abstract. We introduce a new technique for doing the key recovery part of an integral or higher order differential attack. This technique speeds up the key recovery phase significantly and can be applied to any block cipher with S-boxes. We show several properties of this technique, then apply it to PRINCE and report on the improvements in complexity from earlier integral and higher order differential attacks on this cipher. Our attacks on 4 and 6 rounds were the fastest and the winner of PRINCE Challenge's last round in the category of chosen plaintext attack.

Keywords: PRINCE · Lightweight · Block cipher · Key recovery attack · Integral · Higher-order differential

1 Introduction

PRINCE is a lightweight block cipher that was introduced in [1]. The cipher has received a fair share of attention from cryptanalysts in the last years, with many different attacks on round-reduced versions [3–15]. The Prince Challenge website tracks the best attacks and promises cash prizes for attacks that will have a serious impact in real-world applications [2].

In this paper we will revisit two earlier works [12,13] on PRINCE and improve the complexities of the attacks described there. Both papers are concerned with integral attacks, with [12] also giving details of a bit-pattern integral attack on 4 rounds and a higher order differential attack on 7 rounds of PRINCE. We re-use the integral distinguishers described in [4,13].

The improvement we can do lies in the key recovery part. We introduce a new technique to do key recovery, using a binary array. For PRINCE, the size of this array is only 16 bits. Using this technique we can skip the partial trial decryptions to check for balancedness in an integral or higher order differential attack. This technique can be applied to speed up this type of attacks on any block cipher with S-boxes. In addition to using this technique for key recovery we also apply the accelerated key search technique described in [14,15] when partial keys need to be guessed.

The improvements and comparisons to previous attacks are summarized in Table 1. All time complexities are given in terms of number of r-round PRINCE encryptions based on counting the number of S-box look-ups needed. The data

© Springer International Publishing AG 2017
A. Bogdanov (Ed.): LightSec 2016, LNCS 10098, pp. 3–17, 2017.
DOI: 10.1007/978-3-319-55714-4_1

Table 1. Summary of cryptanalytic results on PRINCE

Rounds	Time	Data		Memory	Technique	Ref.
4	2^{64}	16	CP	16	Integral	[4]
	$2^{43.4}$	32	KP	$2^{26.7}$	Diff./Logic	[11]
	5 s	2^{10}	CP	$\ll 2^{27}$	MitM	[11]
	$2^{23.9}$	48	CP	48	Integral	[12]
	$2^{9.7}$	160	CP	160	Integral	[12]
	$2^{7.4}$	64	CP	negl.	Integral	Section 5.1
5	2^{64}	80	CP	16	Integral	[4]
	$2^{24.6}$	96	CP	96	Integral	[12]
	$2^{21.4}$	32	CP	32	Integral	Section 5.2
	2^{13}	2^{13}	CP	32	Integral	Section 5.2
6	$2^{101.1}$	64	KP	2^{34}	MitM	[11]
	$2^{96.8}$	2	KP	negl.	Acc. Exh.	[15]
	$2^{86} + 2^{86} M.A.$[a]	2	KP	$2^{24.6}$	Acc. Exh.	[15]
	2^{64}	2^{16}	CP	2^{16}	Integral	[4]
	$2^{33.7}$	2^{16}	CP	$2^{31.9}$	MitM	[11]
	$2^{32.3}$	$2^{14.6}$	CP	$2^{14.6}$	Integral	[13]
	$2^{28.9}$	$2^{14.9}$	CP	$\ll 2^{27}$	Diff./Logic	[11]
	$2^{36.3}$	$2^{18.6}$	CP	$2^{18.6}$	Integral	[12]
	$2^{24.6}$	2^{13}	CP	2^{13}	Integral	Section 5.3
7	$2^{52.1}$	$2^{34.6}$	CP	$2^{34.6}$	H.-O. Diff.	[12]
	$2^{44.3}$	2^{33}	CP	2^{33}	H.-O. Diff.	Section 5.4
8	2^{124}	2	KP	2^{20}	SitM	[6]
	$2^{122.7}$	2	KP	negl.	Acc. Exh.	[14]
	$2^{109.3}$	2	KP	2^{65}	MitM	[14]
	$2^{66.3}$	2^{16}	CP	$2^{49.9}$	MitM	[11]
	$2^{65.7}$[b]	2^{16}	CP	$2^{68.9}$	MitM	[11]
	2^{60}	2^{53}	CP	2^{30}	MitM	[7]
	$2^{50.7}$[b]	2^{16}	CP	$2^{84.9}$	MitM	[11]
9	2^{64}	2^{57}	CP	$2^{57.3}$	MitM	[7]
	$2^{51.2}$	$2^{46.9}$	CP	$2^{52.2}$	Multiple Diff.	[8]
10	2^{124}	2	KP	negl.	Acc. Exh.	[14]
	$2^{122.2}$	2	KP	$2^{53.3}$	MitM	[14]
	2^{68}[b]	2^{57}	CP	2^{41}	MitM	[11]
	$2^{60.6}$	$2^{57.9}$	CP	$2^{61.5}$	Multiple Diff.	[8]

[a]Memory Access to a table with 2^{25} indexes.
[b]Online Time.

complexities are given as the number of chosen plaintext/ciphertext pairs needed. The results from [12,13] have been transformed into this format, and in some cases slightly corrected, to get a correct comparison.

2 PRINCE Block Cipher

PRINCE is an FX-constructed lightweight block cipher with block size of 64 bits [1]. Two keys are used in PRINCE, both of length 64 bits, one for whitening (K_0) and the other as a round key (K_1) for the core of the structure (see Fig. 1). The round key is used in every round without any key schedule, and the whitening key before the ciphertext (K_0') is derived by applying a simple linear mapping to K_0.

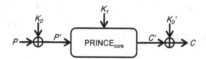

Fig. 1. PRINCE FX construction

The PRINCE$_{core}$ is an AES-like block cipher that employs an involutive 12-round structure. PRINCE$_{core}$ starts with two *xors* with K_1 and a round constant, followed by 5 forward rounds, a middle layer, 5 backward rounds and at the end, two more *xors* with a round constant and K_1. Figure 2 shows the schematic view of PRINCE$_{core}$.

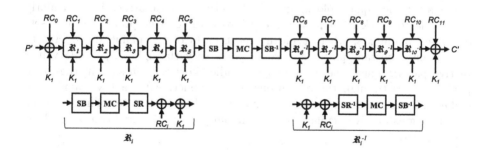

Fig. 2. PRINCE core

The state is defined as a 4×4 matrix similar to AES, but in PRINCE, instead of bytes the cells contain nibbles. Each round of PRINCE$_{core}$ consists of 5 operations: S-box, mix column, shift row, round constant addition and key addition. These are described as follows:

- **S-box** (SB): Every nibble in the state is replaced using a 4-bit S-box.
- **Mix Column** (MC): The state is multiplied with an involutive 64×64 binary matrix. More precisely, this large matrix can be expressed as sixteen 4×4 matrices where each of these mixes four bits in one column of the state.
- **Shift Row** (SR): Row i of the state is cyclically rotated by i positions to the left (same as shift row operation in AES).
- **Round Constant Addition** (RC): A bit-wise xoring with a round constant $RC_i, i = 0, ..., 11$.
- **Key Addition** (AK): A bit-wise xoring with the key K_1.

The two middle rounds contain only three layers, SB, MC and SB^{-1} which makes it an involutive transformation. This transformation can also be separated into four smaller transformations, one for each column in the state.

In the backward rounds, the operations come in the reverse order of the forward rounds, and SB and SR are replaced with SB^{-1} and SR^{-1}. The round constants are also different, but related to the round constants in the forward rounds. The difference $RC_i \oplus RC_{11-i}, i = 0, ..., 11$ is always equal to the constant value $\alpha = $ 0xc0ac29b7c97c50dd.

3 Integral and Higher-Order Differential Distinguishers for PRINCE

In this section we will briefly introduce integral and higher-order differential attacks. For each of the attacks we will revisit two integral and one higher-order differential distinguisher for PRINCE that are used in previous attacks [4,12,13].

3.1 Integral Distinguishers

The integral or square attack was originally designed as a dedicated attack in [16] against the Square block cipher. This cryptanalytic attack is particularly applicable to block ciphers that use S-boxes. Integral cryptanalysis uses sets of chosen plaintexts, where typically most parts of the plaintexts are set to a constant (constant parts) and some parts vary through all possible values (active parts). Then, the cryptanalyst studies how the xor-sum in the given parts changes through the operations of the cipher. After a few rounds, the cipher states still sum up to zero over one set (balanced state). This property will distinguish a given cipher from a random permutation and can be used for key recovery.

3.5-round Integral Distinguisher for PRINCE. The 3.5-round integral distinguisher for PRINCE first used in [4] covers one forward round, two middle rounds and one backward round except its SB^{-1} operation. In this distinguisher we use 2^4 plaintexts which only differ in one nibble and the other 15 nibbles are constant. When one S-box takes all its 2^4 possible inputs and the inputs for all other S-boxes are constant, the states after the above 3.5 rounds (state right before the last SB^{-1} operation) will be balanced, i.e. the xor-sum of these states will be equal to zero.

4.5 Round Integral Distinguisher for PRINCE. The 4.5-round integral distinguisher for PRINCE introduced by Posteuca and Negara in [13] contains two forward rounds, two middle rounds and one backward round except its SB^{-1} operation. In this distinguisher we use 2^{12} plaintexts which only differ in three nibbles in the same column and the other 13 nibbles are constant. When three S-boxes in a column take all their 2^{12} possible inputs and the input for all other S-boxes are constant, the state after 4.5 rounds will be balanced.

For explanations for why these sets are balanced after 3.5 and 4.5 rounds we refer to [4,12,13].

3.2 Higher-Order Differential Distinguisher

The higher-order differential attack is a generalization of differential cryptanalysis. While in a differential attack the difference between only two plaintexts is used, higher-order differential attack studies the propagation of a set of differences between a larger set of plaintexts. Lai, in 1994, laid the groundwork by showing that differentials are a special case of the more general case of higher order derivatives [17] and Knudsen, in the same year, was able to show how the concept of higher order derivatives can be used to mount attacks on block ciphers [18].

Higher-order differential attacks are applicable to ciphers where the bits of the cipher state at some point can be represented as Boolean polynomials of a low algebraic degree. In PRINCE the only non-linear operation is the SB, so the algebraic degree of the output of one round is three. Using this property of PRINCE, in [12] one 5.5-round higher-order differential for PRINCE is presented. This distinguisher calculates the i-th derivative at some selected state and uses a set of 2^i plaintexts, where i plaintext bits vary over all possible values, while the rest of the state is set to an arbitrary constant.

5.5-round Higher-Order Differential Distinguisher for PRINCE. The expression of state variables after 3 SB layers have algebraic degree at most 3^3. Therefore, any 28-th or higher order derivative of the state must be zero. The distinguisher uses two more rounds with no cost in algebraic degree to arrive at a 5.5-round distinguisher.

The distinguisher uses 2^{32} chosen plaintexts, where two columns take all possible input values. As the S-box is bijective, the first SB operation preserves the property that the two selected columns take all 2^{32} possible values. In the next step MC works on columns independently, thus still there are 32 state bits taking all possible combinations. The SR operation will move constant value nibbles into columns with all-valued nibbles, so the MC operation in the second round destroys the property.

Therefore, the distinguisher gets the first two SB layers for free and then it covers another three SB and SB^{-1} operations. So, it gives a balanced state after 5.5 rounds (the state right before SB^{-1} in the sixth round).

4   New Technique for Key Recovery

Assume that the S-boxes used in the target block cipher is n bits. Let A be a 2^n-bit binary array, $A = [a_0, a_1, \ldots, a_{2^n-1}]$. For any such array, we define K_A to be the following set of n-bit values:

$$K_A = \{k \in GF(2)^n | \bigoplus_{i=0}^{2^n-1} a_i \cdot S(k \oplus i) = 0\} \tag{1}$$

For example, for the PRINCE S-box where $n = 4$, if $A = [1, 1, 1, 0, 1, 0, \ldots, 0]$, the only solutions for

$$S(k) \oplus S(k \oplus 1) \oplus S(k \oplus 2) \oplus S(k \oplus 4) = 0$$

is $K_A = \{c\}$.

The computation cost for finding the corresponding K_A for an array of A is $w_A \times 2^n$ S-box evaluations, where w_A denotes the Hamming weight of array A. This is because for each n-bit value of key we have to compute one S-box look-up for each set bit in A.

Assume that we want to attack an R-round cipher using an $(R - 0.5)$-round distinguisher which says that for a set of 2^d chosen plaintexts, the xor-sum of the cipher states after $(R - 0.5)$ rounds is equal to zero. After these $(R - 0.5)$-rounds there is an S-box layer before reaching the ciphertext.

The usual key recovery method would be to guess the 2^n possible values for each of the last round key words in the output of an S-box, and then partially decrypt through the SB operation for every ciphertext. If the xor-sum of these 2^d nibbles are equal to zero we accept the guessed value of subkey as a candidate and if not we reject it. The time complexity for finding key candidates for one n-bit word of the last round key using one set of 2^d ciphertexts is equal to $2^n \times 2^d$ S-box evaluations.

In the following we introduce our technique which is faster than the straightforward method. In our technique we will build an A array for each word in the state from the 2^d ciphertexts. Then for each array, we will find key candidates for the corresponding word of last round key.

At the start of the attack, for each word of state we allocate a 2^n-bit array A initialized to all zeroes. Then we look at the corresponding word in each of the 2^d ciphertexts. When the value of this word is equal to x, we will flip the x-th bit in the corresponding A. After doing this for all the 2^d ciphertexts, we can just find the corresponding set K_A for the created array. The values in K_A are the key candidates for this word of last round key. So for a set of 2^d ciphertexts, instead of 2^{d+n} S-box evaluations, our key recovery method will need about $n_{SB} \times 2^n$ S-box evaluations to find the candidates for each word of the last round key, where n_{SB} denotes the average number of S-box evaluations for the created arrays.

Compared with the usual key recovery method, using A arrays is faster, which helps to reduce the complexity of integral or higher-order differential attacks. Specially when size of data sets are big (d is large), the speed-up factor $\frac{2^d}{n_{SB}}$ of our technique gets bigger.

4.1 Some Features of A Arrays

Here we introduce some facts about possible (A, K_A) values which help us to evaluate the average number of S-box operations needed n_{SB} and also make it smaller.

Lemma 1. *In an actual attack, the weight of A is always even.*

Proof. The set of ciphertexts is of size 2^d, and hence even. We flip exactly one bit in A for each ciphertext, so starting from the all-zero array the weight will always be even after processing an even number of ciphertexts.

Lemma 2. *If $A = [0, \ldots, 0]$ or $A = [1, \ldots, 1]$, then $K_A = GF(2^n)$.*

Proof. In the first case, all terms in the xor-sum in (1) are 0 regardless of k, so the statement is trivially true. The second case follows from the fact SB is a bijective operation.

Lemma 3. *Let $\bar{A}$ be the complement of A, that is, $\bar{A} = [1, 1, ..., 1] \oplus A$. Then $K_{\bar{A}} = K_A$.*

Proof. Since SB is bijective, we know that $\bigoplus_{i=0}^{2^n-1} S(k \oplus i) = 0$ for any fixed k. If the subset of terms selected by A sum to 0 (so $k \in K_A$), the complementary subset of terms must also sum to 0, hence $k \in K_{\bar{A}}$.

Lemma 4. *If the weight of A is 2 or $2^n - 2$, then $K_A = \emptyset$.*

Proof. SB is bijective, so $S(x) \oplus S(y) \neq 0$ for $x \neq y$ and the case of weight 2 is proven. The case for weight $2^n - 2$ follows from Lemma 3.

Using the properties introduced in the above lemmas, it is sufficient to find the key candidates only for arrays where the weight w_A is even and $4 \leq w_A \leq 2^{n-1}$. This technique is possible to apply to any integral or higher-order differential attacks on block ciphers that use S-boxes, but in the following we will just focus on the PRINCE block cipher.

4.2 Using the A Arrays

Having an $(R - 0.5)$-round distinguisher we can do the key-recovery phase on both R-round and $R + 1$-round PRINCE using the technique introduced above. For attacking R rounds we allocate one array to each of the nibbles in a state. Each array will suggest some candidates for one nibble of $K_1 \oplus K_0'$, including the right value. So the corresponding K_A to these arrays can never be empty. In these attacks we will not save the ciphertexts in the memory, so the memory complexity will just be saving the arrays, which is negligible.

For attacking $R + 1$-round PRINCE, instead of a half-round (one SB^{-1} operation), there is one and a half rounds (one SB^{-1} operation and one complete round) between the ciphertext and the end of the distinguisher. For key recovery we then guess one column of $K_0' \oplus K_1$ and partially decrypt the corresponding column in all of the 2^d ciphertexts for one round. Then we build A-arrays for the partially decrypted nibbles and find candidates for 4 corresponding nibbles of K_1. Since we do not know whether the guessed value of $K_0' \oplus K_1$ is the right one or not, the arrays related to these 4 nibbles of K_1 could have a empty set of K_A. In this case, when an array suggests an empty K_A it means the guessed value for $K_0' \oplus K_1$ was wrong. We call this a *false array*.

Both of the R- and $R + 1$-round PRINCE attacks are illustrated in Figs. 3 and 4, respectively.

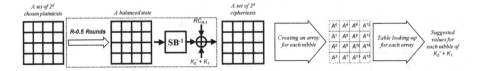

Fig. 3. Attack on R-round PRINCE using $(R - 0.5)$-round distinguisher

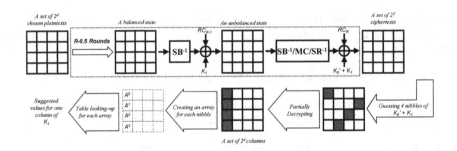

Fig. 4. Attack on $R + 1$-round PRINCE using $(R - 0.5)$-round distinguisher

4.3   Average Number of S-box Evaluations for an Array

For computing the cost of finding key candidates we need to know the average number of S-box evaluations for an array. By using the lemmas, this number will be equal to

$$n_{SB} = 4 \times (P_4 + P_{12}) + 6 \times (P_6 + P_{10}) + 8 \times P_8 \qquad (2)$$

where P_w is the probability that the weight of array A is w.

In fact, the value for P_w depends on the number of texts used to produce the array A. For example, when $d = 4$ then $P_{16} < P_0$ even though there is only one array of weight 0 and one of weight 16. We can evaluate P_w, by using a recursive formula that we explain in the following. Let A_i be the array for one nibble, after processing i ciphertexts in one set. Assume we have processed $i - 1$

nibble values and found that the weight of A_{i-1} is w. By processing one more nibble in the set, we have the relations below for the weight w' of the array A_i:

$$\begin{cases} Pr(w'=1) & = & 1 & w = & 0 \\ Pr(w'=15) & = & 1 & w = & 16 \\ Pr(w'=w-1) & = & \frac{w}{16} & w \neq 0{,}16 \\ Pr(w'=w+1) & = & 1-\frac{w}{16} & w \neq 0{,}16 \end{cases} \quad (3)$$

Let $f_i = [f_i(0), f_i(1), \ldots, f_i(16)]$ be the probability distribution for the weight of the array A_i. In an actual attack, the array A is initialized to all-zeroes, so $f_0 = [1, 0, \ldots, 0]$. Given f_{i-1}, the probability distribution f_i is given as

$$\begin{cases} f_i(0) = \frac{1}{16} \cdot f_{i-1}(1) \\ f_i(j) = (1 - \frac{j-1}{16}) \cdot f_{i-1}(j-1) + \frac{j+1}{16} \cdot f_{i-1}(j+1) \quad 0 < j < 16 \\ f_i(16) = \frac{1}{16} \cdot f_{i-1}(15) \end{cases} \quad (4)$$

The values of P_w to be used in (2) are the values in f_{2^d} when using a set of 2^d chosen plaintexts, and these values can be computed by using (4) recursively. When d is equal to 4, n_{SB} will be 6.37419 and it converges quickly to 6.51904 for larger d's.

4.4 Average Number of Key Candidates for an Array

By running through the all 16-bit arrays with weight of 4, 6 and 8, we can count the number of arrays giving K_A's of the same size. These numbers are summarized in Table 2. For each possible weight w we find the average size of K_A, denoted $\bar{n}_w$, both with and without false arrays.

Table 2. Average number for suggested key candidates

w	number of arrays with $|K_A| =$						average value for $|K_A|, \bar{n}_w$	
	0	1	2	3	4	16	with F.A.	without F.A.
0	0	0	0	0	0	1	16	16
2	120	0	0	0	0	0	0	–
4	392	816	432	160	20	0	1.2308	1.5686
6	3120	3040	1488	288	72	0	0.8951	1.4664
8	4502	4320	2976	640	432	0	1.0816	1.6635
10	3120	3040	1488	288	72	0	0.8951	1.4664
12	392	816	432	160	20	0	1.2308	1.5686
14	120	0	0	0	0	0	0	–
16	0	0	0	0	0	1	16	16

In a set of 2^d ciphertexts produced according to the distinguisher, the average number for $|K_A|$ is equal to

$$|\bar{K}| = \sum_{w=0}^{15} P_w \cdot \bar{n}_w \tag{5}$$

The values of P_w to be used in (5) are the values in f_{2^d} when using a set of 2^d chosen plaintexts. We can now compute the exact value of the expected number of suggested keys from one set of plaintexts in an attack, given by (5). In our attacks with false arrays $|\bar{K}|$ is always 1. In attacks without false arrays $\bar{n}_K$ is about 1.5360 using 2^4 ciphertexts, and $|\bar{K}|$ converges quickly to 1.5453 for larger sets.

5   Cryptanalysis of Round-Reduced PRINCE

In this section we will use the distinguishers from Sect. 3 and the key recovery method introduced in Sect. 4 to cryptanalyze round-reduced PRINCE.

5.1   Attack on 4-round PRINCE

For 4-round PRINCE, we will use the 3.5-round integral distinguisher. One set consists of 16 chosen plaintexts that gets encrypted through 4-round PRINCE. One bit-array A is initialized to all zero for each of the 16 nibbles in a state. For the value x in a nibble, we flip the bit a_x in the corresponding A for each ciphertext as they are produced. Finally we use the arrays to find the key candidates, and repeat with one more set to get unique values. The exact procedure for recovering a unique value for $K_0' \oplus K_1$ using s sets of data is summarized in Algorithm 1. In the algorithm we use $C_i^{j,t}$ to denote i-th nibble in the j-th ciphertext of the t-th set. K^i denotes candidate subkeys for the i-th nibble.

After finding $K_0' \oplus K_1$, we follow the attack in [12] and use a 2.5-round distinguisher starting from the second round of the 3.5-round distinguisher to find the exact value of K_1. The internal states will be balanced after 2.5 rounds, just before the S-box layer in the third round. We use the recovered $K_0' \oplus K_1$ to decrypt the 4-round ciphertexts one round, and follow Algorithm 1 on the cipher states after three rounds to recover K_1. When both $K_0' \oplus K_1$ and K_1 are known it is trivial to find the user-selected key.

Complexity: This attack is without false arrays and each set of data has 2^4 pairs. Each array will suggest on the average $m = 1.5360$ keys. After the first set of data is processed we expect $m^{16} = 2^{9.91}$ key candidates remaining for the whole $K_0' \oplus K_1$. Using another set of data we will only have an expected $(2^{9.91})^2 \times 2^{-64} = 2^{-44.19}$ key candidates remaining for the value of $K_0' \oplus K_1$. With very high probability, only the correct value for $K_0' \oplus K_1$ will remain. So we need only two sets of data for finding $K_0' \oplus K_1$ and similarly another two sets of data for finding K_1.

Algorithm 1. Key recovery attack without false arrays

---

for $i = 0 : 15$ **do**
   $K^i = \mathbb{F}_2^4$;
end for
for $t = 1 : s$ **do**
   for $i = 0 : 15$ **do**
      $A^i = [0, \ldots, 0]$;
   end for
   for $j = 0 : 2^d - 1$ **do**
      for $i = 0 : 15$ **do**
         Put $x = C_i^{j,t}$ and flip the bit a_x^i;
      end for
   end for
   for $i = 0 : 15$ **do**
      Find k^i, the key candidates for A^i;
      $K^i = K^i \cap k^i$;
   end for
end for
Return $K = [K^0, \ldots, K^{15}]$;

The data complexity of the attack is $2^4 \times (2 + 2) = 2^6$ chosen plaintexts and its memory complexity is just saving $16 \times m$ nibbles for storing the initial key candidates and 16 arrays of 16-bits each which is negligible.

The time complexity of this attack will be producing the chosen data (2^6 4-round encryptions), 16 times finding the key candidates for each nibble of $K_0' \oplus K_1$ for each set (on average $2 \times 16 \times 2^4 \times 6.37419$ SB operations), one round partial decryption of second data sets (2^5 one round encryptions) and 16 times finding the key candidates for each nibble of K_1 for each set. In total this is equal to about $2^{7.44}$ 4-round PRINCE encryptions.

5.2 Attack on 5-round PRINCE

For cryptanalyzing 5-round PRINCE, we can use either the 3.5-round or 4.5-round integral distinguishers. Using the 3.5-round distinguisher will lead to lower data complexity, but a higher time complexity than using the 4.5-round distinguisher. We present both attacks below.

Attack with 4.5-round Distinguisher: The attack has a similar procedure to the 4-round one, except that in each set there are 2^{12} ciphertexts instead of 2^4. First we find a unique value for $K_0' \oplus K_1$ using Algorithm 1. Then we can decrypt one round and use the 3.5-round distinguisher to find the value of K_1. For the 3.5-round distinguisher it is not necessary to ask for more data, we can use subsets of size 2^4 that exist in the sets of 2^{12} pairs we already have. Using the recovered value for $K_0' \oplus K_1$ we will partially decrypt only two subsets of 2^4 ciphertexts for one round to reach the internal state after 4 rounds and use them to find the exact value of K_1 with Algorithm 1.

Complexity: This attack is without false arrays and each set of data has 2^{12} pairs. So each array will suggest $m = 1.5453$ keys. After the first set of data is processed we can expect to have $m^{16} = 2^{10.05}$ key candidates for the whole $K_0' \oplus K_1$. Using another set of data we expect to have only $(2^{10.05})^2 \times 2^{-64} = 2^{-43.91}$ key candidates for the value of $K_0' \oplus K_1$. So we need only two sets of data for finding $K_0' \oplus K_1$, and reuse subsets within these to find K_1.

The data complexity of the attack is $2 \times 2^{12} = 2^{13}$ chosen plaintexts and its memory complexity is saving two set of 2^4 data for recovering K_1. The time for producing the chosen data sets is dominating the time complexity in the attack. Hence the time complexity is approximately 2^{13} 5-round PRINCE encryptions.

Attack with 3.5-round Distinguisher: In this attack, we will guess one column of $K_0' \oplus K_1$ and partially decrypt the ciphertexts for one round. The values for four nibbles at the end of the fourth round can be computed for each guessed column. We build A-arrays from these values. Then we will find the corresponding candidates for 4 nibbles of K_1. When the guess for a column of $K_0' \oplus K_1$ is wrong, we may end up with an A array such that K_A is the empty set, that is, we have a false array. In this case we can reject the guessed value for $K_0' \oplus K_1$ as wrong and go to next value. The exact procedure for recovering a unique value for the c-th column of $K_0' \oplus K_1$ and its corresponding 4 nibbles in K_1 is summarized in Algorithm 2.

Algorithm 2. Key recovery attack with false arrays

---

for $K \in \mathbb{F}_2^{16}$ do
  for $i = 0 : 3$ do
    $K_1^i = \mathbb{F}_2^4$;
  end for
  for $t = 1 : s$ do
    for $i = 0 : 3$ do
      $A^i = [0, \ldots, 0]$;
    end for
    for $j = 0 : 2^d - 1$ do
      Using K partially decrypt $C_{4c:4c+3}^{j,t}$ to reach $[x^0, x^1, x^2, x^3]$;
      for $i = 0 : 3$ do
        Flip the bit $a_{x^i}^i$;
      end for
    end for
    for $i = 0 : 3$ do
      Find k^i, the key candidates for A^i;
      $K_1^i = K_1^i \cap k^i$;
      if K_1^i is empty then
        Reject the current value of K and go to next value;
      end if
    end for
  end for
  Return K and $[K_1^0, K_1^1, K_1^2, K_1^3]$;
end for

Complexity: In this attack we may get false arrays and each set of data has 2^4 pairs. Then each array will suggest one key on the average. So after processing the first set of data we will have one candidate for 4 nibbles of K_1 related to the guessed value for 4 nibbles of $K_0' \oplus K_1$. Using another set of data, there will remain only $2^{16} \times 2^{-16} = 1$ key candidate for 4 nibbles of $K_0' \oplus K_1$ and the related 4 nibbles in K_1. For finding the other subkeys related to the other columns we will use these sets of data again, so we need only these two sets.

The data complexity of the attack is $2^4 \times 2 = 2^5$ chosen plaintexts. The memory complexity is saving the 2^5 ciphertexts.

The time complexity is in the worst case (when we never exit early due to empty K_1^i)

$$4 \times 2^{16} \times 2 \times (2^4 \times 4 + 4 \times 2^4 \times 6.519) = 2^{27.91}$$

SB operations which is about $2^{21.59}$ 5-round PRINCE encryptions. Using the accelerating techniques from [14] (which stores S-box evaluations that are not affected by new guesses of $K_1 \oplus K_0'$), the time complexity can be further reduced to $2^{27.76}$ SB operations or $2^{21.44}$ 5-round PRINCE encryptions.

5.3   Attack on 6-round PRINCE

For attacking 6-round PRINCE, we will use the 4.5-round integral distinguisher with partial key guessing following Algorithm 2. With two sets of 2^{12} chosen plaintext/ciphertext pairs, we will guess one column of $K_0' \oplus K_1$, partially decrypt the ciphertexts for one round and build A-arrays, and then find the corresponding values for 4 nibbles of K_1.

This attack will need only two sets of data, so the data complexity of the attack is $2^{12} \times 2 = 2^{13}$ chosen plaintexts. The memory complexity is again saving the ciphertexts. The time complexity will be

$$4 \times 2^{16} \times 2 \times (2^{12} \times 4 + 4 \times 2^4 \times 6.519) = 2^{33.04}$$

SB operations, and by using the accelerating techniques from [14] when guessing the 4 nibbles of $K_0' \oplus K_1$, the time complexity can be reduced to $2^{31.22}$ SB operations or approximately $2^{24.64}$ 6-round PRINCE encryptions.

5.4   Attack to 7-round PRINCE

For the attack on 7-round PRINCE, we use the 5.5-round higher-order differential distinguisher and Algorithm 2 with two sets of 2^{32} pairs of data. Each set of data will be balanced right before the S-box layer in the sixth round, so the key recovery procedure in Algorithm 2 can be applied.

Again this attack will need only two sets of data, so its data complexity is 2^{33} chosen plaintext/ciphertext pairs. Saving the ciphertexts is the substantial memory complexity. The time complexity will be

$$4 \times 2^{16} \times 2 \times (2^{32} \times 4 + 4 \times 2^4 \times 6.519) = 2^{53}$$

SB operations which by applying the accelerating technique the time complexity can be reduced to $2^{51.09}$ SB operations or $2^{44.29}$ 7-round PRINCE encryptions.

6   Conclusion

In this paper we have introduced a technique of using arrays for the key recovery part of an integral or higher order differential attack. In particular, integral and higher order differential attacks on block ciphers with S-boxes will benefit from this technique.

We have applied the faster key recovery to the same integral or higher order differential distinguishers used in earlier attacks on PRINCE. The improvements in complexity, as measured by the number of S-box evaluations, gains a significant factor from the earlier attacks. Our attacks on 4 and 6 rounds were the fastest and the winner of PRINCE Challenge's last round in the category of chosen plaintext attack.

References

1. Borghoff, J., et al.: PRINCE – a low-latency block cipher for pervasive computing applications. In: Wang, X., Sako, K. (eds.) ASIACRYPT 2012. LNCS, vol. 7658, pp. 208–225. Springer, Heidelberg (2012). doi:10.1007/978-3-642-34961-4_14

2. The PRINCE Team: PRINCE challenge. https://www.emsec.rub.de/research/research_startseite/prince-challenge/

3. Abed, F., List, E., Lucks, S.: On the security of the core of PRINCE against biclique and differential cryptanalysis. IACR Cryptology ePrint Archive, Report 2012/712 (2012)

4. Jean, J., Nikolić, I., Peyrin, T., Wang, L., Wu, S.: Security analysis of PRINCE. In: Moriai, S. (ed.) FSE 2013. LNCS, vol. 8424, pp. 92–111. Springer, Heidelberg (2014). doi:10.1007/978-3-662-43933-3_6

5. Soleimany, H., et al.: Reflection cryptanalysis of PRINCE-like ciphers. In: Moriai, S. (ed.) FSE 2013. LNCS, vol. 8424, pp. 71–91. Springer, Heidelberg (2014). doi:10.1007/978-3-662-43933-3_5

6. Canteaut, A., Naya-Plasencia, M., Vayssière, B.: Sieve-in-the-middle: improved MITM attacks. In: Canetti, R., Garay, J.A. (eds.) CRYPTO 2013. LNCS, vol. 8042, pp. 222–240. Springer, Heidelberg (2013). doi:10.1007/978-3-642-40041-4_13

7. Li, L., Jia, K., Wang, X.: Improved meet-in-the-middle attacks on AES-192 and PRINCE. IACR Cryptology ePrint Archive, Report 2013/573 (2013)

8. Canteaut, A., Fuhr, T., Gilbert, H., Naya-Plasencia, M., Reinhard, J.-R.: Multiple differential cryptanalysis of round-reduced PRINCE. In: Cid, C., Rechberger, C. (eds.) FSE 2014. LNCS, vol. 8540, pp. 591–610. Springer, Heidelberg (2015). doi:10.1007/978-3-662-46706-0_30

9. Fouque, P.-A., Joux, A., Mavromati, C.: Multi-user collisions: applications to discrete logarithm, even-mansour and PRINCE. In: Sarkar, P., Iwata, T. (eds.) ASIACRYPT 2014. LNCS, vol. 8873, pp. 420–438. Springer, Heidelberg (2014). doi:10.1007/978-3-662-45611-8_22

10. Dinur, I.: Cryptanalytic time-memory-data tradeoffs for FX-constructions with applications to PRINCE and PRIDE. In: Oswald, E., Fischlin, M. (eds.) EUROCRYPT 2015. LNCS, vol. 9056, pp. 231–253. Springer, Heidelberg (2015). doi:10.1007/978-3-662-46800-5_10

11. Derbez, P., Perrin, L.: Meet-in-the-middle attacks and structural analysis of round-reduced PRINCE. In: Leander, G. (ed.) FSE 2015. LNCS, vol. 9054, pp. 190–216. Springer, Heidelberg (2015). doi:10.1007/978-3-662-48116-5_10

12. Morawiecki, P.: Practical attacks on the round-reduced PRINCE? IACR Cryptology ePrint Archive, Report 2015/245 (2015)
13. Posteuca, R., Negara, G.: Integral cryptanalysis of round-reduced PRINCE cipher. Proc. Rom. Acad. Ser. A Math. Phys. Tech. Sci. Inf. Sci. **16**, 265–269 (2015). Special issue
14. Rasoolzadeh, S., Raddum, H.: Cryptanalysis of PRINCE with minimal data. In: Pointcheval, D., Nitaj, A., Rachidi, T. (eds.) AFRICACRYPT 2016. LNCS, vol. 9646, pp. 109–126. Springer, Cham (2016). doi:10.1007/978-3-319-31517-1_6
15. Rasoolzadeh, S., Raddum, H.: Cryptanalysis of 6-round PRINCE using 2 Known Plaintexts. Presented at ArcticCrypt 2016, also available at IACR Cryptology ePrint Archive. Report 2016/132 (2016)
16. Daemen, J., Knudsen, L., Rijmen, V.: The block cipher Square. In: Biham, E. (ed.) FSE 1997. LNCS, vol. 1267, pp. 149–165. Springer, Heidelberg (1997). doi:10.1007/BFb0052343
17. Lai, X.: Higher order derivatives and differential cryptanalysis. In: Blahut, R.E., Costello Jr., D.J., Maurer, U., Mittelholzer, T. (eds.) Communications and Cryptography, vol. 276, pp. 227–233. Springer, New York (1994)
18. Knudsen, L.R.: Truncated and higher order differentials. In: Preneel, B. (ed.) FSE 1994. LNCS, vol. 1008, pp. 196–211. Springer, Heidelberg (1995). doi:10.1007/3-540-60590-8_16

Differential Attacks on Lightweight Block Ciphers PRESENT, PRIDE, and RECTANGLE Revisited

Cihangir Tezcan[1,2]([⊠]), Galip Oral Okan[1], Asuman Şenol[1], Erol Doğan[1], Furkan Yücebaş[1], and Nazife Baykal[1]

[1] CYDES Laboratory, Department of Cyber Security, Informatics Institute, Middle East Technical University, Ankara, Turkey
cihangir@metu.edu.tr
[2] Department of Mathematics, Middle East Technical University, Ankara, Turkey

Abstract. Differential distribution and linear approximation tables are the main security criteria for S-box designers. However, there are other S-box properties that, if overlooked by cryptanalysts, can result in erroneous results in theoretical attacks. In this paper we focus on two such properties, namely undisturbed bits and differential factors. We go on to identify several inconsistencies in published attacks against the lightweight block ciphers PRESENT, PRIDE, and RECTANGLE and present our corrections.

Keywords: Block cipher · Lightweight · Differential attack · Differential factor · Undisturbed bit

1 Introduction

Confusion layer of symmetric cryptography algorithms mostly consists of substitution boxes (S-boxes) and in order to provide better security against known attacks, S-boxes are selected depending on their cryptographic properties. Low non-linear and differential uniformity [16] provide resistance against linear [15] and differential cryptanalysis [3], respectively and most of the time these are the only properties designers focus on. However, it has been shown that high algebraic degrees and branch numbers make the cipher more resistant against algebraic [7] and cube [9] attacks. Moreover, lack of undisturbed bits [22] provides resistance against truncated [12], impossible [2], and improbable [21] differential cryptanalysis. It was shown in [14] that undisturbed bits are actually linear structures in coordinate functions. Therefore, linear structures should be avoided to be more secure against these kinds of attacks. Resistance against side-channel attacks like differential power analysis [13] can be obtained depending on the number of shares [4] in threshold implementations. Implementation invariant resistance against these attacks can be obtained by using S-boxes with a low transparency order [17], but this alone is not sufficient to ensure a satisfactory

© Springer International Publishing AG 2017
A. Bogdanov (Ed.): LightSec 2016, LNCS 10098, pp. 18–32, 2017.
DOI: 10.1007/978-3-319-55714-4_2

level of security [6]. Finally, it was shown in [24] that S-boxes may have properties called differential factors which partition the key space into two or more disjoint sets that are indistinguishable by differential cryptanalytic techniques.

In this work, we focus on undisturbed bits and differential factors which appear mostly in lightweight ciphers since they generally use small S-boxes. These properties are sometimes overlooked by attackers and designers alike. We analyzed the differential attacks in the literature on lightweight ciphers and we show that the differential attacks on PRESENT, PRIDE, and RECTANGLE require some correction. We first show that the 16-round differential attack of [25] on PRESENT needs to guess 8 more bits of the key to work due to the undisturbed bits. Secondly, we show that the 18-round differential attack of [29] and 19-round differential attack of [26] on PRIDE cannot capture 6 and 4 bits of the key, respectively due to differential factors. Thus, the true time complexities of the exhaustive searches performed at the end of these attacks are greater by a factor of 2^6 and 2^4 compared to the claimed values. Finally, we show that the time complexity of the 19-round related-key differential attack of [19] on the initial version of RECTANGLE can be reduced by a factor of $2^{1.07}$ with the help of two differential factors.

2 Preliminaries

2.1 PRESENT

PRESENT [5] is a 31-round SPN (Substitution Permutation Network) type block cipher with block size of 64 bits that supports 80 and 128-bit secret keys. It has been internationally standardized by ISO/IEC 29192-2:2012 [10] as a lightweight block cipher. The round function of PRESENT, which is depicted in Fig. 1, is the same for both versions of PRESENT and consists of standard operations such as subkey XOR, substitution and permutation. At the beginning of each round, the 64-bit input of the round function is XORed with the subkey. Immediately after the subkey XOR, 16 identical 4×4 S-boxes are used in parallel as a non-linear substitution layer and finally a permutation is performed so as to provide diffusion.

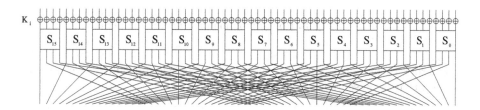

Fig. 1. Round function of PRESENT

2.2 PRIDE

PRIDE [1] is a 20-round SPN type block cipher with a block size of 64 bits and 128-bit secret key. It uses the FX construction [11], where the first half of the secret key is used for pre-whitening and post-whitening. The latter half is used to generate round keys. The overall structure is shown in Fig. 2.

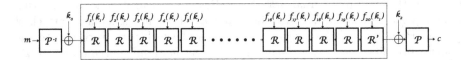

Fig. 2. Overall structure of PRIDE

The first 19 rounds use the same round function $\mathcal{R}$, composed of successive key addition, substitution and linear layers. The substitution layer features 16 identical 4×4 S-boxes in parallel. PRIDE's linear layer is made up of three sublayers, and has been specially designed to run efficiently in software implementations on 8-bit micro-controllers. The last round function $\mathcal{R}'$ omits the linear layer. The round functions are shown in Fig. 3.

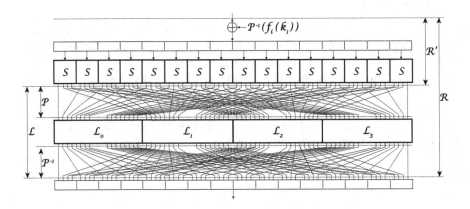

Fig. 3. Round function of PRIDE

In order to be consistent with the previous attacks on PRIDE, we use the notation that is presented in Table 1.

Table 1. PRIDE notation conventions

I_r	The input of the r-th round
X_r	The state after the key addition layer of the r-th round
Y_r	The state after the substitution layer of the r-th round
Z_r	The state after the permutation layer of the r-th round
W_r	The state after the matrix layer of the r-th round
O_r	The output of the r-th round
ΔX	The XOR difference of X and X'

2.3 RECTANGLE

RECTANGLE [28] is a lightweight block cipher with an SPN structure. This algorithm allows lightweight and fast implementations using bit-slice techniques. Its block length is 64 bits and its key length can be 80 bits or 128 bits. The substitution layer consists of 16 identical 4×4 S-boxes applied in parallel. This S-box can be implemented with only 12 basic logical instructions. The permutation layer contains only 3 rotations. 64-bit intermediate values of the cipher state can be showed as 4×16 rectangular array of bits

$$\begin{bmatrix} w_{15} & w_{14} & w_{13} & \cdots & w_0 \\ w_{31} & w_{30} & w_{29} & \cdots & w_{16} \\ w_{47} & w_{46} & w_{45} & \cdots & w_{32} \\ w_{63} & w_{62} & w_{61} & \cdots & w_{48} \end{bmatrix}$$

RECTANGLE has 25 rounds. Each round is composed of three steps: AddRoundkey, SubColumn and ShiftRow. In the AddRoundkey step, the cipher state is XORed with the rightmost 64 bits of the round subkey. In the SubColumn step, the S-box is applied to each column of the cipher state in parallel. In the ShiftRow step, the last three rows are left rotated 1, 12, and 13 bits, respectively. After 25 rounds of iterations, there is a final subkey XOR.

The key schedule of RECTANGLE is composed of three steps. The S-box is the same as in a round transformation. The key arranged as a 5×16 array of bits like in figure:

$$\begin{bmatrix} k_{0,15} & k_{0,14} & k_{0,13} & \cdots & k_{0,0} \\ k_{1,15} & k_{1,14} & k_{1,13} & \cdots & k_{1,0} \\ k_{2,15} & k_{2,14} & k_{2,13} & \cdots & k_{2,0} \\ k_{3,15} & k_{3,14} & k_{3,13} & \cdots & k_{3,0} \\ k_{4,15} & k_{4,14} & k_{4,13} & \cdots & k_{4,0} \end{bmatrix}$$

The 64-bit round subkey is composed of the first 4 rows of the current contents of the key. After this step, the key is updated as follows:

1. Applying S-box to the bits at the 4 uppermost and the 4 rightmost columns
2. Applying a 1-round generalized Feistel transformation
3. XORing a 5-bit round constant with the 5-bit key state

Finally K_{25} is extracted from the updated key state. The round constants are generated by a 5-bit LFSR.

The initial design of RECTANGLE, which is now referred to as REC-0, has a different key schedule and uses the inverse of RECTANGLE's S-box.

2.4 Differential Factors

Definition 1 ([24]). *Let S be a function from $\mathbb{F}_2^n$ to $\mathbb{F}_2^m$. For all $x, y \in \mathbb{F}_2^n$ that satisfy $S(x) \oplus S(y) = \mu$, if we also have $S(x \oplus \lambda) \oplus S(y \oplus \lambda) = \mu$, then we say that the S-box has a* differential factor λ *for the output difference μ. (i.e. μ remains invariant for λ).*

Theorem 1 ([24]). *If a bijective S-box S has a differential factor λ for an output difference μ, then S^{-1} has a differential factor μ for the output difference λ.*

Before showing the effect of differential factors on differential attacks, we recall the definition of advantage.

Definition 2 ([18]). *If an attack on an m-bit key gets the correct value ranked among the top r out of 2^m possible candidates, we say the attack obtained an $(m - log(r))$-bit* advantage *over exhaustive search.*

Theorem 2 ([24]). *In a block cipher let an S-box S contain a differential factor λ for an output difference μ and the partial round key k is XORed with the input of S. If an input pair provides the output difference μ under a partial subkey k', then the same output difference is observed under the partial subkey $k' \oplus \lambda$. Therefore, during a differential attack involving the guess of a partial subkey corresponding to the output difference μ, the advantage of the cryptanalyst is reduced by 1 bit and the time complexity of this key guess step is halved.*

Differential factors of PRESENT, PRIDE and RECTANGLE's S-boxes are provided in Table 2.

2.5 Undisturbed Bits

Definition 3 ([22]). *For a specific input difference of an S-box, if some bits of the output difference remain invariant, then we call such bits* undisturbed.

Undisturbed bits of PRESENT, PRIDE and RECTANGLE's S-boxes are provided in Table 3.

Table 2. Differential factors of PRESENT, PRIDE and RECTANGLE's S-boxes

S-box	0123456789ABCDEF	λ	μ
PRESENT	C56B90AD3EF84712	1	5
PRESENT	C56B90AD3EF84712	F	F
PRIDE	048F15E927ACBD63	1	1
PRIDE	048F15E927ACBD63	8	8
RECTANGLE	65CA1E79B03D8F42	2	4
RECTANGLE	65CA1E79B03D8F42	E	C

Table 3. Undisturbed bits of PRESENT, PRIDE and RECTANGLE's S-boxes

S-box	Input diff.	Output diff.	Output diff.	Input diff.
PRESENT	1001	???0	0101	???0
PRESENT	0001	???1	0001	???1
PRESENT	1000	???1	0100	???1
PRIDE	0001	01??	0001	01??
PRIDE	0010	1???	0010	1???
PRIDE	0011	1???	0011	1???
PRIDE	1000	?0??	1000	?0??
PRIDE	1001	?1??	1001	?1??
RECTANGLE	0001	??1?	0010	?11?
RECTANGLE	0100	??11	0100	?1??
RECTANGLE	0101	??0?	0110	?0??
RECTANGLE	1000	???1	1100	??1?
RECTANGLE	1100	???0	1110	??0?

3   Differential Attacks on Lightweight Block Ciphers

3.1   Differential Attacks on PRESENT

Resistance of PRESENT against differential cryptanalysis is provided by the designers [5] in terms of active S-boxes. The best known differential attack on PRESENT is provided in [25] by adding two rounds to the bottom of the 24 different 14-round differentials which has different input and same output difference. Recently, it was shown in [23] that this attack overlooks 6 differential factors and therefore the number of bits that are actually captured is 6 fewer than what is claimed. In this work we give another correction to this attack due to undisturbed bits.

16-Round Differential Attack. The 16-round differential attack of [25] adds two rounds to the bottom of the 24 different 14-round differentials which has different input and same output difference. These differentials hold with probability $p = 2^{-62}$ and Δ_1 is an example for these differentials

$$\Delta_1 : 0700000000000700 \rightarrow_{14r} 0000000900000009$$

The output difference of the characteristics activates the S-boxes S_0 and S_8 in the round 15 and S_4, S_6, S_8, S_{10}, S_{12}, and S_{14} in the round 16 which is shown in Table 4. Thus, this differential attack captures 32 bits of the key with a time complexity of $2^{33.18}$ 2-round PRESENT encryptions, a data complexity of 2^{64} chosen plaintexts, and a memory complexity of 2^{32} 6-bit counters. This part of the attack works with a success probability of 99.9999939% and then the remaining 48 bits are obtained via exhaustive search which requires 2^{48} 16-round PRESENT encryptions.

Table 4. 16-round differential attack of [25]. Values that need to be obtained are shown in bold.

Rounds	x_{15}	x_{14}	x_{13}	x_{12}	x_{11}	x_{10}	x_9	x_8	x_7	x_6	x_5	x_4	x_3	x_2	x_1	x_0
Differences in Bits																
$X_{1,I}$	0000	0111	0000	0000	0000	0000	0000	0000	0000	0000	0000	0000	0000	0111	0000	0000
14-Round Differential Δ_1																
$X_{14,P}$	0000	0000	0000	0000	0000	0000	0000	1001	0000	0000	0000	0000	0000	0000	0000	1001
$X_{15,S}$	0000	0000	0000	0000	0000	0000	0000	???0	0000	0000	0000	0000	0000	0000	0000	???0
$X_{15,P}$	0000	000?	0000	000?	0000	000?	0000	000?	0000	000?	0000	000?	0000	0000	0000	0000
$X_{16,S}$	0000	????	0000	????	0000	????	0000	????	0000	????	0000	????	0000	**0000**	0000	**0000**

However, the activated S-boxes of the round 16 have the input difference 1 and inverse of PRESENT's S-box has a differential factor $\lambda = 5$ for $\mu = 1$. Thus, $\mu = 1$ coincides with the input difference of these six S-boxes and it was shown in [23] that the advantage of this attack is actually 26 bits instead of 32 bits. This theoretical result is also experimentally verified by removing the first few rounds of the 14-round differential so that it remains within our computational power.

This observation reduces the time complexity of the first part of the attack to $2^{27.18}$ 2-round PRESENT encryptions and the memory complexity to 2^{26} 6-bit counters. However, the time complexity of exhaustive search for the remaining bits of the key is 2^{54} 16-round PRESENT encryptions, instead of 2^{48} as it was claimed.

We further give a correction to this attack due to the undisturbed bits. Since the input difference 9 for the S-box only activates the most significant three bits, it was assumed that we need to capture the values of three S-boxes in the 16-th round. However, we cannot verify the characteristic without knowing the all four bits of the S-box output in the 15-th round. We provided the parts that need to be obtained in bold in Table 4. Thus, the attacker also needs to guess the 16-th round subkeys corresponding to S_0 and S_2. But the attackers advantage increases by 6 instead of 8 bits due to the following property.

Property 1. Inverse of PRESENT's S-box S has the property $lsb(S^{-1}(x)) = lsb(S^{-1}(x \oplus 5))$ where lsb is the least significant bit.

Thus, a correct differential attack on 16-round PRESENT needs to guess 32 key bits in the 16-th round that correspond to the nibbles x_0, x_2, x_4, x_6, x_8, x_{10}, x_{12}, x_{14} and 8 key bits in the 15-th round. However, this attack provides 32-bit advantage to the attacker instead of 40 bits because of the 6 differential factors corresponding to the nibbles x_4, x_6, x_8, x_{10}, x_{12}, x_{14} and the application of Property 1 to the nibbles x_0 and x_2. Thus, the whole 80-bit key can be obtained after an exhaustive search that requires 2^{48} 16-round PRESENT encryptions.

3.2   Differential Attacks on PRIDE

18-Round Differential Attack. An 18-round differential attack on PRIDE is provided in [29] by adding one round to the top and two rounds to the bottom of a 15-round characteristic. This attack is summarized in Table 5.

Since this attack activates 16 S-boxes, authors try to capture corresponding 64-bit round keys which require 2^{66} 18-round PRIDE encryptions and recover the remaining 64 bits via exhaustive search with time complexity of 2^{64} 18-round PRIDE encryptions. However, this attack overlooks both the differential factors and undisturbed bits of PRIDE which can be used to reduce the time complexity of first part of the attack. On the other, the 6 differential factors that are shown in Table 5 prevent the attacker from capturing 6 bits of the key. Hence the exhaustive search at the end of the attack requires 2^{70} 18-round PRIDE encryptions instead of 2^{64}. Thus, the correct time complexity of this attack is 2^{70} 18-round PRIDE encryptions, not 2^{66}.

Table 5. 18-round differential attack of [29]. Differences $\mu = 8$ which have differential factors $\lambda = 8$ are shown in bold.

Rounds	x_{15}	x_{14}	x_{13}	x_{12}	x_{11}	x_{10}	x_9	x_8	x_7	x_6	x_5	x_4	x_3	x_2	x_1	x_0
Differences in Bits																
ΔI_1	0000	0000	0000	0000	0000	????	0000	0000	0000	????	0000	0000	0000	????	0000	0000
ΔX_1	0000	0000	0000	0000	0000	????	0000	0000	0000	????	0000	0000	0000	????	0000	0000
ΔY_1	0000	0000	0000	0000	0000	**1000**	0000	0000	0000	**1000**	0000	0000	0000	**1000**	0000	0000
ΔZ_1	0000	0100	0100	0100	0000	0000	0000	0000	0000	0000	0000	0000	0000	0000	0000	0000
ΔW_1	0100	0000	0000	0000	0000	0000	0000	0000	0000	0000	0000	0000	0000	0000	0000	0000
ΔI_2	0000	1000	0000	0000	0000	0000	0000	0000	0000	0000	0000	0000	0000	0000	0000	0000
15-Round Differential																
ΔX_{17}	0000	0000	0000	0000	0000	**1000**	0000	0000	0000	**1000**	0000	0000	0000	**1000**	0000	0000
ΔY_{17}	0000	0000	0000	0000	0000	????	0000	0000	0000	????	0000	0000	0000	????	0000	0000
ΔZ_{17}	0000	0?00	0?00	0?00	0000	0?00	0?00	0?00	0000	0?00	0?00	0?00	0000	0?00	0?00	0?00
ΔW_{17}	0?00	0?00	0?00	0?00	00?0	???0	0??0	0??0	???0	00?0	0??0	0??0	0??0	0??0	0??0	0??0
ΔI_{18}	00?0	?0??	0??0	0000	0?00	??0?	0??0	0000	0000	????	0???	0000	0000	????	0?00	0000
ΔX_{18}	00?0	?0??	0??0	0000	0?00	??0?	0??0	0000	0000	????	0???	0000	0000	????	0?00	0000
ΔY_{18}	????	????	????	0000	????	????	????	0000	0000	????	????	0000	0000	????	????	0000
ΔO_{18}	????	????	????	0000	????	????	????	0000	0000	????	????	0000	0000	????	????	0000

19-Round Differential Attack. The 18-round attack of [29] neglects the undisturbed bits in PRIDE. This observation has been noted in [26], and the attack has been improved to cover 19 rounds. However, this attack also fails to recognize the implications of the differential factors present in PRIDE's S-box.

The attack leverages the fact that an input difference of 8 yields an S-box output difference of 8 with statistically significant probability in order to identify 109 1-round characteristics that are used to construct 15-round iterative characteristics. Coincidentally, 8 happens to be a differential factor. The only difference amongst the various characteristics is which of the two nibbles holds a value of 8. It follows that the published attack fails to recover 4 bits of the key: two in the second round and another two in the penultimate round. These corrections increase the overall time complexity from 2^{63} to 2^{64} 19-round PRIDE encryptions (Table 6).

Table 6. 19-round differential attack of [26]. Differences $\mu = 8$ which have differential factors $\lambda = 8$ are shown in bold.

Rounds	x_1	x_2	x_3	x_4	x_5	x_6	x_7	x_8	x_9	x_{10}	x_{11}	x_{12}	x_{13}	x_{14}	x_{15}	x_{16}
Differences in Bits																
ΔI_1	????	????	????	0000	????	0000	????	0000	????	????	0000	0000	????	????	0000	0000
ΔX_1	????	????	????	0000	????	0000	????	0000	????	????	0000	0000	????	????	0000	0000
ΔY_1	?00?	00?0	00?0	0000	?00?	0000	00?0	0000	?0??	00?0	0000	0000	?00?	00?0	0000	0000
ΔZ_1	?000	?000	?000	?000	0000	0000	0000	0000	0??0	00?0	??00	0?00	?000	?000	?000	?000
ΔW_1	0000	?000	?000	0000	0000	0000	0000	0000	0000	?000	?000	0000	0000	?000	?000	?000
ΔI_2	0000	0000	0000	0000	?0??	0000	0000	0000	?0??	0000	0000	0000	0000	0000	0000	0000
ΔX_2	0000	0000	0000	0000	?0??	0000	0000	0000	?0??	0000	0000	0000	0000	0000	0000	0000
ΔY_2	0000	0000	0000	0000	**1000**	0000	0000	0000	**1000**	0000	0000	0000	0000	0000	0000	0000
ΔZ_2	0000	1000	1000	0000	0000	0000	0000	0000	0000	0000	0000	0000	0000	0000	0000	0000
ΔW_2	0000	1000	1000	0000	0000	0000	0000	0000	0000	0000	0000	0000	0000	0000	0000	0000
ΔI_3	0000	0000	0000	0000	1000	0000	0000	0000	1000	0000	0000	0000	0000	0000	0000	0000
15-Round Differential																
ΔX_{18}	0000	0000	0000	0000	**1000**	0000	0000	0000	**1000**	0000	0000	0000	0000	0000	0000	0000
ΔY_{18}	0000	0000	0000	0000	?0??	0000	0000	0000	?0??	0000	0000	0000	0000	0000	0000	0000
ΔZ_{18}	0000	?000	?000	0000	0000	0000	0000	0000	0000	?000	?000	0000	0000	?000	?000	0000
ΔW_{18}	?000	?000	?000	?000	0000	0000	0000	0000	??00	000?	??00	0000	?000	?000	?000	?000
ΔI_{19}	?0??	00?0	0000	0000	?00?	0000	0000	00?0	?0??	00?0	0000	0000	?00?	0000	0000	0000
ΔX_{19}	?0??	00?0	0000	0000	?00?	0000	0000	00?0	?0??	00?0	0000	0000	?00?	0000	0000	0000
ΔY_{19}	????	????	0000	0000	????	0000	0000	????	????	????	0000	0000	????	0000	0000	0000
ΔO_{19}	????	????	0000	0000	????	0000	0000	????	????	????	0000	0000	????	0000	0000	0000

20-Round Related-Key Differential Attack. 20-round related-key differential attacks that break the full PRIDE are provided in [8]. One of the attacks tries to capture 68 bits of the key by using an 18-round path and performs 2^{60} encryptions to capture the remaining bits. Due to a single differential factor, this attack's actual time complexity is 2^{61}. Another attack of [8] tries to capture 80 bits of the key by using a 17-round path and performs 2^{48} encryptions to capture the remaining bits. This time there are four differential factors and the

Table 7. One of the 20-round differential attacks of [8]. Differences $\mu = 8$ which have differential factors $\lambda = 8$ are shown in bold.

Rounds	x_1	x_2	x_3	x_4	x_5	x_6	x_7	x_8	x_9	x_{10}	x_{11}	x_{12}	x_{13}	x_{14}	x_{15}	x_{16}
Differences in Bits																
ΔI_1	????	0000	0000	0000	????	0000	0000	0000	0000	0000	0000	0000	0000	0000	0000	0000
ΔX_1	????	0000	0000	0000	????	0000	0000	0000	0000	0000	0000	0000	0000	0000	0000	0000
ΔY_1	**1000**	0000	0000	0000	**1000**	0000	0000	0000	0000	0000	0000	0000	0000	0000	0000	0000
ΔZ_1	1000	1000	0000	0000	0000	0000	0000	0000	0000	0000	0000	0000	0000	0000	0000	0000
ΔW_1	1000	1000	0000	0000	0000	0000	0000	0000	0000	0000	0000	0000	0000	0000	0000	0000
ΔI_1	1000	0000	0000	0000	1000	0000	0000	0000	0000	0000	0000	0000	0000	0000	0000	0000
ΔI_{19}	0000	0000	0000	0000	0000	0000	0000	0000	0000	0000	0000	0000	0000	0000	0000	0000
ΔX_{19}	**1000**	0000	0000	0000	**1000**	0000	0000	0000	0000	0000	0000	0000	0000	0000	0000	0000
ΔY_{19}	????	0000	0000	0000	????	0000	0000	0000	0000	0000	0000	0000	0000	0000	0000	0000
ΔZ_{19}	?000	?000	0000	0000	?000	?000	0000	0000	?000	?000	0000	0000	?000	?000	0000	0000
ΔW_{19}	?000	?000	?000	?000	?00?	?00?	?000	?000	?000	?00?	?000	?000	?000	?000	?000	?000
ΔI_{20}	????	0000	0000	0??0	????	0000	0000	0??0	????	0000	0000	0000	????	0000	0000	0000
ΔX_{20}	????	0000	0000	0??0	????	0000	0000	0??0	????	0000	0000	0000	????	0000	0000	0000
ΔY_{20}	????	0000	0000	????	????	0000	0000	????	????	0000	0000	0000	????	0000	0000	0000
$\oplus \Delta k_0$	????	0000	0000	????	????	0000	0000	????	????	0000	0000	0000	????	0000	0000	0000
ΔC	?00?	?00?	?000	?000	?00?	?00?	?000	?000	?00?	?00?	?000	?000	?00?	?00?	?000	?000

exhaustive search at the end of the attack should be 2^{52} encryptions instead of 2^{48}. This attack is summarized in Table 7. Moreover, like the 18-round attack of [29], these attacks neglect the undisturbed bits of PRIDE's S-box that are provided in Table 3 and therefore an improvement can be made as in the case of 19-round attack of [26]. However, since "PRIDE does not claim any resistance against related-key attacks" [1], these 20-round related-key attacks do not violate the security claims of the designers.

3.3   Differential Attacks on RECTANGLE

A 19-round related-key differential attack on the initial version of RECTANGLE, which is now referred to as REC-0, is presented in [19] (also published in Chinese [20]). Due to this attack and the software performance, the designers revised the key schedule.

19-Round Related-Key Differential Attack. In order to obtain related-key differential characteristics, differences of the 2nd round and the 16th round subkeys ΔK_2 and ΔK_{16} are fixed in [19]. Then the input and output differences ΔI_2 and ΔO_{18} are fixed as in Table 8 and 1254 characteristics with a total probability of $2^{60.5}$ is obtained with MILP based methods. 19 rounds are attacked by adding two rounds to the top and the bottom of these characteristics and the attack is summarized in Table 8.

The attack of [19] collects data using 2^x structures having the difference ΔI_0 and it is expected that $2^{x+34.54}$ pairs satisfy ΔO_{18}. The key guess part of the attack consists of 4 steps which are partial encryption of the 1st round, partial

Table 8. 19-round differential attack of REC-0. Output differences $\mu = 4$ that have differential factors $\lambda = 2$, and input differences $\mu = 2$ that have differential factors $\lambda = 4$ are shown in bold.

Rounds	x_{15}	x_{14}	x_{13}	x_{12}	x_{11}	x_{10}	x_9	x_8	x_7	x_6	x_5	x_4	x_3	x_2	x_1	x_0
Differences in Bits																
ΔI_0	0000	????	????	????	0000	????	????	????	????	????	0000	0000	????	0000	0000	0000
ΔO_0	0000	**0?00**	??00	?000	0000	000?	001?	0?10	**0?00**	?000	0000	0000	000?	0000	0000	0000
ΔI_1	0000	0000	0000	0000	0000	??1?	????	0000	0000	0000	0000	0000	??0?	0000	0000	0000
ΔO_1	0000	0000	0000	0000	0000	0001	0010	0000	0000	0000	0000	0000	0101	0000	0000	0000
15-Round Differential Δ_1																
ΔI_{17}	0000	0000	0000	0000	0000	0000	0001	0000	0000	0000	0000	0000	0000	0000	0000	0100
ΔO_{17}	0000	0000	0000	0000	0000	0000	????	0000	0000	0000	0000	0000	0000	0000	0000	?1??
ΔI_{18}	0000	0000	?000	0100	0100	00?0	00*?	0000	000*	?000	0?00	0000	0000	0000	**00?0**	000?
ΔO_{18}	0000	0000	????	?1??	?1??	????	????	0000	????	????	????	0000	0000	0000	????	????

encryption of the 2nd round, partial decryption of the 18th round, and partial decryption of the 17th round. These steps have approximate time complexities of $2^{x+40.54}$, $2^{x+39.54}$, $2^{x+38.54}$, and $2^{x+28.54}$ 19-round REC-0 encryptions, respectively.

Since REC-0 uses the inverse S-box of RECTANGLE, it has a differential $\lambda = 4$ for $\mu = 2$ by Theorem 1. Since these differential factors are two rounds away from the characteristic, Theorem 2 do not apply. However, we can still use the differential factors of the round 1 to reduce the time complexity of the attack due to the following property.

Property 2. The differential factor $\lambda = 4$ for $\mu = 2$ flips the value of the bit that corresponds to $\mu = 2$. Namely, the second bits from the right of $S(x)$ and $S(y \oplus 4)$ are the same (similarly for $S(y)$ and $S(x \oplus 4)$).

Property 2 allows us to guess only half of the keys that correspond to the two S-boxes x_{14} and x_7 in the first round. Therefore, if we start guessing keys from these two S-boxes, we reduce the time complexity of the first step of the attack of [19] by a factor of 2^2. However, since the differential factors flips the values of the bits according to Property 2, we need to also try the complements of the two key bits $K_0^{(3,10)} = K_1^{(3,3)}$ and $K_0^{(0,16)} = K_1^{(0,3)}$ in step 2 to avoid missing the correct key. We do not make any changes on the steps 3 and 4 of the attack because the inverse of Rec-0 does not have property like Property 2. Thus, the differential factors at round 18 do not have any effect on the attack. Steps of our modified attack have time complexities of $2^{x+38.29}$, $2^{x+39.29}$, $2^{x+38.55}$, and $2^{x+28.54}$ 19-round encryptions, respectively. If we choose $x = 26$ as in [19], we get a time complexity of $2^{66.35}$ 19-round encryptions compared to $2^{67.42}$ of the original attack. Details of our modified attack is provided in Appendix A.

Table 9. 14-round difference propagation of [27]. Output differences which have differential factors are shown in bold, which are $\mu = 2$ for the S-box and $\mu = 4$ for its inverse.

Input difference of round 0	Output difference of round 13
0000000000000000	0000000000000000
0010000100000000	000000000000**0010**
0000000100000000	000**1**000000000000
0000000000000000	0000000000000000

18-Round Differential Attack. Revising the key schedule of REC-0 made RECTANGLE more secure against related-key attacks and the above 19-round related-key differential attack is not applicable to RECTANGLE. In the single-key scenario, designers provided in [27] a 14-round difference propagation with probability $2^{-62.83}$ and it is presented in Table 9. Designers claim that they can mount an attack on 18-round RECTANGLE using this 14-round characteristic without giving the exact details of this attack. This is the highest number of rounds the designers can break.

Since RECTANGLE replaced the S-box of REC-0 with its inverse, the 14-round characteristic contains two differential factors as shown in Table 9. Therefore attacks on RECTANGLE using this or similar characteristics should consider the effects of differential factors. The time complexity of the 18-round attack is given as $2^{78.67}$ 18-round encryptions for an 80-bit seed key and $2^{126.66}$ 18-round encryptions for a 128-bit seed key. However, these complexities can be marginally larger in practice due to these two differential factors.

4   Conclusion

In this work, we have shown that there exist properties of S-boxes other than difference distribution and linear approximation that are fundamental to the security of lightweight block ciphers. In general, verifying theoretical attacks experimentally is infeasible due to the time, data, and memory complexity involved. Nevertheless, we were able to verify the theoretical results we have put forward through a series of experiments using reduced versions of the attacks in question. We believe that cryptanalysis would benefit from the practice of verifying theoretical results by experimenting on the reduced versions.

Acknowledgment. The work of Cihangir Tezcan was supported by The Scientific and Technological Research Council of Turkey (TÜBİTAK) under the grant 115E447 titled "Quasi-Differential Factors and Time Complexity of Block Cipher Attacks".

A   Modified 19-Round Related-Key Attack on REC-0

Step 1: Guess the value of a part of subkey bits of K_0.

1. Guess $K_0^{(14)}$ and compute the output difference of the 14rd S-box for each remaining plaintext pair; i.e. $S(P^{(14)} \oplus K_0^{(14)}) \oplus S(P'^{(14)} \oplus K_0^{(14)} \oplus \Delta K_0^{(14)})$. This step has time complexity $2 \cdot 2^{x+34.54} \cdot 2^3 \cdot \frac{1}{16} \cdot \frac{1}{19} = 2^{x+30.29}$ If the difference does not have the form ?000, discard the pair. Then the number of expected remaining pairs is $2^{x+28.54}$.

2. Guess $K_0^{(7)}$ and compute the output difference of the 7th S-box for each remaining plaintext pair; i.e. $S(P^{(7)} \oplus K_0^{(7)}) + S(P'^{(7)} \oplus K_0^{(7)} \oplus \Delta K_0^{(7)})$. This step has time complexity $2 \cdot 2^{x+31.54} \cdot 2^6 \cdot \frac{1}{16} \cdot \frac{1}{19} = 2^{x+30.29}$. If the difference does not have the form ?000, discard the pair. Then the number of expected remaining pairs is $2^{x+28.54}$.

3. Repeatedly guess $K_0^{(3)}$, $K_0^{(6)}$, $K_0^{(8)}$, $K_0^{(9)}$, $K_0^{(10)}$, $K_0^{(12)}$, $K_0^{(13)}$. There are $2^{x+8.54}$ right pairs left. This step has time complexity $2 \cdot (2^{x+38.54} \cdot 2^{x+39.54} \cdot 2^{x+40.54} \cdot 2^{x+41.54} \cdot 2^{x+42.54} \cdot 2^{x+43.54} \cdot 2^{x+44.54}) \cdot \frac{1}{16} \cdot \frac{1}{19} = 2^{x+38.29}$.

Step 2: Guess the value of a part of subkey bits of K_0 by guessing some bits of K_0 and K_1.

1. Since many bits of K_1 are obtained from K_0 directly by shifting and adding constant, we only need to guess some bits for a column in K_1. For the 3rd column of K_1, by the key schedule we have
$(K_1^{(0,3)}, K_1^{(1,3)}, K_1^{(2,3)}, K_1^{(3,3)}) = (K_0^{(0,16)}, K_0^{(1,14)}, K_0^{(2,12)}, K_0^{(3,10)})$ Therefore, we need to guess $K_0^{(0,16)} = K_1^{(0,3)}$ and we also need $K_0^{(3,10)} = K_1^{(3,3)}$ because $K_1^{(3,3)}$ was flipped when we apply Substitution operation to $K_1^{(2,7)}$, $K_1^{(3,10)}$ are flipped when we apply Substitution operation to $K_1^{(2,15)}$ because of Property 2. Then the number of expected remaining pairs is $2^{x+4.54}$.

2. Guess the bits $K_0^{(1,1)}$, $K_0^{(2,19)}$, $K_0^{(3,17)}$, and then check up whether $S(I_1^{(10)} \oplus K_1^{(10)}) \oplus S(I'^{(10)} \oplus K_1^{(10)} \oplus \Delta K_1^{(10)}) = 1000$. On average, there are $2^{x+0.54}$ right pairs left.

3. Similarly, as the previous step, guess the bits $K_0^{(0,2)}$, $K_1^{(1,9)}$, $K_0^{(2,18)}$, $K_0^{(3,16)}$, then there are $2^{x-3.46}$ right pairs left on average.

In step 2, time complexity is $2 \cdot (2^{x+45.54} \cdot 2^{x+44.54} \cdot 2^{x+44.54}) \cdot \frac{1}{16} \cdot \frac{1}{19} = 2^{x+39.29}$.

Step 3: Guess the value of a part of subkey bits of K_{19}. This step is identical to the Step 3 of [19] and has a time complexity of $2^{38.55}$.

Step 4: The involved secret bits of K_{18} have guessed in Step 1–3, and we do not need to guess any other secret bits. Add one to the corresponding counter, if there is a right pair left. This step is identical to the Step 3 of [19] and has a time complexity of $2^{28.54}$.

Step 5: If the counter is larger than 1, keep the guess of the subkey bits as the candidates of the right subkeys. For each survived candidate, compute the seed key by doing an exhaustive search for other secret bits.

Therefore, the total time complexity is $2^{66.35}$ 19-round REC-0 encryptions, data complexity is 2^{62} chosen plaintexts since $x = 26$, and the memory complexity is 2^{72} key counters.

References

1. Albrecht, M.R., Driessen, B., Kavun, E.B., Leander, G., Paar, C., Yalçın, T.: Block ciphers – focus on the linear layer (feat. PRIDE). In: Garay, J.A., Gennaro, R. (eds.) CRYPTO 2014. LNCS, vol. 8616, pp. 57–76. Springer, Heidelberg (2014). doi:10.1007/978-3-662-44371-2_4

2. Biham, E., Biryukov, A., Shamir, A.: Cryptanalysis of skipjack reduced to 31 rounds using impossible differentials. J. Cryptol. **18**(4), 291–311 (2005)

3. Biham, E., Shamir, A.: Differential cryptanalysis of DES-like cryptosystems. J. Cryptol. **4**(1), 3–72 (1991)

4. Bilgin, B., Nikova, S., Nikov, V., Rijmen, V., Stütz, G.: Threshold implementations of all 3 × 3 and 4 × 4 S-boxes. In: Prouff, E., Schaumont, P. (eds.) CHES 2012. LNCS, vol. 7428, pp. 76–91. Springer, Heidelberg (2012). doi:10.1007/978-3-642-33027-8_5

5. Bogdanov, A., Knudsen, L.R., Leander, G., Paar, C., Poschmann, A., Robshaw, M.J.B., Seurin, Y., Vikkelsoe, C.: PRESENT: an ultra-lightweight block cipher. In: Paillier, P., Verbauwhede, I. (eds.) CHES 2007. LNCS, vol. 4727, pp. 450–466. Springer, Heidelberg (2007). doi:10.1007/978-3-540-74735-2_31

6. Chakraborty, K., Sarkar, S., Maitra, S., Mazumdar, B., Mukhopadhyay, D., Prouff, E.: Redefining the transparency order. Cryptology ePrint Archive, Report 2014/367 (2014)

7. Courtois, N.T., Pieprzyk, J.: Cryptanalysis of Block ciphers with overdefined systems of equations. In: Zheng, Y. (ed.) ASIACRYPT 2002. LNCS, vol. 2501, pp. 267–287. Springer, Heidelberg (2002). doi:10.1007/3-540-36178-2_17

8. Dai, Y., Chen, S.: Cryptanalysis of full pride block cipher. Cryptology ePrint Archive, Report 2014/987 (2014). http://eprint.iacr.org/2014/987

9. Dinur, I., Shamir, A.: Cube attacks on tweakable black box polynomials. In: Joux, A. (ed.) EUROCRYPT 2009. LNCS, vol. 5479, pp. 278–299. Springer, Heidelberg (2009). doi:10.1007/978-3-642-01001-9_16

10. ISO/IEC 29192–2:2012: Information technology - security techniques - lightweight cryptography - part 2: Block ciphers (2011)

11. Kilian, J., Rogaway, P.: How to protect DES against exhaustive key search (an analysis of DESX). J. Cryptol. **14**(1), 17–35 (2001)

12. Knudsen, L.R.: Truncated and higher order differentials. In: Preneel, B. (ed.) FSE 1994. LNCS, vol. 1008, pp. 196–211. Springer, Heidelberg (1995). doi:10.1007/3-540-60590-8_16

13. Kocher, P., Jaffe, J., Jun, B.: Differential power analysis. In: Wiener, M. (ed.) CRYPTO 1999. LNCS, vol. 1666, pp. 388–397. Springer, Heidelberg (1999). doi:10.1007/3-540-48405-1_25

14. Makarim, R.H., Tezcan, C.: Relating undisturbed bits to other properties of substitution boxes. In: Eisenbarth, T., Öztürk, E. (eds.) LightSec 2014. LNCS, vol. 8898, pp. 109–125. Springer, Cham (2015). doi:10.1007/978-3-319-16363-5_7

15. Matsui, M.: Linear cryptanalysis method for DES cipher. In: Helleseth, T. (ed.) EUROCRYPT 1993. LNCS, vol. 765, pp. 386–397. Springer, Heidelberg (1994). doi:10.1007/3-540-48285-7_33

16. Nyberg, K.: Differentially uniform mappings for cryptography. In: Helleseth, T. (ed.) EUROCRYPT 1993. LNCS, vol. 765, pp. 55–64. Springer, Heidelberg (1994). doi:10.1007/3-540-48285-7_6

17. Prouff, E.: DPA attacks and S-boxes. In: Gilbert, H., Handschuh, H. (eds.) FSE 2005. LNCS, vol. 3557, pp. 424–441. Springer, Heidelberg (2005). doi:10.1007/11502760_29

18. Selçuk, A.A.: On probability of success in linear and differential cryptanalysis. J. Cryptol. 21(1), 131–147 (2008)

19. Shan, J., Hu, L., Song, L., Sun, S., Ma, X.: Related-key differential attack on round reduced rectangle-80. Cryptology ePrint Archive, Report 2014/986 (2014). http://eprint.iacr.org/2014/986

20. Shan, J., Hu, L., Song, L., Sun, S., Ma, X.: Related-key differential attack on 19-round reduced rectangle-80. J. Cryptol. Res. 2(1), 54 (2015). http://www.jcr.cacrnet.org.cn:8080/mmxb/EN/abstract/abstract73.shtml

21. Tezcan, C.: The improbable differential attack: cryptanalysis of reduced round CLEFIA. In: Gong, G., Gupta, K.C. (eds.) INDOCRYPT 2010. LNCS, vol. 6498, pp. 197–209. Springer, Heidelberg (2010). doi:10.1007/978-3-642-17401-8_15

22. Tezcan, C.: Improbable differential attacks on present using undisturbed bits. J. Comput. Appl. Math. 259, 503–511 (2014)

23. Tezcan, C.: Differential factors revisited: corrected attacks on PRESENT and SERPENT. In: Güneysu, T., Leander, G., Moradi, A. (eds.) LightSec 2015. LNCS, vol. 9542, pp. 21–33. Springer, Cham (2016). doi:10.1007/978-3-319-29078-2_2

24. Tezcan, C., Özbudak, F.: Differential factors: improved attacks on SERPENT. In: Eisenbarth, T., Öztürk, E. (eds.) LightSec 2014. LNCS, vol. 8898, pp. 69–84. Springer, Cham (2015). doi:10.1007/978-3-319-16363-5_5

25. Wang, M.: Differential cryptanalysis of reduced-round PRESENT. In: Vaudenay, S. (ed.) AFRICACRYPT 2008. LNCS, vol. 5023, pp. 40–49. Springer, Heidelberg (2008). doi:10.1007/978-3-540-68164-9_4

26. Yang, Q., Hu, L., Sun, S., Qiao, K., Song, L., Shan, J., Ma, X.: Improved differential analysis of block cipher PRIDE. In: Lopez, J., Wu, Y. (eds.) ISPEC 2015. LNCS, vol. 9065, pp. 209–219. Springer, Cham (2015). doi:10.1007/978-3-319-17533-1_15

27. Zhang, W., Bao, Z., Lin, D., Rijmen, V., Yang, B., Verbauwhede, I.: Rectangle: a bit-slice lightweight block cipher suitable for multiple platforms. Cryptology ePrint Archive, Report 2014/084 (2014). http://eprint.iacr.org/2014/084

28. Zhang, W., Bao, Z., Lin, D., Rijmen, V., Yang, B., Verbauwhede, I.: Rectangle: a bit-slice lightweight block cipher suitable for multiple platforms. Sci. China Inf. Sci. 58(12), 1–15 (2015)

29. Zhao, J., Wang, X., Wang, M., Dong, X.: Differential analysis on block cipher pride. Cryptology ePrint Archive, Report 2014/525 (2014). http://eprint.iacr.org/

Impossible Differential Cryptanalysis of 16/18-Round Khudra

Ferhat Karakoç[1(✉)], Öznur Mut Sağdıçoğlu[1], Mehmet Emin Gönen[1,2], and Oğuzhan Ersoy[3]

[1] TÜBİTAK - BİLGEM - UEKAE, PK 74, 41470 Gebze, Kocaeli, Turkey
{ferhat.karakoc,oznur.sagdicoglu,mehmet.gonen}@tubitak.gov.tr
[2] Gebze Technical University, Gebze, Kocaeli, Turkey
[3] Boğaziçi University, Istanbul, Turkey
oguzhan.ersoy@boun.edu.tr

Abstract. Khudra is a recently proposed lightweight block cipher specifically dedicated for Field Programmable Gate Arrays (FPGAs) implementation. It is a 4-branch type-2 generalized Feistel structure (GFS) of 18 rounds with 64-bit block size and 80-bit security margin. This paper studies the security of Khudra against impossible differential cryptanalysis. In the single-key scenario, the best impossible differential attack given by the designers works for 11 rounds with 2^{57} chosen plaintexts and 2^{61} encryptions. In this paper, by exploiting the structure of Khudra and the redundancy in its key schedule, we significantly improve previously known results. First, we propose an impossible differential attack on 14-round Khudra with $2^{54.06}$ chosen plaintexts, $2^{50.26}$ encryptions and 2^{49} memory. Then, we extend the attack by including pre-whitening keys with $2^{59.03}$ known plaintexts, $2^{67.06}$ time and $2^{59.03}$ memory complexities. Finally, we present an impossible differential attack against 16-round Khudra where whitening-keys are omitted. The 16-round attack requires $2^{49.58}$ chosen plaintexts, $2^{79.26}$ encryptions and 2^{64} memory. To the best of our knowledge, these attacks are the best known attacks in the single-key scenario.

Keywords: Khudra · Generalized feistel structure · Lightweight · Impossible differential cryptanalysis

1 Introduction

In recent years, *lightweight cryptography* has become a subject undergoing intense study in the area of cryptography. The underlying reason comes from growing demand on secure resource-constrained devices, like RFID tags and sensors in wireless network. Therefore, designing secure and efficient lightweight block cipher engages interest of both industrial and academic communities. In the last decade, several lightweight block ciphers have been proposed such as RoadRunneR [2], SIMON and SPECK [3], PRESENT [5], PRINCE [6],

© Springer International Publishing AG 2017
A. Bogdanov (Ed.): LightSec 2016, LNCS 10098, pp. 33–44, 2017.
DOI: 10.1007/978-3-319-55714-4_3

KATAN/KTANTAN [9], LED [12], ITUbee [14], Khudra [16], TWINE [20] and LBlock [22].

While most of the lightweight algorithms aim efficiency in software and ASIC-based platforms, Khudra is specifically designed for FPGAs. In the SPACE 2014 conference, Kolay and Mukhopadhyay introduced Khudra a 4-branch type-2 GFS of 18 rounds with 64-bit block size and 80-bit key size [16]. Key schedule is simply composed of 16-bit partitions of the main key where 32-bit pre-whitening, 32-bit post-whitening and 32-bit round keys are generated.

Although Khudra is a very recent design, there have been several studies regarding its security margin [10,17,18,21,23]. In [17], the authors investigate Khudra in a related-key scenario. They mount rectangle attack on 16-round version of the algorithm without whitening layers, and time complexity of $2^{78.68}$ memory accesses, $2^{59.77}$ encryptions and $2^{57.72}$ decryptions and data complexity of $2^{57.82}$ chosen plaintexts are required. Another related-key attack is applied in [23] where impossible differential attack is used against full round of the algorithm. The workload of the attack are $2^{68.46}$ encryption operations, 2^{63} chosen plaintexts and 2^{64} memory. Third related key attack is given in [10]. The authors present rectangle and differential attacks on 16- and 18-round versions of the algorithm. Moreover, in the paper there is an impossible differential attack on 14-round version of the algorithm. The details regarding the complexities of these attacks are given in Table 1.

There are also single-key scenario attacks presented in [18,21]. The first attack in the single key model was given in [21] where a meet-in-the-middle type attack is applied. It works on 14-round version of the algorithm with $2^{66.19}$ time, 2^{51} data and $2^{64.8}$ memory complexities. Finally, in [18], the previous attack is improved by reducing the memory complexity from $2^{64.8}$ to $2^{32.8}$. Also, the authors introduce a new guess-and-determine type attack on 14 rounds with 2 known plaintext-ciphertext pairs and 2^{64} time complexity. In addition, the authors found 2^{40} weak keys for the full cipher.

This paper studies the security of Khudra against impossible differential cryptanalysis which is a form of differential cryptanalysis. It was introduced by Knudsen and Biham et al. to analyze DEAL [15] and Skipjack [4], respectively. The attack uses differentials that hold with probability zero to derive the right key by discarding the wrong keys which lead to the impossible differential. There is no harm to say that GFSs are vulnerable to impossible differential attack because of the slow diffusion.

The best impossible differential attack found by the designers works on 11-round version of the algorithm with 2^{57} chosen plaintexts and 2^{61} encryptions. In [7], several Feistel structures are analyzed regarding differential propagation, including CAST [1], MARS [8] and RC6 [19] ciphers. Since Khudra is a RC6-like block cipher, 9-round impossible characteristic for such a structure given in [7] can be adapted. With the help of this characteristic, we attack 14 rounds of Khudra with data complexity of $2^{54.06}$ chosen plaintexts, time complexity of $2^{50.26}$ encryptions and memory complexity of 2^{49}. Then, we extend the attack by including pre-whitening keys with $2^{59.03}$ data, $2^{67.06}$ time and $2^{59.03}$ memory complexities. Finally, we present an impossible differential attack against 16-round Khudra where whitening-keys are omitted. The 16-round attack requires $2^{49.58}$ chosen plaintexts, $2^{79.26}$ encryptions of Khudra and 2^{64} memory.

We summarize all cryptanalytic results of Khudra in the Table 1.

Table 1. Comparison of the known attacks against Khudra.

Rounds	Data	Time	Memory	Attack type	Source
16^a	$2^{57.82}$ CP	$2^{59.77}$	negligible	RK-R	[17]
14^b	2^{57} CP	$2^{69.3}$	negligible	RK-ID	[10]
16	2^{53} CP	$2^{64.08}$	negligible	RK-R	[10]
18^a	2^{53} CP	$2^{63.97}$	negligible	RK-R	[10]
18	2^{63} CP	$2^{68.46}$	2^{64}	RK-ID	[23]
14^a	2^{51} CP	$2^{66.19}$	$2^{64.8}$	MITM	[21]
14^a	2^{51} CP	$2^{66.19}$	$2^{32.8}$	MITM	[18]
14^b	2 KP	2^{64}	negligible	GD	[18]
14^a	$2^{54.06}$ CP	$2^{50.26}$	2^{49}	ID	Sect. 3
14^c	$2^{59.03}$ KP	$2^{67.06}$	$2^{59.03}$	ID	Sect. 3
16^a	$2^{49.58}$ CP	$2^{79.26}$	2^{64}	ID	Sect. 4

[a]without whitening keys, [b]without pre-whitening key, [c]without post-whitening key, KP: known plaintexts, CP: chosen plaintexts, RK: related key, R: rectangle attack, ID: impossible differential attack, MITM: meet in the middle, GD: guess and determine.

Our paper is organized as follows. Section 2 provides a brief description of Khudra. Section 3 presents an attack on 14-round cipher. In Sect. 4, we improve the attack to 16-round version of Khudra. We conclude our paper in Sect. 5.

2 Definition of Khudra

Notation: Throughout the paper we use the following notation. We show the 16 bit partitions of 80-bit master key K as k_i where $K = k_0\|k_1\|k_2\|k_3\|k_4$. $x^{(i,j)}$ denotes j-th left-most 16 bits of i-th round output for $j \in 0, 1, 2, 3$ and $i \geq 1$. We use ΔX to denote the difference of X and X'. The difference used in this paper is the XOR ($\oplus$) difference, i.e., $\Delta X = X \oplus X'$. $a_{(m)}$ is used to represent a in m bits (e.g. $0_{(16)}$ is the 16-bit string of 0). $RC_i = 0\|i_{(6)}\|00\|i_{(6)}\|0$ for $i \in 0, ..., 35$ are the round constants. We use F_L^i and F_R^i to distinguish the left and the right F functions in i-th round.

Khudra: Khudra is a 4-branch type-2 GFS of 18 rounds [13]. Addition to 18 rounds, the cipher includes pre- and post-whitening layers. Whitening and round keys are generated from the master key in a very simple way. The block size and key length of the cipher is 64 and 80 bits, respectively. The pseudo code of the

Algorithm 1. Khudra encryption operation.

1: **Input:** Plaintext $P = P_0\|P_1\|P_2\|P_3$ and Key K
2: **Output:** Ciphertext $C = C_0\|C_1\|C_2\|C_3$
3: $k_0\|k_1\|k_2\|k_3\|k_4 \leftarrow K$.
4: $x^{(0,0)}\|x^{(0,1)}\|x^{(0,2)}\|x^{(0,3)} \leftarrow (P \oplus (k_0\|0_{(16)}\|k_1\|0_{(16)}))$.
5: **for** r=1 to 18 **do**
6:     $x^{(r,0)} \leftarrow F(x^{(r-1,0)}) \oplus x^{(r-1,1)} \oplus k_{(2r-2) \bmod 5} \oplus RC_{2r-2}$
7:     $x^{(r,1)} \leftarrow x^{(r-1,2)}$
8:     $x^{(r,2)} \leftarrow F(x^{(r-1,2)}) \oplus x^{(r-1,3)} \oplus k_{(2r-1) \bmod 5} \oplus RC_{2r-1}$
9:     $x^{(r,3)} \leftarrow x^{(r-1,0)}$
10: **end for**
11: $C \leftarrow (x^{(18,0)}\|x^{(18,1)}\|x^{(18,2)}\|x^{(18,3)}) \oplus (0_{(16)}\|k_4\|0_{(16)}\|k_3)$

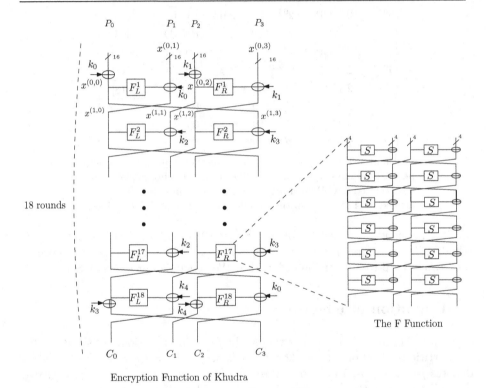

Encryption Function of Khudra

Fig. 1. The structure of Khudra

encryption operation is given in Algorithm 1. Figure 1 shows the structure of Khudra.

The function F is a 6-round 4 branch type-2 generalized Feistel Structure and uses 4-bit PRESENT's S-box S [5] given in Table 2. Note that since key is not included in F, the function can be considered as a 16-bit S-box.

Table 2. 4-bit S-box

x	0 1 2 3 4 5 6 7 8 9 A B C D E F
S[x]	C 5 6 B 9 0 A D 3 E F 8 4 7 1 2

Since round constants does not affect our attack, we refer to [16] for the constants and other details of the cipher.

3   Impossible Differential Attack on 14 Rounds

In this section, we present impossible differential attacks on 14 rounds of Khudra with and without pre-whitening keys (for both versions post-whitening keys are omitted). First, we show the attack excluding whitening keys. Then, we briefly explain how to extend the attack to cover pre-whitening keys.

To attack on 14-round Khudra with and without pre-whitening layer we use the generic 9-round distinguisher on 4-branch type-2 GFS

$$0_{(16)}0_{(16)}0_{(16)}\alpha_{(16)} \xrightarrow{9 \text{ rounds}} 0_{(16)}0_{(16)}\alpha_{(16)}0_{(16)}$$

where α represents a 16-bit non-zero difference. When the input difference is $0_{(16)}0_{(16)}0_{(16)}\alpha_{(16)}$ and the output difference is $0_{(16)}0_{(16)}\alpha_{(16)}0_{(16)}$, $\Delta x^{(4,3)}$ and $\Delta x^{(5,2)}$ becomes $\alpha_{(16)}$. It means that output of F_R^5 have to have zero-difference. As seen in Fig. 2, input of F_R^5 have a non-zero difference with probability of 1. Since F is a permutation, it is impossible that its output has zero difference while there is a none-zero difference in the input. With this contradiction we have an impossible distinguisher on 9 rounds.

We add 3 rounds to the top and 2 rounds to the bottom of the distinguisher to attack on 14 rounds.

As seen in Fig. 3, if the plaintext pair (P, P') and corresponding ciphertext pair (C,C') satisfies the following conditions

- $\Delta x^{(0,2)} = \Delta x^{(14,0)}$
- $\Delta x^{(1,0)} = 0$
- $\Delta x^{(14,3)} = 0$
- $\Delta x^{(13,3)} = 0$

the probability that a wrong key causes the impossible differential for 9 rounds is 2^{-48} because of the three conditions $\Delta x^{(2,2)} = 0$, $\Delta x^{(3,0)} = 0$ and $\Delta x^{(12,3)} = 0$.

The key parts used to check these conditions are k_0, k_1 and k_2 which have 48-bit length in total. Thus, the required number of plaintext pairs (M) which can be used in the attack can be calculated as

$$M \geq |k| \times 2^c \times ln(2) = 48 \times 2^{48} \times ln(2) \approx 2^{53.06}$$

where $|k|$ is the length of guessed key and c is the number of conditions in bits to eliminate all wrong candidates for k_0, k_1 and k_2. A plaintext pair having the condition $\Delta x^{(1,0)} = 0$ can be used in the attack with a probability of

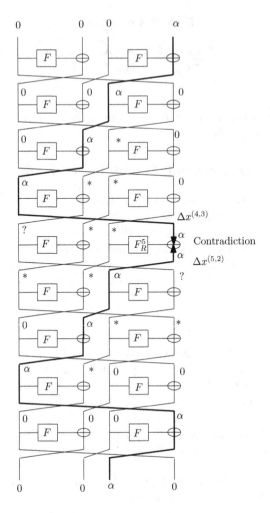

0 : zero-difference
α : a non-zero difference
* : non-zero difference
? : zero or non-zero difference

Fig. 2. A 9-round impossible differential characteristic

2^{-48}, because the corresponding ciphertext pairs should satisfy the conditions $\Delta x^{(0,2)} = \Delta x^{(14,0)}$, $\Delta x^{(14,3)} = 0$ and $\Delta x^{(13,3)} = 0$. Note that these conditions can be checked without any key information. Thus, $2^{53.06+48} = 2^{101.06}$ plaintext pairs satisfying $\Delta x^{(1,0)} = 0$ are required. Let a structure be the set of 2^{48} plaintexts where $F(x^{(0,0)}) \oplus x^{(0,1)}$ are the same for all plaintexts. Using one structure, approximately 2^{95} plaintext pairs can be constructed. To have $2^{101.06}$ pairs, 67 structures are needed. After having required amount of plaintext-ciphertext pairs

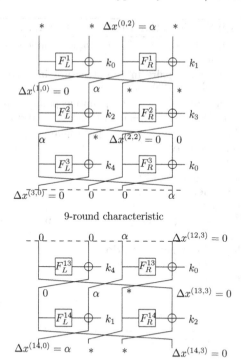

9-round characteristic

Fig. 3. 14-round impossible differential attack.

we apply the attack as given in Algorithm 2. In the attack, we use the following well-known property of invertible S-boxes.

Property 1. [11] Given an input difference and an output difference of an invertible S-box, there is on average one input that satisfies these differences.

In the attack, we use $67 \times 2^{48} = 2^{54.06}$ chosen plaintexts and about 2^{49} memory to store the candidate keys and plaintexts. While we are calculating time complexity of the attack, we assume that 1 F calculation and 1 table look-up for Property 1 have similar complexity cost. Step 5, 6, 7 and 12 dominates the complexity of the attack.

In the Step 5, since the input and the output difference of F_R^{13} are known we can find the input of F_R^{13} by using the Property 1 with just 1 table look-up. In Step 6, we can get k_1 without any effort as k_1 is the sum of $F_L^{14}(x^{(13,0)})$, $x^{(13,1)}$ and $x^{(14,0)}$. Note that $F_L^{14}(x^{(13,0)})$ can be calculated in Step 3. In step 7, in order to get $\Delta x^{(2,2)}$ we need to calculate F_R^1 and F_R^2 for pairs. But easily F_R^1 can be obtained in Step 3. Thus in Step 7, 2 F computations will be needed. Finally in Step 12, F_L^1 can be computed in Step 3, we have just 1 F computation for F_L^2.

Thus in these steps, 4 F function computations are performed 67×2^{47} times. This computation cost can be approximated to $\frac{4 \times 67 \times 2^{47}}{14 \times 2} \approx 2^{50.26}$ 14-round encryption operations. The cost of 2^{32} encryption operations to find the other

---

Algorithm 2. Impossible differential attack on 14 rounds.

1: Store all possible values of k_0, k_1 and k_2 in a table (candidate table).
2: **for** each of 67 structures **do**
3:     Store plaintext-ciphertext pairs in the structure in a hash table (Table A) indexed by $x^{(14,3)}$, $x^{(13,3)}$ and $x^{(0,2)} \oplus x^{(14,0)}$.
4:     **for** each of approximately $2^{95-48} = 2^{47}$ plaintext pairs where the conditions are satisfied $\Delta x^{(0,2)} = \Delta x^{(14,0)}$, $\Delta x^{(14,3)} = 0$ and $\Delta x^{(13,3)} = 0$ **do**
5:         With the knowledge of input and output difference of F_R^{13} find the input of F_R^{13} ($x^{(12,2)}$) by using Property 1.
6:         Compute k_1 from $x^{(12,2)}$.
7:         Compute $\Delta x^{(2,2)}$ by using k_1.
8:         **if** $\Delta x^{(2,2)} = 0$ **then**
9:             Compute $\Delta x^{(2,1)}$
10:             Find $x^{(2,0)}$ by using Property 1 with the input and output difference of F_L^3.
11:             **for** each possible value for k_0 **do**
12:                 Compute k_2 and remove (k_0, k_1, k_2) from the candidate table.
13:             **end for**
14:         **end if**
15:     **end for**
16: **end for**

---

key parts k_3 and k_4 does not add a considerable effect on the time complexity of the attack.

3.1 Extending the Attack with Pre-whitening Keys

In order to include pre-whitening keys, a modified version of the attack can be used. Because of the whitening keys, $\Delta x^{(1,0)} = 0$ condition cannot be satisfied directly from the choice of plaintext pairs. Therefore, it should be added to the elimination part of wrong keys. In that case, a wrong key causes the impossible differential with a probability of 2^{-64} instead of 2^{-48}. Hence, the required number of plaintext pairs (M) which can be used in the attack can be calculated as

$$M \geq |k| \times 2^e \times ln(2) = 48 \times 2^{64} \times ln(2) \approx 2^{69.06}$$

Thus, in order to mount the attack, $2^{69.06+48} = 2^{117.06}$ plaintext pairs are required. Approximately $2^{59.03}$ plaintexts are enough to generate that much of pairs. Since there is no condition on the plaintexts, the type of the attack falls into known plaintext model.

In this attack, approximately $2^{59.03}$ memory is required to store the candidate keys and plaintexts. The time complexity suffers from the same dominating parts with different number of plaintext pairs. The number of F computations becomes 7. Then, the time complexity can be computed as $\frac{2^{69.06} \times 7}{14 \times 2} \approx 2^{67.06}$ 14-round encryption operations.

4   Impossible Differential Attack on 16 Rounds of Khudra

In this section, we improve the attack for 16-round Khudra using the 9-round impossible differential used in the previous section. In the attack, we assume that the whitening keys are omitted. Because of the key schedule of Khudra, the round keys are used in the same order in every 5 rounds. This helps us to increase the number of rounds attacked. We add 3 and 4 rounds to the top and bottom of the distinguisher, respectively.

To attack on 16-round Khudra, we first construct 3 structures which contain 2^{48} plaintexts where $x^{(1,0)}$ is fixed and $x^{(0,0)}$, $x^{(0,2)}$ and $x^{(0,3)}$ takes all possible values as seen in Fig. 4.

Using each structure, we are able to generate 2^{95} plaintext pairs. The probability that a wrong subkey survives after elimination with one pair is $1 - 2^{-96}$. As we have $3 \cdot 2^{95} \approx 2^{96.58}$ pairs,

$$2^{80} \times (1 - 2^{-96})^{2^{96.58}} \approx 2^{77.84}$$

values of the 80-bit target key remain as the output of the attack algorithm given in Algorithm 3. We perform exhaustive search for the remaining keys.

Algorithm 3. Impossible differential attack on 16 rounds.

1: **for** each possible value of k_0 **do**
2:      Store all possible values of k_1, k_2, k_3, k_4 in Table A.
3:      **for** each of 3 structures **do**
4:          **for** each plaintext and ciphertext pairs in the structure **do**
5:              Compute $F_R^{15}(x^{(14,2)}) \oplus x^{(15,2)}$ and $F_R^{16}(x^{(15,2)}) \oplus x^{(16,2)} \oplus x^{(0,2)}$ and store the pairs in a hash table (Table B) indexed by the computed values.
6:          **end for**
7:          **for** each plaintext pairs generated from Table B which satisfies the conditions $\Delta(F_R^{15}(x^{(14,2)}) \oplus x^{(15,2)}) = 0$ and $\Delta(F_R^{16}(x^{(15,2)}) \oplus x^{(16,2)}) = \Delta x^{(0,2)}$ **do**
8:              Compute $\Delta x^{(2,1)}$ that is the output difference of F_L^3.
9:              By using Property 1 with the knowledge of input and output difference pair of F_L^3, find $x^{(2,0)}$.
10:              Compute k_2.
11:              Find $x^{(1,2)}$ by using Property 1 and derive k_1.
12:              Compute the input and output differences of F_R^{14} .
13:              Extract the input $x^{(13,2)}$ by using Property 1.
14:              Compute k_3 from $x^{(13,2)}$.
15:              Compute input and output difference pair of F_R^{13}.
16:              Find $x^{(12,2)}$ from the difference pair.
17:              Extract k_4 and remove computed value for k_1, k_2, k_3, k_4 from Table A.
18:          **end for**
19:      **end for**
20:      For k_0 and each key in Table A check the keys using two plaintext-ciphertext pairs. Output the key as the correct key which satisfies the pairs.
21: **end for**

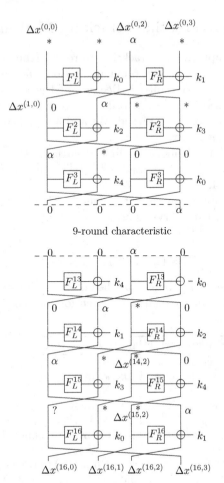

Fig. 4. 16-round impossible differential attack.

The complexity of the attack is calculated as follows. Time complexity is dominated by Step 8-17 where 8 F function computations are performed $2^{16+64.58}$ times in total. The time for these step is equivalent to approximately $\frac{2^{16+64.58} \cdot 8}{32} = 2^{78.58}$ 16-round Khudra encryption operations. Considering the brute force attack for the remaining keys, the total time complexity of the 80-bit key recovery is approximately $2^{78.58} + 2^{77.84} = 2^{79.26}$ encryption operations. The data complexity of the attack is $3 \cdot 2^{48} \approx 2^{49.58}$ chosen plaintexts. In Step 2 and 5, we use tables of size 2^{64} and 2^{48}, respectively. Thus, the memory complexity is about 2^{64}.

5   Conclusion

In this paper, we study the security of the block cipher Khudra against impossible differential cryptanalysis. The best impossible differential attack found by the designers works on 11-round version of the algorithm. By using 9-round impossible differential, first, we attack 14 rounds of Khudra. Then, we extend the attack by including pre-whitening keys. Finally, we present impossible differential attack against 16-round Khudra without whitening-keys. To the extent of our knowledge, these attacks are the best known attacks in a single-key scenario.

References

1. Adams, C., Gilchrist, J.: The CAST-256 encryption algorithm. Technical report (1999)
2. Baysal, A., Şahin, S.: RoadRunneR: a small and fast bitslice block cipher for low cost 8-bit processors. In: Güneysu, T., Leander, G., Moradi, A. (eds.) Light-Sec 2015. LNCS, vol. 9542, pp. 58–76. Springer, Cham (2016). doi:10.1007/978-3-319-29078-2_4
3. Beaulieu, R., Shors, D., Smith, J., Treatman-Clark, S., Weeks, B., Wingers, L.: The SIMON and SPECK families of lightweight block ciphers. IACR Cryptology ePrint Archive 2013, 404 (2013). http://eprint.iacr.org/2013/404
4. Biham, E., Biryukov, A., Shamir, A.: Cryptanalysis of skipjack reduced to 31 rounds using impossible differentials. In: Stern, J. (ed.) EUROCRYPT 1999. LNCS, vol. 1592, pp. 12–23. Springer, Heidelberg (1999). doi:10.1007/3-540-48910-X_2
5. Bogdanov, A., Knudsen, L.R., Leander, G., Paar, C., Poschmann, A., Robshaw, M.J.B., Seurin, Y., Vikkelsoe, C.: PRESENT: an ultra-lightweight block cipher. In: Paillier, P., Verbauwhede, I. (eds.) CHES 2007. LNCS, vol. 4727, pp. 450–466. Springer, Heidelberg (2007). doi:10.1007/978-3-540-74735-2_31
6. Borghoff, J., et al.: PRINCE – a low-latency block cipher for pervasive computing applications. In: Wang, X., Sako, K. (eds.) ASIACRYPT 2012. LNCS, vol. 7658, pp. 208–225. Springer, Heidelberg (2012). doi:10.1007/978-3-642-34961-4_14
7. Bouillaguet, C., Dunkelman, O., Fouque, P.-A., Leurent, G.: New insights on impossible differential cryptanalysis. In: Miri, A., Vaudenay, S. (eds.) SAC 2011. LNCS, vol. 7118, pp. 243–259. Springer, Heidelberg (2012). doi:10.1007/978-3-642-28496-0_15
8. Burwick, C., Coppersmith, D., DAvignon, E., Gennaro, R., Halevi, S., Jutla, C., Matyas, S.M., OConnor, L., Peyravian, M., Safford, D., et al.: The Mars Encryption Algorithm. IBM, 27 August 1999
9. Cannière, C., Dunkelman, O., Knežević, M.: KATAN and KTANTAN — a family of small and efficient hardware-oriented block ciphers. In: Clavier, C., Gaj, K. (eds.) CHES 2009. LNCS, vol. 5747, pp. 272–288. Springer, Heidelberg (2009). doi:10.1007/978-3-642-04138-9_20
10. Dai, Y., Chen, S.: Security analysis of Khudra: a lightweight block cipher for FPGAs. Secur. Commun. Netw. **9**(10), 1173–1185 (2016). http://dx.doi.org/10.1002/sec.1409
11. Dunkelman, O., Keller, N., Shamir, A.: Improved single-key attacks on 8-Round AES-192 and AES-256. In: Abe, M. (ed.) ASIACRYPT 2010. LNCS, vol. 6477, pp. 158–176. Springer, Heidelberg (2010). doi:10.1007/978-3-642-17373-8_10

12. Guo, J., Peyrin, T., Poschmann, A., Robshaw, M.: The LED block cipher. In: Preneel, B., Takagi, T. (eds.) CHES 2011. LNCS, vol. 6917, pp. 326–341. Springer, Heidelberg (2011). doi:10.1007/978-3-642-23951-9_22
13. Hoang, V.T., Rogaway, P.: On generalized feistel networks. In: Rabin, T. (ed.) CRYPTO 2010. LNCS, vol. 6223, pp. 613–630. Springer, Heidelberg (2010). doi:10.1007/978-3-642-14623-7_33
14. Karakoç, F., Demirci, H., Harmancı, A.E.: ITUbee: a software oriented lightweight block cipher. In: Avoine, G., Kara, O. (eds.) LightSec 2013. LNCS, vol. 8162, pp. 16–27. Springer, Heidelberg (2013). doi:10.1007/978-3-642-40392-7_2
15. Knudsen, L.: DEAL - a 128-bit Block Cipher. Technical report no. 151 (1998)
16. Kolay, S., Mukhopadhyay, D.: Khudra: a new lightweight block cipher for FPGAs. In: Chakraborty, R.S., Matyas, V., Schaumont, P. (eds.) SPACE 2014. LNCS, vol. 8804, pp. 126–145. Springer, Cham (2014). doi:10.1007/978-3-319-12060-7_9
17. Ma, X., Qiao, K.: Related-key rectangle attack on round-reduced khudra block cipher. In: Qiu, M., Xu, S., Yung, M., Zhang, H. (eds.) NSS 2015. LNCS, vol. 9408. Springer, Cham (2015). doi:10.1007/978-3-319-25645-0_22
18. Özen, M., Çoban, M., Karakoç, F.: A guess-and-determine attack on reduced-round khudra and weak keys of full cipher. IACR Cryptology ePrint Archive 2015, 1163 (2015). http://eprint.iacr.org/2015/1163
19. Rivest, R.L., Robshaw, M., Sidney, R., Yin, Y.L.: The RC6TM block cipher. In: First Advanced Encryption Standard (AES) Conference (1998)
20. Suzaki, T., Minematsu, K., Morioka, S., Kobayashi, E.: *TWINE*: a lightweight block cipher for multiple platforms. In: Knudsen, L.R., Wu, H. (eds.) SAC 2012. LNCS, vol. 7707, pp. 339–354. Springer, Heidelberg (2013). doi:10.1007/978-3-642-35999-6_22
21. Tolba, M., Abdelkhalek, A., Youssef, A.M.: Meet-in-the-middle attacks on round-reduced khudra. In: Chakraborty, R.S., Schwabe, P., Solworth, J. (eds.) SPACE 2015. LNCS, vol. 9354, pp. 127–138. Springer, Cham (2015). doi:10.1007/978-3-319-24126-5_8
22. Wu, W., Zhang, L.: LBlock: a lightweight block cipher. In: Lopez, J., Tsudik, G. (eds.) ACNS 2011. LNCS, vol. 6715, pp. 327–344. Springer, Heidelberg (2011). doi:10.1007/978-3-642-21554-4_19
23. Yang, Q., Hu, L., Sun, S., Song, L.: Related-key impossible differential analysis of full khudra. IACR Cryptology ePrint Archive 2015, 840 (2015). http://eprint.iacr.org/2015/840

Distinguishing Attacks on (Ultra-)Lightweight WG Ciphers

Mabin Joseph[1,2]($\boxtimes$), Gautham Sekar[2,3],
and R. Balasubramanian[2,3]

[1] Indira Gandhi Centre for Atomic Research, Kalpakkam, Tamil Nadu, India
`mebinjp@gmail.com`
[2] Homi Bhabha National Institute, Training School Complex,
Anushakti Nagar, Mumbai 400094, India
[3] The Institute of Mathematical Sciences, Taramani, Chennai, Tamil Nadu, India
`gautham.sekar@gmail.com`, `balu@imsc.res.in`

Abstract. The Welch-Gong (WG) family of stream ciphers include two subfamilies, which we call WG-A and WG-B, of patented (ultra-) lightweight ciphers designed by Gong et al. The Waterloo Commercialization Office, Canada, has included the WG-A in an RFID anti-counterfeiting system and has proposed the WG-B for securing 4G networks. The WG-A and WG-B ciphers support 80- and 128-bit keys, respectively. In this paper, we detect input-output correlations in the nonlinear transformations used by these ciphers. Exploiting these, we show distinguishing attacks that require, to nearly ensure success, between $2^{22.20}$ and $2^{29.07}$ keystream samples for WG-A and not more than $2^{56.84}$ keystream samples for WG-B. We are not aware of any prior attacks on these ciphers.

Keywords: WG · Lightweight cipher · Distinguishing attack

1 Introduction

Lightweight ciphers. Recently there has been a considerable surge in the popularity of lightweight ciphers due to the advent of Internet of Things. Such ciphers typically use linear feedback shift registers (LFSRs), especially in constrained hardware environments. To augment the linear complexity of the keystream, LFSR-based ciphers use balanced nonlinear functions—the resulting keystream generator is called a nonlinear filter generator and well-known examples are the generators of the WG family of ciphers.

The WG family of ciphers. The WG ciphers are based on the WG transformations [17] which are balanced nonlinear filter functions. The possibility of using the WG transformations for cryptographic purposes was first explored by Gong et al. [9]. The transformations are defined over finite fields of orders 2^5, 2^7, 2^8, 2^{16} and 2^{29}; the corresponding ciphers are respectively denoted by WG-5

© Springer International Publishing AG 2017
A. Bogdanov (Ed.): LightSec 2016, LNCS 10098, pp. 45–59, 2017.
DOI: 10.1007/978-3-319-55714-4_4

Table 1. Attacks on the WG family of stream ciphers

Year	Cipher	Key size (in bits)	IV size (in bits)	Type of attack	Requirements	Success rate (%)
2005	WG-29[a]	80	80	Key recovery [20]	$2^{31.3}$ chosen IVs, $O(2^{32.69})$ time	99.95
2007	WG-29[b]	80, 96, 112, 128[c]	32, 64 or same as key size[c]	Key recovery [16]	$O(2^{45.04})$ data, $O(2^{65.71})$ time	99.99
2012	WG-7	80	81	Distinguishing [14]	$O(2^{13.5})$ data	99.99
2012	WG-7	80	81	Key recovery [14]	$O(2^{19.38})$ data, $O(2^{27})$ time	100
2014	WG-8	80	80	Key recovery [2]	2^{21} chosen IVs, $O(2^{23.29})$ time	99.99
2015	WG-29[b]	128	128	Key recovery [3]	$O(2^{89})$ time, $O(2^{48})$ memory	63.21
2015	WG-5 ($d = 7$)	80	80	Key recovery [15]	$O(2^{15})$ data, $O(2^{30})$ time	100
2015	WG-5 ($d = 15$)	80	80	Key recovery [15]	$O(2^{15})$ data, $O(2^{30})$ time	100
2015	WG-7	80	81	Key recovery [15]	$O(2^{14})$ data, $O(2^{25})$ time	100
2015	WG-8	80	80	Key recovery [15]	$O(2^{22})$ data, $O(2^{48})$ time	100
2015	WG-16	128	128	Key recovery [15]	$O(2^{63})$ data, $O(2^{106})$ time	100
2016	WG-A	80	80	Distinguishing (This paper)	Up to $2^{33.46}$ bits, less than $O(2^{29.07})$ time	99.99
2016	WG-B	128	128	Distinguishing (This paper)	Up to $2^{61.87}$ bits, less than $O(2^{56.84})$ time	99.99

[a]ECRYPT eSTREAM Phase 1 version.
[b]ECRYPT eSTREAM Phase 2 version.
[c]Attack works for any combination of key size and IV size.

[1], WG-7 [10], WG-8 [6], WG-16 [5] and WG-29 [13]. Beginning with WG-29 (a well-received entrant to the ECRYPT eSTREAM project [4] designed by Nawaz et al.), the WG ciphers have been studied extensively, over a period spanning more than a decade. Table 1 lists the ciphers and results of their best known security evaluations.

The WG-A and WG-B,[1] designed by Gong et al. [7], are subfamilies of the WG family and comprise of patented (# US8953784 B2) variants of the WG-8

---

[1] We follow this nomenclature to distinguish between the patented and unpatented variants of WG-8 and WG-16.

Communications in Computer and Information Science 667

Commenced Publication in 2007
Founding and Former Series Editors:
Alfredo Cuzzocrea, Dominik Ślęzak, and Xiaokang Yang

More information about this series at http://www.springer.com/series/7899

Linda Barone · Mario Monteleone
Max Silberztein (Eds.)

Automatic Processing of Natural-Language Electronic Texts with NooJ

10th International Conference, NooJ 2016
České Budějovice, Czech Republic, June 9–11, 2016
Revised Selected Papers

Springer

Editors
Linda Barone
Università degli Studi di Salerno
Fisciano
Italy

Max Silberztein
Université de Franche-Comté
Besançon
France

Mario Monteleone
Università degli Studi di Salerno
Fisciano
Italy

ISSN 1865-0929   ISSN 1865-0937 (electronic)
Communications in Computer and Information Science
ISBN 978-3-319-55001-5   ISBN 978-3-319-55002-2 (eBook)
DOI 10.1007/978-3-319-55002-2

Library of Congress Control Number: 2017933872

Printed on acid-free paper

This Springer imprint is published by Springer Nature
The registered company is Springer International Publishing AG
The registered company address is: Gewerbestrasse 11, 6330 Cham, Switzerland

and WG-16, respectively [7]. WG-A has 3 constituent ultra-lightweight ciphers, each corresponding to a unique *decimation factor* or *d*. Each of these ciphers supports an 80-bit key and an 80-bit initialization vector. Likewise, WG-B comprises of 31 lightweight ciphers, each using a 128-bit key and a 128-bit initialization vector. The designs of WG-A and WG-B are remarkably simple and the ciphers are well suited for hardware applications. At TechConnect World Innovation Conference 2015, the Waterloo Commercialization Office had exhibited an RFID system for anti-counterfeiting enabled with WG-A [19]. Furthermore, information available through the website of the Waterloo Commercialization Office suggests that WG-B is proposed for securing 4G networks [18]. Consequently, there appear to be good chances for these ciphers to be commercially deployed on a wide scale.

Contributions of this paper. We present linear distinguishing attacks on WG-A and WG-B families of ciphers. The attacks on WG-A are highly practical, requiring fewer than $2^{29.07}$ keystream samples for nearly guaranteed success, and have been experimentally verified. Our attacks on WG-B, however, are not very practical and require up to $2^{56.84}$ keystream samples to nearly guarantee success. The security claim of the designers of WG-A and WG-B suggests that these ciphers offer better security compared to their predecessors (this is attributed to the decimation factor). Table 1 shows that our attacks refute this claim.[2]

Organisation of the paper. The remaining paper is organised as follows. Section 2 describes the ciphers along with the notation and convention that we follow. We present our motivational observations for WG in Sect. 3. The biases in the keystream distribution are computed in Sect. 4 and our distinguishing attacks are presented in Sect. 5. In Sect. 6, we discuss how the remaining members of the WG family fare against linear distinguishing attacks. We conclude in Sect. 7. Appendix A explains the computation of a probability associated with our attacks on WG-A and WG-B.

2   Specifications of the Ciphers

Table 2 lists the notation and convention that we follow.

2.1   WG-A

The ultra-lightweight cipher WG-A uses an 80-bit key K and an 80-bit initialization vector IV. The internal state of WG-A consists of a 20-stage LFSR (the stages of which are denoted by $s_A[\cdot]$) defined over the finite field $\mathbb{F}_{2^8}$. The cipher uses an 8-bit nonlinear WG transformation $W_A : \mathbb{F}_{2^8} \to \mathbb{F}_2$. The 256 elements of the finite field $\mathbb{F}_{2^8}$ are generated by the primitive polynomial $R_A(x) = x^8 + x^4 + x^3 + x^2 + 1$ over $\mathbb{F}_2$. Let ω be a root of the primitive polynomial. Any element of $\mathbb{F}_{2^8}$ can be represented as an 8-bit binary vector

---

[2] To facilitate comparisons, we reasonably assume that the success rates of the attacks on WG-16 and WG-B are equal.

Table 2. Notation and convention

Symbol/notation	Meaning
$\mathbb{F}_{2^n}$	Finite field of order 2^n
$s[i+k]$	$(k+1)$th LFSR stage at time i
$x_{(j)}$	jth bit of x where $j=0$ denotes the least significant bit
$\boxplus_8$	Addition in $\mathbb{F}_{2^8}$
$\boxdot_8$	Multiplication in $\mathbb{F}_{2^8}$
$x^n, x \in \mathbb{F}_{2^8}$	$\underbrace{x \boxdot_8 x \boxdot_8 x \boxdot_8 \cdots \boxdot_8 x}_{n}$
$\boxplus_{16}$	Addition in $\mathbb{F}_{2^{16}}$
$\boxdot_{16}$	Multiplication in $\mathbb{F}_{2^{16}}$
$x^n, x \in \mathbb{F}_{2^{16}}$	$\underbrace{x \boxdot_{16} x \boxdot_{16} x \boxdot_{16} \cdots \boxdot_{16} x}_{n}$
$\oplus$	Exclusive OR

$(a_7 a_6 \ldots a_0)$ corresponding to $a_7\omega^7 + a_6\omega^6 + \cdots + a_0$. The feedback polynomial of the LFSR is given by $l_A(x) = x^{20} + x^{11} + x^9 + \omega^{38}$, where ω^{38} corresponds to the binary vector (10010100). The WG transformation, whose input is the 20th LFSR stage, is comprised of a permutation P_A and a trace function T_A. The permutation takes an 8-bit input x and outputs $q_A(x \boxplus_8 1) \boxplus_8 1$, where $q_A(x) = x \boxplus_8 x^9 \boxplus_8 x^{57} \boxplus_8 x^{73} \boxplus_8 x^{71}$. Likewise, the trace function takes an 8-bit input x and outputs $x \boxplus_8 x^2 \boxplus_8 x^{2^2} \boxplus_8 \cdots \boxplus_8 x^{2^7}$. The trace function acts on $P_A(x)$ to yield $W_A(x)$ as $T_A(P_A(x))$. For better security of the cipher, the designers propose to have x^d (see Table 2) instead of x, where d is the decimation factor, as the input to the WG transformation [7]. Although the value of d is not mentioned in the patent document, Mandal et al. identify three values (13, 19 and 61) as "optimal" choices [11]. These values, they argue, impart the best cryptographic properties such as maximum algebraic degree, maximum algebraic immunity, largest possible nonlinearity and smallest possible additive correlation to the output of W_A. Denote by WG-A_d the cipher corresponding to d. Then, WG-A_d operates in two phases: initialization and keystream generation.

Initialization: The LFSR is initially loaded with K and IV and updated for 40 clock cycles.

Algorithm 1. Initialization of WG-A_d

```
1: for i = 1 to 10 do
2:   s_A[2i] = (IV_(8i+3), IV_(8i+2), IV_(8i+1), IV_(8i), K_(8i+3), K_(8i+2), K_(8i+1), K_(8i));
3:   s_A[2i+1] = (IV_(8i+7), IV_(8i+6), IV_(8i+5), IV_(8i+4), K_(8i+7), K_(8i+6), K_(8i+5), K_(8i+4));
4: endfor
5: for i = 1 to 40 do
6:   s_A[i+20] = s_A[i+11] ⊕ s_A[i+9] ⊕ (s_A[i] ⊡_8 ω^38) ⊕ P_A((s_A[i+19])^d);
7: endfor
```

Algorithm 2. Keystream generator of WG-A$_d$

1: $i = 0$;
2: **do** until enough keystream is generated
3:    $z_{A(i)} = W_A((s_A[i + 19])^d)$;
4:    $s_A[i + 20] = s_A[i + 11] \oplus s_A[i + 9] \oplus (s_A[i] \boxdot_8 \omega^{38})$;
5:    $i \leftarrow i + 1$;

Keystream generation: During the $(i+1)$th cycle of keystream generation, one keystream bit $z_{A(i)}$ is generated. The keystream generation process of WG-A$_d$ is shown in Fig. 1.

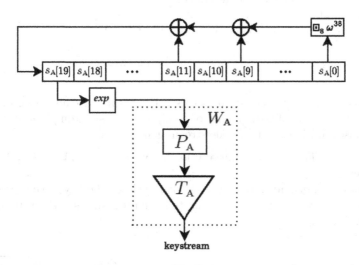

Fig. 1. Keystream generation of WG-A$_d$; *exp* computes $(s_A[19])^d$

2.2   WG-B

The structure of the lightweight cipher WG-B is very similar to that of WG-A. Here, the key K and the initialization vector IV are of length 128 bits each. The LFSR has 32 stages (which are denoted by $s_B[\cdot]$) and is defined over the finite field $\mathbb{F}_{2^{16}}$. The elements of $\mathbb{F}_{2^{16}}$ are generated by β, a primitive root of the polynomial $R_B(x) = x^{16} + x^5 + x^3 + x^2 + 1$ over $\mathbb{F}_2$. The feedback polynomial is given by $l_B(x) = x^{32} + x^{13} + x^3 + \beta^2 + 1$. The permutation is of 16-bit values and is given by $P_B(x) = q_B(x \boxplus_{16} 1) \boxplus_{16} 1$, where $q_B(x) = x \boxplus_{16} x^{2049} \boxplus_{16} x^{2111} \boxplus_{16} x^{2113} \boxplus_{16} x^{63552}$. The trace function and the nonlinear filter function are from $\mathbb{F}_{2^{16}}$ to $\mathbb{F}_2$ and are given by:

$$T_B(x) = x \boxplus_{16} x^2 \boxplus_{16} x^{2^2} \boxplus_{16} \cdots \boxplus_{16} x^{2^{15}},$$
$$W_B(x) = T_B(P_B(x)).$$

Algorithm 3. Initialization of WG-B$_d$

1: **for** $i = 1$ to 16 **do**
2:   $s_\mathrm{B}[i] = (IV_{(8i+7)}, IV_{(8i+6)}, \ldots, IV_{(8i)}, K_{(8i+7)}, K_{(8i+6)}, \ldots, K_{(8i)})$;
3:   $s_\mathrm{B}[i + 16] = s_\mathrm{B}[i]$;
4: **endfor**
5: **for** $i = 1$ to 64 **do**
6:   $s_\mathrm{B}[i + 32] = s_\mathrm{B}[i + 13] \oplus s_\mathrm{B}[i + 3] \oplus (s_\mathrm{B}[i] \boxdot_{16} (\beta^2 + 1)) \oplus P_\mathrm{B}((s_\mathrm{B}[i + 31])^d)$;
7: **endfor**

Algorithm 4. Keystream generator of WG-B$_d$

1: $i = 0$;
2: **do** until enough keystream is generated
3:   $z_{\mathrm{B}(i)} = W_\mathrm{B}((s_\mathrm{B}[i + 31])^d)$;
4:   $s_\mathrm{B}[i + 32] = s_\mathrm{B}[i + 13] \oplus s_\mathrm{B}[i + 3] \oplus (s_\mathrm{B}[i] \boxdot_{16} (\beta^2 + 1))$;
5:   $i \leftarrow i + 1$;

As for WG-A, optimal decimation factors (31 in total) have also been identified for WG-B in [11] and WG-B$_d$ refers to the cipher corresponding to d. It operates in two phases: initialization and keystream generation.

Initialization: The LFSR is initially loaded with K and IV and updated for 64 clock cycles.

Keystream generation: During $(i + 1)$th cycle of the keystream generation phase, one keystream bit $z_{\mathrm{B}(i)}$ is generated. Figure 2 shows the keystream generation of WG-B$_d$.

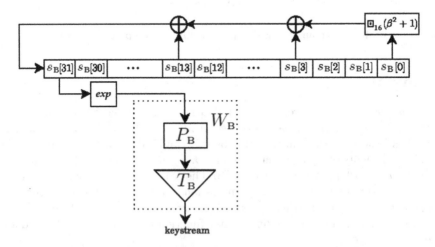

Fig. 2. Keystream generation of WG-B$_d$; *exp* computes $(s_\mathrm{B}[19])^d$

3   Motivational Observation

The sizes of the inputs to W_A and W_B render an exhaustive search over the input space feasible. Performing the search, we detect d independent input-output correlations in the WG transformations. The bitwise correlation probabilities for $W_A(x^{61})$ and $W_B(x^{157})$ are listed in Tables 3(a) and 4(a), respectively. Similarly, the probabilities that $W_A(x^{61}) = (x \boxdot_8 \omega^{38})_{(i)}$ and $W_B(x^{157}) = (x \boxdot_{16} (\beta^2 + 1))_{(i)}$, for several values of i, are listed in Tables 3(b) and 4(b), respectively. All the results presented in this paper are based on the polynomial basis representation of the field elements.

Tables 3(a), 3(b), 4(a) and 4(b) suggest that the WG transformations can be linearly approximated—using this, we state and prove Theorems 1 and 2.

Theorem 1. *If the conditions*

$$W_A(x^d) = x_{(i)}, \tag{1}$$
$$W_A(x^d) = (x \boxdot_8 \omega^{38})_{(i)}, \tag{2}$$

are satisfied for any $i \in \{0, 1, \ldots, 7\}$*, then the keystream of WG-A_d satisfies* $z_{A(t+1)} \oplus z_{A(t-8)} \oplus z_{A(t-10)} \oplus z_{A(t-19)} = 0$ *for* $t \geq 19$.

Proof. The recurrence relation of the constituent LFSR of WG-A_d can be deduced from its feedback polynomial as:

$$s_A[t + 20] = s_A[t + 11] \oplus s_A[t + 9] \oplus (s_A[t] \boxdot_8 \omega^{38}), \text{ for } t \geq 0. \tag{3}$$

From (3), we get:

$$s_A[t + 20]_{(i)} = s_A[t + 11]_{(i)} \oplus s_A[t + 9]_{(i)} \oplus (s_A[t] \boxdot_8 \omega^{38})_{(i)}, \tag{4}$$

Table 3. WG: Probabilities that (a) $W_A(x^{61}) = x_{(i)}$ and (b) $W_A(x^{61}) = (x \boxdot_8 \omega^{38})_{(i)}$, for several values of i

	(a)		(b)
i	$\Pr\left(W_A(x^{61}) = x_{(i)}\right)$	i	$\Pr\left(W_A(x^{61}) = (x \boxdot_8 \omega^{38})_{(i)}\right)$
0	$0.5 + 2^{-4.68}$	0	$0.5 - 2^{-5.00}$
1	$0.5 + 2^{-6.00}$	1	$0.5 + 2^{-4.00}$
2	$0.5 + 2^{-5.00}$	2	$0.5 - 2^{-7.00}$
3	$0.5 - 2^{-6.00}$	3	$0.5 + 2^{-4.00}$
4	$0.5 - 2^{-5.00}$	4	$0.5 + 2^{-7.00}$
5	$0.5 - 2^{-4.00}$	5	$0.5 - 2^{-6.00}$
6	$0.5 + 2^{-6.00}$	6	$0.5 + 2^{-6.00}$
7	$0.5 + 2^{-6.00}$	7	$0.5 - 2^{-3.83}$

Table 4. WG: Probabilities that (a) $W_B(x^{157}) = x_{(i)}$ and (b) $W_B(x^{157}) = (x \boxdot_{16} (\beta^2 + 1))_{(i)}$, for several values of i

	(a)			(b)
i	$\Pr\left(W_B(x^{157}) = x_{(i)}\right)$		i	$\Pr\left(W_B(x^{157}) = (x \boxdot_{16} (\beta^2 + 1))_{(i)}\right)$
0	$0.5 + 2^{-9.79}$		0	$0.5 - 2^{-10.8}$
1	$0.5 + 2^{-12.4}$		1	$0.5 + 2^{-10.1}$
2	$0.5 + 2^{-10.8}$		2	$0.5 - 2^{-9.17}$
3	$0.5 + 2^{-8.96}$		3	$0.5 - 2^{-9.48}$
4	$0.5 + 2^{-10.2}$		4	$0.5 - 2^{-9.48}$
5	$0.5 - 2^{-13.0}$		5	$0.5 + 2^{-13.0}$
6	$0.5 + 2^{-14.0}$		6	$0.5 + 2^{-8.51}$
7	$0.5 + 2^{-10.4}$		7	$0.5 - 2^{-13.0}$
8	$0.5 - 2^{-9.75}$		8	$0.5 - 2^{-7.91}$
10	$0.5 - 2^{-9.48}$		10	$0.5 - 2^{-13.0}$
11	$0.5 + 2^{-9.19}$		11	$0.5 + 2^{-13.0}$
12	$0.5 + 2^{-11.7}$		12	$0.5 + 2^{-13.0}$
13	$0.5 - 2^{-9.00}$		13	$0.5 - 2^{-9.42}$
14	$0.5 - 2^{-11.0}$		14	$0.5 + 2^{-10.1}$
15	$0.5 + 2^{-10.5}$		15	$0.5 + 2^{-10.1}$

for any $i \in \{0, 1, \ldots, 7\}$, $t \geq 19$. Substituting (1) and (2) in (4) yields:

$$W_A((s_A[t + 20])^d) = W_A((s_A[t + 11])^d) \oplus W_A((s_A[t + 9])^d) \oplus W_A((s_A[t])^d), \quad (5)$$

for $t \geq 19$. Since $z_{A(t)} = W_A((s_A[t + 19])^d)$, (5) reduces to:

$$z_{A(t+1)} \oplus z_{A(t-8)} \oplus z_{A(t-10)} \oplus z_{A(t-19)} = 0, \text{ for } t \geq 19.$$

The proof completes. $\qquad\qquad\square$

Theorem 2. *If the conditions*

$$W_B(x^d) = x_{(i)}, \quad (6)$$
$$W_B(x^d) = (x \boxdot_{16} (\beta^2 + 1))_{(i)}, \quad (7)$$

are satisfied for any $i \in \{0, 1, \ldots, 15\}$, *then the keystream of WG-B_d satisfies* $z_{B(t+1)} \oplus z_{B(t-18)} \oplus z_{B(t-28)} \oplus z_{B(t-31)} = 0$ *for* $t \geq 31$.

Proof. The LFSR of WG-B_d is given by the following recursion:

$$s_B[t + 32] = s_B[t + 13] \oplus s_B[t + 3] \oplus (s_B[t] \boxdot_{16} (\beta^2 + 1)), \text{ for } t \geq 0. \quad (8)$$

For the ith bit, (8) becomes:

$$s_B[t + 32]_{(i)} = s_B[t + 13]_{(i)} \oplus s_B[t + 3]_{(i)} \oplus (s_B[t] \boxdot_{16} (\beta^2 + 1))_{(i)}, \quad (9)$$

for any $i \in \{0, 1, \ldots, 15\}, t \geq 31$. Substituting (6) and (7) in (9), we get:

$$W_{\mathrm{B}}((s_{\mathrm{B}}[t+32])^d) = W_{\mathrm{B}}((s_{\mathrm{B}}[t+13])^d) \oplus W_{\mathrm{B}}((s_{\mathrm{B}}[t+3])^d) \oplus W_{\mathrm{B}}((s_{\mathrm{B}}[t])^d), \text{ for } t \geq 31. \tag{10}$$

Since $z_{\mathrm{B}(t)} = W_{\mathrm{B}}((s_{\mathrm{B}}[t+31])^d)$, (10) reduces to:

$$z_{\mathrm{B}(t+1)} \oplus z_{\mathrm{B}(t-18)} \oplus z_{\mathrm{B}(t-28)} \oplus z_{\mathrm{B}(t-31)} = 0, \text{ for } t \geq 31.$$

This completes the proof. $\qquad\qquad\qquad\qquad\qquad\qquad\qquad\qquad\qquad\qquad\square$

4 Bias Estimation

Using the results of Sect. 3, we proceed to compute $\Pr(\hat{z}_{\mathrm{A}} = 0)$ and $\Pr(\hat{z}_{\mathrm{B}} = 0)$, where

$$\hat{z}_{\mathrm{A}} = z_{\mathrm{A}(t+1)} \oplus z_{\mathrm{A}(t-8)} \oplus z_{\mathrm{A}(t-10)} \oplus z_{\mathrm{A}(t-19)}, \, t \geq 19,$$
$$\hat{z}_{\mathrm{B}} = z_{\mathrm{B}(t+1)} \oplus z_{\mathrm{B}(t-18)} \oplus z_{\mathrm{B}(t-28)} \oplus z_{\mathrm{B}(t-31)}, \, t \geq 31.$$

4.1 Biases in the Keystream of WG-A$_{61}$

If $\Pr\left(W_{\mathrm{A}}(x^d) = x_{(i)}\right) = p_i$ and $\Pr\left(W_{\mathrm{A}}(x^d) = (x \boxdot_8 \omega^{38})_{(i)}\right) = q_i$ then:

$$\Pr(\hat{z}_{\mathrm{A}} = 0) = p_i^3 q_i + 3(1-p_i)^2 p_i q_i + 3p_i^2(1-p_i)(1-q_i) + (1-p_i)^3(1-q_i). \tag{11}$$

Equation (11) follows from a simple application of the Matsui's Piling-up Lemma [12]. Nevertheless, to make it convenient for the reader, we detail the derivation in Appendix A. The value of $\Pr(\hat{z}_{\mathrm{A}} = 0)$ varies with i and the probability for which $|\Pr(\hat{z}_{\mathrm{A}} = 0) - 0.5|$ is maximised is considered as its best estimation. The values of p_i and q_i for $d = 61$ are listed in Tables 3(a) and 3(b), respectively. Among the available choices of i, the following linear approximations, corresponding to $i = 5$, maximise the bias.

$$W_{\mathrm{A}}(x^{61}) \approx x_{(5)},$$
$$W_{\mathrm{A}}(x^{61}) \approx (x \boxdot_8 \omega^{38})_{(5)}.$$

Since $\Pr\left(W_{\mathrm{A}}(x^{61}) = x_{(5)}\right) = 0.5 - 2^{-4}$ and $\Pr\left(W_{\mathrm{A}}(x^{61}) = (x \boxdot_8 \omega^{38})_{(5)}\right) = 0.5 - 2^{-6}$, the best estimation of the probability that $\hat{z}_{\mathrm{A}}$ equals zero is $0.5 + 2^{-15}$.

4.2 Biases in the Keystream of WG-B$_{157}$

If $\Pr\left(W_{\mathrm{B}}(x^d) = x_{(i)}\right) = p_i$ and $\Pr\left(W_{\mathrm{B}}(x^d) = (x \boxdot_{16} (\beta^2 + 1))_{(i)}\right) = q_i$ then $\Pr(\hat{z}_{\mathrm{B}} = 0)$ is again given by the RHS of (11). The values of p_i and q_i for $d = 157$ are listed in Tables 4(a) and 4(b), respectively. If the keystream bits are generated by WG-B$_{157}$, the probability that $\hat{z}_{\mathrm{B}}$ equals zero is estimated to be $0.5 - 2^{-33.36}$ based on the following linear approximations:

$$W_{\mathrm{B}}(x^{157}) \approx x_{(3)},$$
$$W_{\mathrm{B}}(x^{157}) \approx (x \boxdot_{16} (\beta^2 + 1))_{(3)}.$$

4.3　Improvements to the Bias Estimations

The probabilities $\Pr(\hat{z}_A = 0)$ and $\Pr(\hat{z}_B = 0)$ of Sects. 4.1 and 4.2 were calculated, in each case, with one of the input bits of the WG transformations. Since multiple input bits of W_A and W_B are correlated to the corresponding output bits, we explore the possibility to obtain a better estimation of the probabilities by combining input bits. The probabilities $\Pr\left(W_A(x^{61}) = \bigoplus_{i \in S} x_{(i)}\right)$ and $\Pr\left(W_A(x^{61}) = \bigoplus_{i \in S} (x \boxdot_8 \omega^{38})_{(i)}\right)$, where $S \subseteq \{0, 1, \ldots, 7\}$ for WG-A$_{61}$ and equivalently for WG-B$_{157}$, were experimentally calculated with arbitrary choices of S. The correlation probabilities which further improved the estimated keystream biases of WG-A$_{61}$ and WG-B$_{157}$ are given below.

$$\Pr(W_A(x^{61}) = \bigoplus_{i \in S_1} x_{(i)}) = 0.5 - 2^{-3.83}, \tag{12}$$

$$\Pr(W_A(x^{61}) = \bigoplus_{i \in S_1} (x \boxdot_8 \omega^{38})_{(i)}) = 0.5 + 2^{-4}, \tag{13}$$

$$\Pr(W_B(x^{157}) = \bigoplus_{i \in S_2} x_{(i)}) = 0.5 + 2^{-6.83}, \tag{14}$$

$$\Pr(W_B(x^{157}) = \bigoplus_{i \in S_2} (x \boxdot_{16} (\beta^2 + 1))_{(i)}) = 0.5 - 2^{-8}, \tag{15}$$

where $S_1 = \{0, 3, 5, 6\}$ and $S_2 = \{1, 3, 5, 6, 8, 9, 14, 15\}$. Assigning the probabilities of (12) and (13) respectively for p_i and q_i, (11) yields $\Pr(\hat{z}_A = 0) = 0.5 - 2^{-12.49}$ for WG-A$_{61}$. Similarly, the assignments $p_i = 0.5 + 2^{-6.83}$ and $q_i = 0.5 - 2^{-8}$ yield $\Pr(\hat{z}_B = 0) = 0.5 - 2^{-25.49}$ for WG-B$_{157}$. The WG-A and WG-B families are restricted to ciphers corresponding to the optimal d; the values of $\Pr(\hat{z}_A = 0)$ and $\Pr(\hat{z}_B = 0)$ for all these ciphers are listed in Tables 5(a) and 5(b), respectively.

Table 5. Probabilities that (a) $\hat{z}_A = 0$ and (b) $\hat{z}_B = 0$, for each of the WG-A$_d$ and WG-B$_d$ ciphers

(b) WG-B$_d$

d	$\Pr(\hat{z}_B = 0)$	d	$\Pr(\hat{z}_B = 0)$	d	$\Pr(\hat{z}_B = 0)$
157	$0.5 - 2^{-25.49}$	2137	$0.5 - 2^{-24.01}$	5213	$0.5 + 2^{-26.23}$
409	$0.5 - 2^{-25.74}$	2251	$0.5 + 2^{-24.90}$	6043	$0.5 + 2^{-26.03}$
451	$0.5 - 2^{-25.21}$	2473	$0.5 - 2^{-26.09}$	7673	$0.5 - 2^{-25.04}$
469	$0.5 + 2^{-26.52}$	2741	$0.5 - 2^{-25.07}$	7771	$0.5 - 2^{-26.19}$
1057	$0.5 + 2^{-25.36}$	3223	$0.5 - 2^{-25.86}$	10651	$0.5 - 2^{-26.32}$
1187	$0.5 - 2^{-26.20}$	3419	$0.5 - 2^{-26.48}$	10667	$0.5 - 2^{-25.38}$
1327	$0.5 - 2^{-26.43}$	3449	$0.5 - 2^{-25.62}$	13631	$0.5 - 2^{-25.99}$
1393	$0.5 + 2^{-25.55}$	3581	$0.5 - 2^{-25.59}$	14327	$0.5 - 2^{-25.66}$
1397	$0.5 - 2^{-25.29}$	4411	$0.5 - 2^{-26.19}$	32767	$0.5 + 2^{-26.57}$
1771	$0.5 + 2^{-25.51}$	4681	$0.5 + 2^{-26.17}$		
1933	$0.5 + 2^{-25.38}$	4789	$0.5 - 2^{-26.56}$		

(a) WG-A$_d$

d	$\Pr(\hat{z}_A = 0)$
13	$0.5 - 2^{-9.25}$
19	$0.5 + 2^{-12.68}$
61	$0.5 - 2^{-12.49}$

5 Attack Complexities

In this section, we compute the complexities of our distinguishing attacks on WG-A and WG-B using the results of Sect. 4. Let n denote the number of $\hat{z}_A$'s available to the attacker, D' denote the distribution of $Z := \sum_n \hat{z}_A$, $p' = \Pr(\hat{z}_A = 0)$, D denote the distribution of Z given that WG-A$_{61}$ is an ideal cipher and $p = 0.5$. If the $\hat{z}_A$'s are independent and identically distributed random variables (i.i.d.), then Z has a binomial distribution. The means (μ', μ) and standard deviations (σ', σ) of the distributions D', D are given by: $\mu' = np'$, $\mu = np$, $\sigma' = \sqrt{np'(1-p')}$ and $\sigma = \sqrt{np(1-p)}$.

If n is large (a commonly used rule of thumb is that $np > 5$ and $n(1-p) > 5$), one can approximate each binomial distribution with the normal distribution with the same mean and standard deviation. Given this, if $|\mu' - \mu| > 3.62(\sigma' + \sigma) \Rightarrow n > 13.1/(p' - 0.5)^2 = 2^{28.69}$, the cipher WG-A$_{61}$ can be distinguished from an ideal cipher with 99.99% success rate (since the cumulative distribution function gives the value 0.9999 at $\mu + 3.62\sigma$) and 0.01% false positive rate. Similarly, $2^{54.69}$ keystream samples ($\hat{z}_B$) are required to distinguish WG-B$_{157}$ from an ideal cipher, with a success probability of 0.9999. In order to generate the keystream samples $\hat{z}_A$ and $\hat{z}_B$, in the worst case, the attacker collects 21 keystream bits and 33 keystream bits, respectively per (K, IV) pair (but actually 4 bits will suffice). The data complexities of our distinguishing attacks on the other members of the WG-A and WG-B families are respectively listed in Tables 6(a) and 6(b)—in each case, the success rate is 99.99%.

Table 6. Data requirements of our attacks (corresponding to 0.9999 success probability) on the WG-A$_d$ and WG-B$_d$ ciphers

(b) WG-B$_d$

(a) WG-A$_d$

d	$\log_2(\# samples)$		d	$\log_2(\# samples)$		d	$\log_2(\# samples)$
157	54.69		2137	51.74		5213	56.16
409	55.19		2251	53.51		6043	55.78
451	54.13		2473	55.90		7673	53.78
469	56.76		2741	53.85		7771	56.09
1057	54.43		3223	55.43		10651	56.35
1187	56.11		3419	56.66		10667	54.47
1327	56.57		3449	54.95		13631	55.70
1393	54.80		3581	54.89		14327	55.03
1397	54.30		4411	56.09		32767	56.84
1771	54.73		4681	56.06			
1933	54.47		4789	56.82			

d	$\log_2(\# samples)$
13	22.20
19	29.07
61	28.69

5.1 Experimental Verification

From Table 6(a), it is clear that the distinguishing attacks on WG-A are of practical complexities. In order to verify our analysis, we simulated the attacks on WG-A$_{13}$, WG-A$_{19}$ and WG-A$_{61}$. In each case, the keystream bits, as per the data requirement given in Table 6(a), were generated from 2^{20} (K, IV) pairs chosen uniformly at random with each pair generating 10^3 keystream bits and the required probability was computed.[3] This process was repeated 10^4 times. The mean probabilities for WG-A$_{13}$, WG-A$_{19}$ and WG-A$_{61}$ were found to be $0.5 - 2^{-9.40}$, $0.5 + 2^{-15.10}$ and $0.5 - 2^{-12.51}$, respectively. The theoretical and experimental results for WG-A$_{13}$ and WG-A$_{61}$ agree very well; the reason why the agreement is not as pronounced in the case of WG-A$_{19}$ is being currently investigated.

6   Discussion

In [14], Orumiehchiha et al. report a linear distinguishing attack, that is similar to our attacks, on WG-7. Our investigations, in fact, show that every member of the WG family, with the sole exception of the WG-29, is vulnerable to such linear attacks. The low correlation immunity and the low resilience of the WG transformations allow us to identify linear approximations of the kind provided in Sect. 4.3.

For WG-29, the input size of the WG transformation is too large to perform an exhaustive search over the input space using a general purpose computer. Nawaz et al. report that it is 1-order resilient and can be approximated by linear functions [13]. Therefore, the possibility of the existence of a set, similar to the set S of Sect. 4.3, that renders WG-29 vulnerable to linear distinguishing attacks cannot be eliminated.

7   Conclusions

In this paper, we have showed distinguishing attacks on the stream ciphers WG-A and WG-B. To nearly guarantee success, the attacks require between $2^{22.20}$ and $2^{29.07}$ keystream samples for WG-A, and fewer than $2^{56.84}$ keystream samples for WG-B. Let $T_{A,ini}$ and $T_{A,kga}$ respectively denote the run-times of the initialization algorithm and keystream generation algorithm of WG-A. Then, assuming that one sample is collected per (K, IV) pair, our attacks on the WG-A ciphers each requires at the most $2^{29.07}(T_{A,ini} + 21 \cdot T_{A,kga})$ time.[4] Likewise, our attacks on the WG-B ciphers each requires at the most $2^{56.84}(T_{B,ini} + 33 \cdot T_{B,kga})$ time, where $T_{B,ini}$ and $T_{B,kga}$ are the respective run-times of the initialization algorithm and keystream generation algorithm of WG-B. For a success rate of

---

[3] In this paper, to compute the time complexity of our distinguishing attacks we assume that the attacker collects one keystream sample per (K, IV) pair. It is reasonable to expect the results of our simulations to agree with simulations performed with 2^{30} (K, IV) pairs chosen uniformly at random and one keystream sample per (K, IV) pair.

[4] An inherent assumption is that the decimation factor has no bearing on the run-time of the cipher.

60%, the attacks on WG-A and WG-B respectively require not more than $2^{21.47}$ and $2^{49.24}$ keystream samples, and equivalent time. To the best of our knowledge, these are the first attacks on the WG-A as well as the WG-B.

The low nonlinearity and the low correlation immunity of the WG transformations appear to be the main causes of these attacks. As pointed out in [6] and [8], increasing the number of tap positions of the LFSRs used in the WG ciphers may increase the complexity of the distinguishing attacks. For instance, if there are 9 tap positions instead of 3 in the LFSR of WG-A$_{61}$, our attack will require $2^{62.65}$ keystream samples for a success rate of 99.99%. Nevertheless, to preclude these attacks, we recommend using filter functions having good correlation immunity.

Acknowledgements. The authors would like to thank the anonymous reviewers of LightSec 2016 for their comments and suggestions.

A   Derivation of the Probability $\Pr(\hat{z}_A = 0)$

Let us define the Boolean variables Y_1, Y_2, Y_3, Y_4 and Y_5 as follows:

$$Y_1 = W_A((s_A[t+20])^d) \oplus s_A[t+20]_{(i)}\,,$$
$$Y_2 = W_A((s_A[t+11])^d) \oplus s_A[t+11]_{(i)}\,,$$
$$Y_3 = W_A((s_A[t+9])^d) \oplus s_A[t+9]_{(i)}\,,$$
$$Y_4 = W_A((s_A[t])^d) \oplus (s_A[t] \boxdot_8 \omega^{38})_{(i)}\,,$$
$$Y_5 = z_{A(t+1)} \oplus z_{A(t-8)} \oplus z_{A(t-10)} \oplus z_{A(t-19)}\,,$$

for any $i \in \{0,1,\ldots,7\}$, $t \geq 19$. From Theorem 1, we construct the Boolean truth table given in Table 7.

From Sect. 4.1, we get:

$$\Pr(Y_1 = 0) = p_i\,, \tag{16}$$
$$\Pr(Y_2 = 0) = p_i\,, \tag{17}$$
$$\Pr(Y_3 = 0) = p_i\,, \tag{18}$$
$$\Pr(Y_4 = 0) = q_i\,, \tag{19}$$
$$\Pr(Y_5 = 0) = \Pr(\hat{z}_A = 0)\,. \tag{20}$$

We assume that the events corresponding to Y_1, Y_2, Y_3 and Y_4 are independent and the events corresponding to the rows of the truth table given in Table 7 are mutually exclusive. Then, the truth table given in Table 7 and (16)–(20) yield:

$$\Pr(\hat{z}_A = 0) = p_i^3 q_i + 3(1-p_i)^2 p_i q_i + 3p_i^2(1-p_i)(1-q_i) + (1-p_i)^3(1-q_i)\,. \qquad \square$$

Table 7. Truth table that satisfies the relation between the Boolean variables Y_1, Y_2, Y_3, Y_4 and Y_5

Y_1	Y_2	Y_3	Y_4	Y_5
0	0	0	0	0
0	0	0	1	1
0	0	1	0	1
0	0	1	1	0
0	1	0	0	1
0	1	0	1	0
0	1	1	0	0
0	1	1	1	1
1	0	0	0	1
1	0	0	1	0
1	0	1	0	0
1	0	1	1	1
1	1	0	0	0
1	1	0	1	1
1	1	1	0	1
1	1	1	1	0

References

1. Aagaard, M., Gong, G., Mota, R.K.: Hardware implementations of the WG-5 cipher for passive RFID tags. In: IEEE International Symposium on Hardware-Oriented Security and Trust, Proceedings of HOST 2013, pp. 29–34 (2013). doi:10.1109/HST.2013.6581561
2. Ding, L., Jin, C., Guan, J., Wang, Q.: Cryptanalysis of lightweight WG-8 stream cipher. IEEE Trans. Inf. Foren. Secur. **9**(4), 645–652 (2014). doi:10.1109/TIFS.2014.2307202
3. Ding, L., Jin, C., Guan, J., Zhang, S., Cui, T., Han, D., Zhao, W.: Cryptanalysis of WG family of stream ciphers. Comput. J. **58**(10), 2677–2685 (2015). doi:10.1093/comjnl/bxv024
4. ECRYPT: The eSTREAM project. http://www.ecrypt.eu.org/stream
5. Fan, X., Gong, G.: Specification of the stream cipher WG-16 based confidentiality and integrity algorithms. University of Waterloo Technical report, CACR 2013–06 (2013). http://cacr.uwaterloo.ca/techreports/2013/cacr2013-06.pdf
6. Fan, X., Mandal, K., Gong, G.: WG-8: a lightweight stream cipher for resource-constrained smart devices. In: Singh, K., Awasthi, A.K. (eds.) QShine 2013. LNICSSITE, vol. 115, pp. 617–632. Springer, Heidelberg (2013). doi:10.1007/978-3-642-37949-9_54
7. Gong, G., Aagaard, M., Fan, X.: Lightweight stream cipher cryptosystems. US Patent 8,953,784 (2015). https://www.google.com/patents/US8953784

8. Gong, G., Aagaard, M., Fan, X.: Resilience to distinguishing attacks on WG-7 cipher and their generalizations. Cryptogr. Commun. **5**(4), 277–289 (2013). doi:10. 1007/s12095-013-0089-7

9. Gong, G., Youssef, A.M.: Cryptographic properties of the Welch-Gong transformation sequence generators. IEEE Trans. Inf. Theory **48**(11), 2837–2846 (2002). doi:10.1109/TIT.2002.804043

10. Luo, Y., Chai, Q., Gong, G., Lai, X.: A lightweight stream cipher WG-7 for RFID encryption and authentication. In: IEEE Global Telecommunications Conference, Proceedings of GLOBECOM 2010, pp. 1–6 (2010). doi:10.1109/GLOCOM.2010. 5684215

11. Mandal, K., Gong, G., Fan, X., Aagaard, M.: Optimal parameters for the WG stream cipher family. Cryptogr. Commun. **6**(2), 117–135 (2013). doi:10.1007/ s12095-013-0091-0

12. Matsui, M.: Linear cryptanalysis method for DES cipher. In: Helleseth, T. (ed.) EUROCRYPT 1993. LNCS, vol. 765, pp. 386–397. Springer, Heidelberg (1994). doi:10.1007/3-540-48285-7_33

13. Nawaz, Y., Gong, G.: WG: a family of stream ciphers with designed randomness properties. Inf. Sci. **178**(7), 1903–1916 (2008). doi:10.1016/j.ins.2007.12.002

14. Orumiehchiha, M.A., Pieprzyk, J., Steinfeld, R.: Cryptanalysis of WG-7: a lightweight stream cipher. Cryptogr. Commun. **4**(3), 277–285 (2012). doi:10.1007/ s12095-012-0070-x

15. Rønjom, S.: Powers of subfield polynomials, cyclic codes and algebraic attacks with applications to the WG stream ciphers. In: International Workshop on Coding and Cryptography, WCC 2015 (2015). https://hal.inria.fr/hal-01276274

16. Rønjom, S., Helleseth, T.: Attacking the filter generator over $GF(2^m)$. In: Carlet, C., Sunar, B. (eds.) WAIFI 2007. LNCS, vol. 4547, pp. 264–275. Springer, Heidelberg (2007). doi:10.1007/978-3-540-73074-3_20

17. Seon, N.J., Golomb, S.W., Gong, G., Lee, H.K., Gaal, P.: Binary pseudorandom sequences of period $2^n - 1$ with ideal autocorrelation. IEEE Trans. Inf. Theory **44**(2), 814–817 (1998). doi:10.1109/18.661528

18. Waterloo Commericalization Office: Lightweight Security Algorithm for 4G Networks. https://uwaterloo.ca/research/waterloo-commercialization-office-watco/ business-opportunities-industry/lightweight-security-algorithm-4g-networks

19. TechConnect World, Innovation Conference, Expo: A Secure RFID System for Product Anti-Counterfeiting. http://www.techconnectworld.com/World2015/ participate/innovation/pop.html?id=205

20. Wu, H., Preneel, B.: Resynchronization attacks on WG and LEX. In: Robshaw, M. (ed.) FSE 2006. LNCS, vol. 4047, pp. 422–432. Springer, Heidelberg (2006). doi:10.1007/11799313_27

Cryptanalysis of QTL Block Cipher

Mustafa Çoban[1,2], Ferhat Karakoç[2(✉)], and Mehmet Özen[1]

[1] Department of Mathematics, Faculty of Arts and Sciences,
Sakarya University, Adapazarı, Sakarya, Turkey
`ozen@sakarya.edu.tr`
[2] TÜBİTAK - BİLGEM - UEKAE, PK 74, 41470 Gebze, Kocaeli, Turkey
`{mustafa.coban,ferhat.karakoc}@tubitak.gov.tr`

Abstract. QTL is an ultra-lightweight block cipher designed for extremely constrained devices. The cipher has two versions, QLT-64 and QTL-128 supporting key lengths of 64 and 128 bits, respectively. In this paper, we present the first third party cryptanalysis of QTL. We first introduce related key distinguishers for full versions of the cipher. We propose attacks on full QTL in single key model by using the related key distinguishers. With these attacks we are able to reduce the security of QTL-64 and QTL-128 by 16 bits. We also enumerate 2^{48} weak keys and propose a practical key recovery attack on full QTL-64 for these keys. This attack requires 2^{16} data and recovers the key in a time complexity of 2^{32} encryptions. We also give some observations disprove designers' claims about number of active S-boxes and actual value of differential branch number.

Keywords: Cryptography · Lightweight block cipher · Related-key attacks · Self-similarity cryptanalysis · QTL cipher

1 Introduction

Lightweight cryptography is a hot topic in the crypto community because of the industrial needs. A lot of lightweight block ciphers have been proposed for the usage in constrained platforms. Some of them are PRIDE [1], SIMON and SPECK [2], PRESENT [5], LED [7], ITUBEE [10], PRINTCIPHER [11], Prince [6].

QTL is a recently published ultra-lightweight and competitive block cipher according to the performance results given in the design paper [12]. The cipher has a block size of 64 bits and supports key lengths of 64 and 128 bits for two variants QTL-64 and QTL-128, respectively. The cipher is based on a variant of generalized Feistel structure and QTL-64 (QTL-128) consists of 16 (20) rounds. In each round, a 64-bit round key is used. Because of having a very simple key schedule, round constants are used to differentiate the round functions.

In this paper, we present the first third party cryptanalysis of QTL in single key and related key scenarios. We first introduce related key distinguishers with a probability of one using complementation property [8] for full cipher in spite of designers' claim on the security against related key attacks. By using the

© Springer International Publishing AG 2017
A. Bogdanov (Ed.): LightSec 2016, LNCS 10098, pp. 60–68, 2017.
DOI: 10.1007/978-3-319-55714-4_5

technique given in [3], we present attacks on both versions of full QTL which exploits the related key distinguishers. The time complexity of the attacks on full QTL-64 and full QTL-128 is 2^{48} and 2^{112} encryption operations, respectively. We also observe that the round constants of QTL-64 have a property which reduces the security of the cipher dramatically. By the help of this observation we are able to mount a practical attack on full QTL-64 for 2^{48} out of 2^{64} keys performing 2^{32} encryptions. The attack requires only 2^{16} chosen plaintexts and negligible memory. We experimentally confirmed the attack and found the correct key in a few minutes using a standard PC. Finally, we present our results about the number of differentially active S-Boxes and differential branch numbers which are smaller than the ones given by the designers.

We organized the paper as follows. In Sect. 2, we introduce the notations used in the paper and give the definition of QTL. In Sect. 3, we present full round related key distinguishers and by using these distinguishers, we introduce attacks in single key model on full QTL. We define 2^{48} weak keys for QTL-64 and propose a very practical key recovery attack on full QTL-64 in Sect. 4. In Sect. 5, we give our observations on the number of differentially active S-boxes in three-round characteristic and differential branch number. Section 6 concludes the paper.

2   Definition of QTL

2.1   Notation

Throughout the paper, we use the following notation. X_j^i denotes the left-most j-th 16 bits of i-th round input where $0 \leq j \leq 3$ and $0 \leq i \leq 15$ (19) for QTL-64 (QTL-128). K_j and RK_j are used for the left-most j-th 16 bits of master key K and round key RK where K_0 and RK_0 are the left-most 16 bits of K and RK, respectively. CON_1^i and CON_2^i represent 8-bit parts of ith round constant.

2.2   QTL

QTL [12] is a recently published ultra-lightweight block cipher. It has a variant of Generalized Feistel Network structure and has two versions QTL-64 and QTL-128 supporting 64 and 128-bit key lengths, respectively. Both versions have a block size of 64 bits and use the same round function. The number of rounds for QTL-64 and QTL-128 are 16 and 20, respectively. In one round, 64-bit round key is used. While for QTL-64 round keys are the master key K, for QTL-128 the left and right halves of 128-bit master key are used in odd and even rounds, respectively. 64-bit round key is divided into four 16 bits to be used in four F functions as seen in Fig. 1.

The output of i-th round is computed as:

- $X_0^{i+1} = F_2(X_2^i, RK_1, CON_2^i) \oplus X_3^i$
- $X_2^{i+1} = F_1(X_0^i, RK_0, CON_1^i) \oplus X_1^i$
- $X_1^{i+1} = F_1(X_2^{i+1}, RK_2, CON_1^i) \oplus X_0^i$
- $X_3^{i+1} = F_2(X_0^{i+1}, RK_3, CON_2^i) \oplus X_2^i$

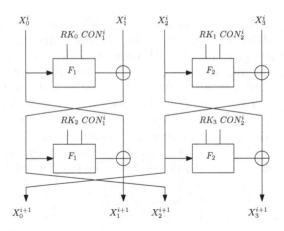

Fig. 1. i-th round function

where the input of first round (X^0) is the plaintext P and the ciphertext C is $X_2^r\|X_1^r\|X_0^r\|X_3^r$ where r is 16 (20) for QTL-64 (QTL-128).

F_1 and F_2 permutations pictured in Fig. 2 are S-P-S Networks.

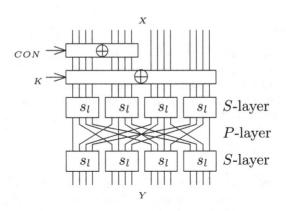

Fig. 2. F_l function where $l \in \{1,2\}$

The only difference between F_1 and F_2 is the usage of different S-boxes. The S-boxes s_1 and s_2 used in F_1 and F_2 are the PRESENT S-box [5] and one of the S-boxes used in mCRYPTON [13], respectively. Note that the left-most bits entering the S-boxes are the most significant bits. In F permutation, 8-bit round constant part and 16-bit round key part are xored to the left most 8 bits and 16 bits of the input, respectively. The result is divided into four 4 bits and for each 4 bits the S-box is applied. Then the bit permutation given in Table 1 is performed. Finally, the S-box operation is again used on the bit permutation output to produce the output of F permutation.

Table 1. Bit permutation. Note that the left most bit position is 0.

Bit position in the input	0	1	2	3	4	5	6	7	8	9	10	11	12	13	14	15
Bit position in the output	0	4	8	12	1	5	9	13	2	6	10	14	3	7	11	15

The S-boxes and round constants are given in Tables 2 and 3, respectively. A detailed description of the algorithm can be found in [12].

Table 2. S-boxes

Input	0	1	2	3	4	5	6	7	8	9	a	b	c	d	e	f
Output of s_1	c	5	6	b	9	0	a	d	3	e	f	8	4	7	1	2
Output of s_2	4	f	3	8	d	a	c	0	b	5	7	e	2	6	1	9

Table 3. Round constants

	i	0	1	2	3	4	5	6	7	8	9	10	11	12	13	14	15	16	17	18	19
For QTL-64	CON_1^i	00	01	02	03	04	05	06	07	08	09	0a	0b	0c	0d	0e	0f				
	CON_2^i	10	11	12	13	14	15	16	17	18	19	1a	1b	1c	1d	1e	1f				
For QTL-128	CON_1^i	00	01	02	03	04	05	06	07	08	09	0a	0b	0c	0d	0e	0f	10	11	12	13
	CON_2^i	14	15	16	17	18	19	1a	1b	1c	1d	1e	1f	20	21	22	23	24	25	26	27

3   Single Key Recovery Attacks from Related Key Distinguishers

The designers claim that QTL is also secure against related key attacks giving bounds on the number of active S-boxes in the related key scenario. However, because of the complementation property [8] of QTL, we show that by encrypting different plaintexts under related keys both versions of QTL can be distinguished from a random permutation trivially. In addition, by following the idea in [3] we use the related key distinguishers to attack on full QTL in single key scenario. We present the related key distinguishers and the attack only for QTL-64, the same distinguishers and a similar attack are also valid for QTL-128.

Let δ be any non-zero 16-bit value, $P = P_0\|P_1\|P_2\|P_3$, and $P' = (P_0 \oplus \delta)\|(P_1 \oplus \delta)\|(P_2 \oplus \delta)\|(P_3 \oplus \delta)$ be two plaintexts. C and C' are the corresponding ciphertexts of P and P' under key K and $K' = K \oplus (\delta\|\delta\|\delta\|\delta)$, respectively. Since the 16-bit inputs of F functions and 16-bit round key parts will have the same difference, the xor operations cancel the differences and the output of F functions have zero-differences with a probability of 1. It is trivial to see from the definition of the cipher that each round output have the same difference $\delta\|\delta\|\delta\|\delta$. As a result, the probability of having the equation $C \oplus C' = \delta\|\delta\|\delta\|\delta$ is 1 while it is expected to be 2^{-64} for a random permutation.

Here for each non-zero value of δ we have a deterministic distinguisher that is we have $2^{|\delta|} - 1 = 2^{16} - 1$ distinguishers in total. By using these distinguishers, we are able to reduce the security of QTL-64 by 16 bits applying the attack given in Algorithm 1.

Algorithm 1. Single key recovery attack by using related key distinguishers

---

1: Take a plaintext P_0
2: **for** each possible value of δ **do**
3:    Get corresponding ciphertext C_δ for $P_0 \oplus (\delta\|\delta\|\delta\|\delta)$.
4:    Store δ and $C_\delta \oplus (\delta\|\delta\|\delta\|\delta)$ in a hash table T index by $C_\delta \oplus (\delta\|\delta\|\delta\|\delta)$.
5: **end for**
6: **for** each possible value of K_1, K_2, K_3 **do**
7:    Compute C encrypting P_0 with the key $(0^{16}\|K_1\|K_2\|K_3)$.
8:    Search C in Table T.
9:    **if** a match is found **then**
10:       Return $(\delta\|(K_1 \oplus \delta)\|(K_2 \oplus \delta)\|(K_3 \oplus \delta))$ as the correct key where δ is the value in the matching row in Table T.
11:    **end if**
12: **end for**

In Algorithm 1, Table T has 2^{16} values and 2^{48} computed ciphertexts are searched in the table. Thus 2^{64} possible match is checked in Step 9. Since the probability of the condition in this step is 2^{-64}, Step 10 is reached approximately two times, one for the correct key and one for a wrong key.

The complexity of the attack is 2^{48} encryptions which can be seen easily from the attack algorithm. The attack requires 2^{16} chosen plaintexts and needs 2^{16} (64+16)-bit memory.

With this attack we give another example which shows that although related key attack model is sometimes controversial and some cipher proposals ignore .this type of attacks, it may be important to design a cipher regarding related key attacks to make the ciphers secure against single key attacks.

4 A Key Recovery Attack on QTL-64 for Weak Keys

Because of the simple and symmetric structure of the key schedule, round constants were used to break the similarity between round functions to prevent the cipher from self similarity attacks such as slide [4] and reflection [9].

We propose a practical key recovery attack on full QTL-64 by exploiting the symmetry in rounds and a relation between round constants. Our attack resembles the attack on reduced-round ITUBEE in a related key scenario given in [14]. For some reduced-round ITUBEE, the xor difference of the first i-th and last i-th round constants have same difference. [14] uses this property to make all non-linear parts in the cipher passive in a related key scenario. Like ITUBEE, round function of QTL-64 has a symmetric structure except for round constant operation. Full QTL-64 has the same property on round constants which is for $0 \leq i \leq 15$ $(CON_1^i\|CON_2^i) \oplus (CON_1^{15-i}\|CON_2^{15-i}) = 0x0F0F$. By using this property and giving a 16-bit condition on the key, we are able to attack on full QTL-64. Because of the 16-bit condition, our attack works only for 2^{48} out of 2^{64} keys. We call the keys having the property $K_0 \oplus K_2 = K_1 \oplus K_3$ as weak keys. For these keys, we present a practical key recovery attack on the full cipher.

Let $P = P_0\|P_1\|P_2\|P_3$ and $C = C_0\|C_1\|C_2\|C_3$ be a plaintext and the corresponding ciphertext produced by QTL-64 under a weak key $K = K_0 \| K_1 \| K_2 \| (K_1 \oplus (K_0 \oplus K_2))$. $F_1(X, K_0, CON_1^i)$ equals to $F_1(X \oplus 0x0F00 \oplus K_0 \oplus K_2, K_2, CON_1^{15-i})$ since the inputs of the S-P-S layer for the two inputs are the same $(X \oplus K_0 \oplus (CON_1^i\|0x00)) = (X \oplus 0x0F00 \oplus K_0 \oplus K_2 \oplus K_2 \oplus (CON_1^{15-i}\|0x00))$ (remember that $CON_1^i \oplus CON_1^{15-i} = 0x0F$). A similar result can be found as $F_2(X, K_1, CON_2^i) = F_2(X \oplus 0x0F00 \oplus K_0 \oplus K_2, K_3, CON_2^{15-i})$. Because of these two equations, encryption of $P' = (C_0 \oplus 0x0F00 \oplus K_0 \oplus K_2)\|(C_1 \oplus 0x0F00 \oplus K_0 \oplus K_2)\|(C_2 \oplus 0x0F00 \oplus K_0 \oplus K_2)\|(C_3 \oplus 0x0F00 \oplus K_0 \oplus K_2)$ under the same weak key gives the ciphertext with the equation $C' = (P_0 \oplus 0x0F00 \oplus K_0 \oplus K_2)\|(P_1 \oplus 0x0F00 \oplus K_0 \oplus K_2)\|(P_2 \oplus 0x0F00 \oplus K_0 \oplus K_2)\|(P_3 \oplus 0x0F00 \oplus K_0 \oplus K_2)$ with a probability of 1 as seen in Fig. 3.

We mount a practical key recovery attack by using this distinguisher. The attack procedure is given in Algorithm 2.

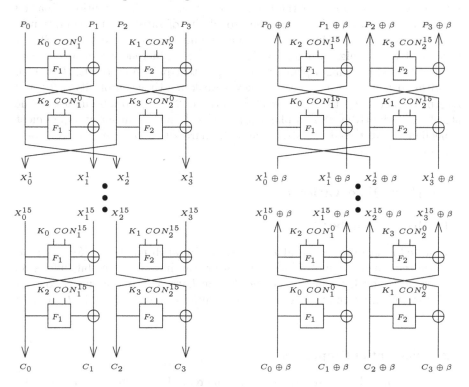

Fig. 3. Distinguisher on full QTL-64. $\beta = (0x0F00 \oplus K_0 \oplus K_2)$.

Algorithm 2. Practical Key Recovery Attack on QTL-64 for weak keys

---

1: **Input:** One plaintext-ciphertext pair $(P = P_0\|P_1\|P_2\|P_3, C = C_0\|C_1\|C_2\|C_3)$
2: **Output:** 64-bit key $(K = (K_0\|K_1\|K_2\|K_3))$
3: **for** all possible values of 16-bit $(K_0 \oplus K_2)$ **do**
4:    Compute $\beta = 0x0F00 \oplus K_0 \oplus K_2$.
5:    Ask to the encryption oracle for the ciphertext $C' = C'_0\|C'_1\|C'_2\|C'_3$ of $P' = (C_0 \oplus \beta)\|(C_1 \oplus \beta)\|(C_2 \oplus \beta)\|(C_3 \oplus \beta)$.
6:    **if** $(C'_0 \oplus P_0) = (C'_1 \oplus P_1) = (C'_2 \oplus P_2) = (C'_3 \oplus P_3) = \beta$ **then**
7:       **for** all possible values of (K_0, K_1) **do**
8:          **if** 64-bit key $(K_0, K_1, K_0 \oplus (K_0 \oplus K_2), K_1 \oplus (K_0 \oplus K_2))$ satisfies a (P, C) pair **then**
9:             Output the key
10:         **end if**
11:      **end for**
12:   **end if**
13: **end for**

In Step 5 in Algorithm 2, 2^{16} query to the encryption oracle are performed for all possible values of $K_0 \oplus K_2$. For the correct value of $K_0 \oplus K_2$, the condition in Step 6 will be satisfied if the unknown key is a weak key. On the other hand, if the guess is not correct or the key is not a weak key, the condition is passed with a probability of 2^{-64}. Thus, the probability of satisfying the condition in Step 6 more than one times is 2^{-48}, that is only for the correct guess Step 7 is reached with a high probability. In Step 8, 2^{32} different values for K_0 and K_1 are checked by using a plaintext and ciphertext pair. As a result, the attack algorithm detects whether or not the key is weak in a time complexity of 2^{16} and returns correct key if the key is weak performing 2^{32} encryption queries. In the attack, 2^{16} adaptively chosen plaintexts are used and the memory requirement is negligible. We tested the attack on a standard PC and were able to recover the key in a few minutes.

5 Other Observations

5.1 Branch Number

It is stated in the proposal that the differential branch number in F_1 and F_2 is 5. Since the output values of one active S-box can have only one-bit difference, the second S-box layer in the F_1 and F_2 can have only one active S-box. By this observation we conclude that the differential branch number in F_1 and F_2 is only 2.

5.2 Differential Properties

Designers claimed that any three-round differential characteristic has at least 21 active S-boxes. We found the following three-round differential characteristic

Table 4. 3-round differential characteristic in hexadecimal form

First round input difference	0003	0004	0008	0800
Intermediate difference in first round	0007	0003	0000	0008
Second round input difference	0000	0000	0007	0008
Intermediate difference in second round	0000	0000	0000	0007
Third round input difference	0000	0000	0000	0007
Intermediate difference in third round	0000	0000	0007	0000
Third round output difference	0007	0000	0000	0008

which contains only 10 active S-boxes. This shows that the result about differential active S-boxes for any consecutive three-round is much lower than the number given by designers. In Table 4, we present a 3-round differential characteristic with 10 active S-Boxes:

In the differential characteristic, there are two active F_1 and three active F_2 functions. In the first round, two F_1 and one F_2 functions are active. We pass first F_1 and F_2 with the differential path $0003 \xrightarrow{S} 0001 \xrightarrow{P,S} 0003$ and $0008 \xrightarrow{S} 0004 \xrightarrow{P,S} 0800$, respectively. We pass second F_1 with $0007 \xrightarrow{S} 0001 \xrightarrow{P,S} 0003$. In the second round, one F_2 function is active. First F_2 function in second round and second F_2 function in third round have the same differential trail which is $0007 \xrightarrow{S} 0001 \xrightarrow{P,S} 0008$. All active F_i functions in this characteristic have 2 active S-boxes. Therefore, it has 10 active S-boxes. This result shows there is a differential path having less number of active S-boxes than the minimum number of S-boxes claimed by the designers.

6   Conclusion

We have analyzed the security of QTL. We have introduced related key distinguishers for full two versions of the cipher in contrast to the claims of designers. We have also proposed attacks taking advantage of the related key distinguishers by using the technique given in [3]. With these attacks we have shown that QTL-64 and QTL-128 provides at most 48 and 112-bit security, respectively. Although QTL-64 has 16 rounds (actually each round consists of two rounds) and uses S-P-S structure in each F functions, we present a practical key recovery attack on full QTL-64 for 2^{48} weak keys showing that a wrong choice for round constants can reduce the security of the cipher dramatically. Moreover, we disprove the claims of the designers about number of active differential S-boxes and branch number.

References

1. Albrecht, M.R., Driessen, B., Kavun, E.B., Leander, G., Paar, C., Yalçın, T.: Block ciphers – focus on the linear layer (feat. PRIDE). In: Garay, J.A., Gennaro, R. (eds.) CRYPTO 2014. LNCS, vol. 8616, pp. 57–76. Springer, Heidelberg (2014). doi:10.1007/978-3-662-44371-2_4

2. Beaulieu, R., Shors, D., Smith, J., Treatman-Clark, S., Weeks, B., Wingers, L.: The SIMON and SPECK lightweight block ciphers. In: Proceedings of the 52nd Annual Design Automation Conference, San Francisco, CA, USA, 7–11 June 2015, pp. 175:1–175:6. ACM (2015)

3. Biham, E.: New types of cryptanalytic attacks using related keys. J. Cryptology 7(4), 229–246 (1994)

4. Biryukov, A., Wagner, D.: Slide attacks. In: Knudsen, L. (ed.) FSE 1999. LNCS, vol. 1636, pp. 245–259. Springer, Heidelberg (1999). doi:10.1007/3-540-48519-8_18

5. Bogdanov, A., et al.: PRESENT: an ultra-lightweight block cipher. In: Paillier, P., Verbauwhede, I. (eds.) CHES 2007. LNCS, vol. 4727, pp. 450–466. Springer, Heidelberg (2007). doi:10.1007/978-3-540-74735-2_31

6. Borghoff, J., et al.: PRINCE – a low-latency block cipher for pervasive computing applications. In: Wang, X., Sako, K. (eds.) ASIACRYPT 2012. LNCS, vol. 7658, pp. 208–225. Springer, Heidelberg (2012). doi:10.1007/978-3-642-34961-4_14

7. Guo, J., Peyrin, T., Poschmann, A., Robshaw, M.: The LED block cipher. In: Preneel, B., Takagi, T. (eds.) CHES 2011. LNCS, vol. 6917, pp. 326–341. Springer, Heidelberg (2011). doi:10.1007/978-3-642-23951-9_22

8. Hellman, M.E., Merkle, R.C., Schroeppel, R., Washington, L., Diffie, W., Pohlig, S., Schweitzer, P.: Results of an Initial Attempt to Cryptanalyze the NBS Data Encryption Standard. Information Systems Laboratory, Stanford University (1976)

9. Kara, O.: Reflection cryptanalysis of some ciphers. In: Chowdhury, D.R., Rijmen, V., Das, A. (eds.) INDOCRYPT 2008. LNCS, vol. 5365, pp. 294–307. Springer, Heidelberg (2008). doi:10.1007/978-3-540-89754-5_23

10. Karakoç, F., Demirci, H., Harmancı, A.E.: ITUbee: a software oriented lightweight block cipher. In: Avoine, G., Kara, O. (eds.) LightSec 2013. LNCS, vol. 8162, pp. 16–27. Springer, Heidelberg (2013). doi:10.1007/978-3-642-40392-7_2

11. Knudsen, L., Leander, G., Poschmann, A., Robshaw, M.J.B.: PRINTCIPHER: a block cipher for IC-printing. In: Mangard, S., Standaert, F.-X. (eds.) CHES 2010. LNCS, vol. 6225, pp. 16–32. Springer, Heidelberg (2010). doi:10.1007/978-3-642-15031-9_2

12. Li, L., Liu, B., Wang, H.: QTL: a new ultra-lightweight block cipher. Microprocess. Microsyst. (2016)

13. Lim, C.H., Korkishko, T.: mCrypton – a lightweight block cipher for security of low-cost RFID tags and sensors. In: Song, J.-S., Kwon, T., Yung, M. (eds.) WISA 2005. LNCS, vol. 3786, pp. 243–258. Springer, Heidelberg (2006). doi:10.1007/11604938_19

14. Soleimany, H.: Self-similarity cryptanalysis of the block cipher ITUBEE. IET Inf. Secur. 9(3), 179–184 (2015)

A Brief Comparison of Simon and Simeck

Stefan Kölbl$^{(\boxtimes)}$ and Arnab Roy

DTU Compute, Technical University of Denmark, Kongens Lyngby, Denmark
{stek,arroy}@dtu.dk

Abstract. Simeck is a new lightweight block cipher design based on combining the design principles of the Simon and Speck block cipher. While the design allows a smaller and more efficient hardware implementation, its security margins are not well understood. The lack of design rationals of its predecessors further leaves some uncertainty on the security of Simeck.

In this work we give a short analysis of the impact of the design changes by comparing the upper bounds on the probability of differential and linear trails with Simon. We also give a comparison of the effort of finding those bounds, which surprisingly is significantly lower for Simeck while covering a larger number of rounds at the same time.

Furthermore, we provide new differentials for Simeck which can cover more rounds compared to previous results on Simon and study how to choose good differentials for attacks and show that one can find better differentials by building them from a larger set of trail with initially lower probability.

We also provide experimental results for the differentials for Simon32 and Simeck32 which show that there exist keys for which the probability of the differential is significantly higher than expected.

Based on this we mount key recovery attacks on 19/26/33 rounds of Simeck32/48/64, which also give insights on the reduced key guessing effort due to the different set of rotation constants.

Keywords: SIMON · SIMECK · Differential cryptanalysis · Block cipher

1 Introduction

Simeck is a family of lightweight block ciphers proposed in CHES'15 by Yang, Zhu, Suder, Aagaard and Gong [13]. The design combines the Simon and Speck block ciphers proposed by NSA [4], which leads to a more compact and efficient implementation in hardware. The block cipher Simon is built by iterating a very simple round function which uses bitwise AND and rotation while the block cipher Speck uses modular addition as non-linear operations. The designers of Simeck chose a different set of rotation constants from Simon to construct the round function.

The efficiency of Simon and Speck on hardware and software platform has a natural appeal to use similar design principles for constructing efficient primitives. The designers of Simon and Speck do not provide rationales for the original choices apart from implementation aspects. These modifications are likely to

© Springer International Publishing AG 2017
A. Bogdanov (Ed.): LightSec 2016, LNCS 10098, pp. 69–88, 2017.
DOI: 10.1007/978-3-319-55714-4_6

have an impact on the security margins, which often are already small for light-weight designs and can be a delicate issue. Hence it is important to understand the effect of the parameter change on the security of SIMON like design.

The SIMON block cipher family has been studied in various paper [1,2,5,9, 10,12] and the attacks covering the most rounds are based on differential and linear cryptanalysis, which therefore will also be the focus of this work. However very few analyses [7] were done to study the choice of parameters for SIMON and SPECK and their effect on the security of these block ciphers.

Our Results. In this paper we give a first analysis on the impact of these design changes by comparing the bounds for differential and linear trails with the corresponding variants of SIMON. An unexpected advantage for SIMECK is, that it takes significantly less time to find those while also covering more rounds (see Table 1). Additionally we investigate strategies to find differentials which have a high probability and are more suitable for efficient attacks.

Surprisingly, we can find differentials with higher probability for SIMECK32 by not using the input and output difference from the best differential trails. Furthermore, we also provide new differentials which cover 4 and 5 rounds for SIMECK48 and SIMECK64 respectively which also have a slightly higher probability compared to previous results on SIMON.

We verified the estimated probability with experiments for both SIMON32 and SIMECK32 to confirm our model and also noticed that for some keys a surprisingly large number of valid pairs can be found.

This is followed by key-recovery attacks for reduced round versions of SIMECK (see Table 6). These attacks are similar to previous work [5] done on SIMON and give insight into the lower complexity for the key recovery process for SIMECK as we need to guess fewer key bits.

Table 1. A comparison between the number of rounds for which upper bounds on the probability of differential and linear trails exist, the probability of differentials utilized in attacks and the best differential attacks on SIMON and SIMECK. Results contributed by this work are marked in bold.

Cipher	Rounds	Upper Bounds		Differentials		Key Recovery
		differential	linear	Rounds	$\Pr(\alpha \to \beta)$	
SIMON32/64	32	**32**	**32**	13	$2^{-28.79}$ [5]	21 [11]
SIMECK32/64	32	**32**	**32**	13	$\mathbf{2^{-27.28}}$	22 [8]
SIMON48/96	36	**19**	**20**	16	$2^{-44.65}$ [10]	24 [11]
SIMECK48/96	36	**36**	**36**	20	$\mathbf{2^{-43.65}}$	26 [8]
SIMON64/128	44	15 [7]	**17**	21	$2^{-60.21}$ [10]	29 [11]
SIMECK64/128	44	**40**	**41**	26	$\mathbf{2^{-60.02}}$	35 [8]

2   The SIMECK Block Cipher

SIMECK2n is a family of block ciphers with n-bit word size, where $n = 16, 24, 32$. Each variant has a block size of $2n$ and key size of $4n$ giving the three variants of SIMECK: SIMECK32/64, SIMECK48/96 and SIMECK64/128. As for each block size there is only one key size we will omit the key size usually.

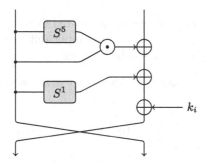

Fig. 1. The round function of SIMECK.

The block cipher is based on the *Feistel* construction and the round function f is the same as in SIMON apart from using $(5, 0, 1)$ for the rotation constants (as depicted in Fig. 1). The key-schedule on the other hand is similar to SPECK, reusing the round function to update the keys. The key K is split into four words (t_2, t_1, t_0, k_0) and the round keys $k_0, \ldots, k_{r-1}$ are given by:

$$k_{i+1} = t_i$$
$$t_{i+3} = k_i \oplus f(t_i) \oplus C \tag{1}$$

3   Preliminaries

Differential cryptanalysis is a powerful tool for analyzing block ciphers using a chosen plaintext attack. The idea is to find a correlation between the difference of a pair of plaintexts and the corresponding pair of ciphertexts. Resistance to differential cryptanalysis is an important design criteria but it is difficult, especially for designs like SIMON, to proof the resistance against it.

Definition 1. *A differential trail Q is a sequence of difference patterns*

$$Q = (\alpha_0 \xrightarrow{f_0} \alpha_1 \xrightarrow{f_1} \cdots \alpha_{r-1} \xrightarrow{f_{r-1}} \alpha_r). \tag{2}$$

In general, as the key is unknown to an attacker, we are interested in the probability that a random pair of inputs follows such a differential trail and the goal for the attacker is to find a correlation between input and output difference with high probability.

Definition 2. *The probability of a differential trail Q is defined as*

$$\Pr(\alpha_0 \xrightarrow{f_0} \alpha_1 \xrightarrow{f_1} \cdots \alpha_{r-1} \xrightarrow{f_{r-1}} \alpha_r) = \prod_{t=0}^{r-1} \Pr(\alpha_t \to \alpha_{t+1}) \tag{3}$$

and gives the probability that a random input follows the differential trail. The last equality holds if we assume independent rounds.

In most attack scenarios we are not interested in the probability of a differential trail, as we are only interested in the input difference α_0 and the output difference α_r, but not what happens in between.

Definition 3. *The probability of a* differential *is the sum of all r round differential trails*

$$\Pr(\alpha_0 \xrightarrow{f} \alpha_r) = \sum_{\alpha_1,\dots,\alpha_{r-1}} (\alpha_0 \xrightarrow{f_0} \alpha_1 \xrightarrow{f_1} \cdots \alpha_{r-1} \xrightarrow{f_{r-1}} \alpha_r) \tag{4}$$

which have the same input and output difference.

4   Analysis of SIMON and SIMECK

In [7] the differential and linear properties of SIMON were studied, including variants using a different set of rotation constants. Following up on this work, we can use the same methods to analyze the round function of SIMECK. This allows us to find lower bounds for the probability of a differential trail resp. square correlation of a linear trail for a given number of rounds.

4.1   Diffusion

An important criteria for the quality of a round function in a block cipher is the amount of diffusion it provides, i.e. how many rounds r it takes until each bit at the input effects all bits of the output. For SIMON this was already studied in [7] for the whole parameter set and we only explicitly state the comparison to SIMECK here in Table 2.

Table 2. Number of rounds required for full diffusion.

Wordsize	32-bit	48-bit	64-bit
SIMON	7 Rounds	8 Rounds	9 Rounds
SIMECK	8 Rounds	9 Rounds	11 Rounds

4.2   Bounds on the Best Differential Trails

We carried out experiments for the parameter set of SIMECK using CryptoSMT[1] to find the optimal differential and linear trails for SIMECK32, SIMECK48 and SIMECK64 and compare it with the results on SIMON. The results of this experiment are given in Fig. 2. The bounds on the square correlation for linear trails are given in the Appendix.

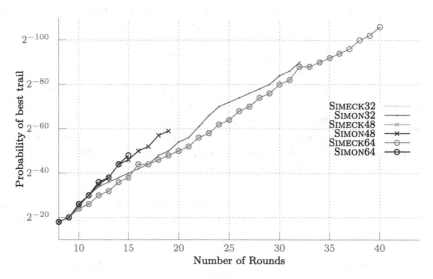

Fig. 2. Lower bounds on the probability of the best differential trails for variants of SIMON and SIMECK. For the different variants of SIMECK the bounds are the same.

While the bounds for SIMON32 and SIMECK32 are still comparable we noticed a significant difference for the larger variants. While the required number of rounds for SIMON48, such that the probability of the best trail is less than 2^{-48}, is 16, SIMECK48 achieves the same property only after 20 rounds. It is also interesting to note that the bounds for the different word sizes of SIMECK are the same, which is not the case for SIMON.

In our experiments we noticed that the different set of rotation constants plays a huge role in the running time of the SMT solver. For instance finding the bounds in Fig. 2 took 51 h for SIMON32 and 10 h for SIMECK32[2]. Especially for larger block sizes it allows us to provide bounds for a significant larger number of rounds including full SIMECK48. For SIMON64 computing the bounds up to 15 rounds takes around 19 h, while the same process only takes around 30 min for SIMECK64. We computed the bounds for SIMECK64 up to round 40 in around 53 h.

---

[1] CryptoSMT https://github.com/kste/cryptosmt Version: 70794d83.
[2] Using Boolector 2.0.1. running on an Intel Xeon X5650 2.66 GHz 48 GB RAM (1 core).

4.3 Differential Effect in SIMON and SIMECK

As noted in previous works SIMON shows a strong differential resp. linear hull effect, which invalidates an often made assumption that the probability of the best trail can be used to estimate the probability of the best differential. Therefore bounds on differential and linear trails have to be treated with caution. The choice of constants for SIMON-like round functions also plays a role in this as shown in [7].

One approach to find good differentials is to first find the best trail for a given number of rounds of SIMECK using CryptoSMT [6] and then find a large set of trails with the same input and output difference. However, as we will see later this will not always give the highest probability differential. The results of these experiments are summarized in Table 3.

If we compare those with previous results on SIMON we can cover more rounds. The best previous differential attack by Wang, Wang, Jia and Zhao [11] utilizes a 13-round differential for SIMON32, a 16-round differential for SIMON48 and a 21-round differential for SIMON64. We show that with the same or slightly better probability (Table 1) differentials can be found for a higher number of rounds for both SIMECK48 and SIMECK64.

Table 3. Overview of the differentials we found for SIMECK which can likely be used to mount attacks. The probability is given by summing up all trails up to probability 2^{max} taking a time T.

Cipher	Rounds	$Q = (\alpha \rightarrow \beta)$	$\log_2(p)$	max	T
SIMECK32	13	$(8000, 4011) \rightarrow (4000, 0)$	-27.28	-49	17 h
SIMECK48	20	$(20000, 450000) \rightarrow (30000, 10000)$	-43.65	-98	135 h
SIMECK48	20	$(400000, e00000) \rightarrow (400000, 200000)$	-43.65	-74	93 h
SIMECK48	21	$(20000, 470000) \rightarrow (50000, 20000)$	-45.65	-100	130 h
SIMECK64	25	$(2, 40000007) \rightarrow (40000045, 2)$	-56.78	-90	110 h
SIMECK64	26	$(0, 4400000) \rightarrow (8800000, 400000)$	-60.02	-121	120 h

While we let our experiments run for a few days, the probability only improves marginally after a short time. For instance, for SIMECK32 and SIMECK48 the estimates after three minutes are only 2^{-2} lower than the final results and after two hours the improvements are very small. Some additional details on the differential utilized in the key-recovery attack on SIMECK48 can be found in the Appendix 9, including the exact running times to obtain the results.

4.4 Choosing a Good Differential for Attacks

For an attack we want a differential with a high probability, but also the form of the input and output difference can have an influence on the resulting attack complexity. Ideally we want differentials with a sparse input/output difference resp. of the form $(x, 0) \rightarrow (0, x)$. When expanding such a differential it leads to a truncated differential with fewer unknown bits which reduces the complexity in the key recovery part of the attack as will be seen later.

The best differential trail of the form $(x, 0) \rightarrow (0, x)$ only has a probability of 2^{-42} for SIMECK32 resp. 2^{-47} for SIMON32. The corresponding differential improves the probability to $\approx 2^{-36.7}$, but is still unlikely to be useful for an attack. If we relax the restriction and allow differentials of the form $(x, x) \rightarrow (0, x)$ we can find differential trails with a probability of 2^{-38} (the same bound exists for SIMON32). However, the corresponding differentials still seem impractical for an attack. As both this approaches fail for finding good differentials we do not impose any restrictions on the form of the input resp. output difference of the differentials.

Table 4. Number of differential trails for 13-round SIMECK32.

$\Pr(\alpha \xrightarrow{f^{13}} \beta)$	Trails
2^{-32}	640
2^{-33}	128
2^{-34}	31616
2^{-35}	49152

We looked at all 40 rotation invariant differentials constructed from the best differential trail with probability 2^{-32} for SIMECK32 (see Table 4). There are only two possible distributions for the trails contributing to the differential, which we denote as Type 1 and Type 2 (see Fig. 3 and Table 8). There are 8 trails of Type 1, all with at least one word having 0 difference, and the corresponding differential gives a slightly higher probability. For a list of these differentials see Table 7.

However, by expanding our search we could find a better differential. By not using the optimal differential trail we can find the differential $(8000, 4011) \rightarrow (4000, 0)$ which has a higher probability even though the best trail contributing only has a probability of 2^{-36}. This is due to the higher number of trails contributing to this specific differential (see Type 3 in Fig. 3 respectively Table 8).

For 20-round SIMECK48 the best trails with pattern only has a probability of 2^{-62} and for $(x, x) \rightarrow (0, x)$ it is 2^{-54}. The corresponding differentials are not usable for an attack in this case. Therefore, we again do not impose any of these restrictions and use the 20-round trails with highest probability. For SIMECK48 there are 768 such trails with a probability of 2^{-50} (32 rotation invariant) and we choose the one where the input and output difference is most sparse.

For SIMECK64 the best differentials we found are also based on the best trail and given in Table 3.

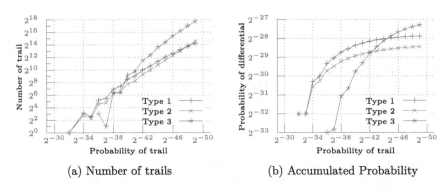

(a) Number of trails   (b) Accumulated Probability

Fig. 3. Distribution of trails contributing to the differentials for 13 rounds of SIMECK32 and the accumulated probability by summing up all trails up to a specific probability.

4.5 Experimental Verification

While the previous approach can give a good estimate for the probability one can expect for a differential, it is not entirely clear how good these approximations are. As both SIMON32 and SIMECK32 allow us to run experiments on the full codebook we can verify the probabilities at least for these variants. For a random function we expect that the number of valid pairs are a Poisson distribution.

Definition 4. *Let X be a Poisson distributed random variable representing the number of pairs (a, b) with values in $\mathbb{F}_2^n$ following a differential $Q = (\alpha \xrightarrow{f} \beta)$, that means $f(a) \oplus f(a \oplus \alpha) = \beta$, then*

$$\Pr(X = l) = \frac{1}{2}(2^n p)^l \frac{e^{-(2^n p)}}{l!} \tag{5}$$

where p is the probability of the differential.

We ran experiments for both SIMON32 and SIMECK32 reduced to 13 rounds by encrypting the full code book for a large number of random keys. The differential we used for SIMON32 is $(0, 40) \rightarrow (4000, 0)$, which is also used in the best attack so far [11] and has an estimated probability of $2^{-28.56}$. The expected number of valid pairs is $\mathbf{E}(X) \approx 5.425$. We encrypted the full code book using 202225 random master keys and counted the number of unique pairs. The full distribution is given in Fig. 4. The distribution follows the model in Eq. 5, but we observe some unusual high number of pairs for some keys. For example the key $K = (k_0, k_1, k_2, k_3) = (\texttt{8ec1}, \texttt{1cf8}, \texttt{e84a}, \texttt{cee2})$ gives 1082 pairs following the differential. If 13 rounds of SIMON32 would behave like a random function, this would only occur with an extremely low probability $\Pr(X = 1082) \ll 2^{-1000}$.

For SIMECK32 we used the new differential $(8000, 4011) \rightarrow (4000, 0)$ with $\mathbf{E}(X) \approx 13.175$. Again, we encrypt the full code book for 134570 random keys and the distribution follows our model as can be seen in Fig. 5. Similar, to SIMON for some keys a surprisingly large number of valid pairs can be found. In both

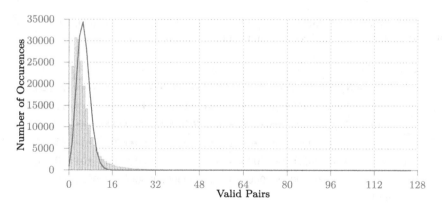

Fig. 4. Distribution of how many times we observe l valid pairs for the differential $(0,40) \xrightarrow{f^{13}} (4000,0)$ for SIMON32 using a random key.

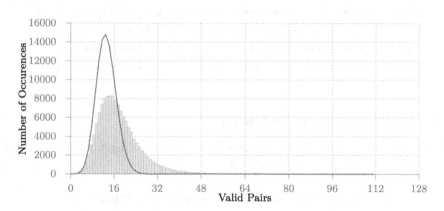

Fig. 5. Distribution of how many times we observe l valid pairs for the differential $(8000,4011) \xrightarrow{f^{13}} (4000,0)$ for SIMECK32 using a random key.

cases our method provides a good estimate for the probability of a differential and we can use Eq. 5 for estimating the number of pairs.

5 Recovering the Key

In the following subsection we describe the key recovery attack on SIMECK48 based on the differential given in Table 3. Extending this differential both in forward and backward directions gives the truncated differential shown in Table 5 which will be used in the attack. The input difference to round r is denoted as Δ^r and k_r denotes the round key for round r. The difference in the left resp. right part of the state we denote as ΔL^r and ΔR^r.

Table 5. Truncated differential obtained by extending $(400000, e00000) \xrightarrow{20}$ $(400000, 200000)$ in both directions until all bits are unknown.

Round	ΔL	ΔR	*	*
−5	***0***0****************	************************	22	24
−4	***000000***0***********	***0***0****************	17	22
−3	***00000000000***0****1*	***000000***0***********	11	17
−2	***0000000000000000***01	***00000000000***0****1*	6	11
−1	111000000000000000000000	***0000000000000000***01	0	6
0	010000000000000000000000	111000000000000000000000	0	0
20 rounds				
20	010000000000000000000000	001000000000000000000000	0	0
21	1*10000000000000000*000	010000000000000000000000	2	0
22	***000000000000*000***01	1*100000000000000000*000	7	2
23	***0000000*000***0****1*	***000000000000*000***01	12	7
24	***00*000***0***********	***0000000*000***0****1*	18	12
25	***0***0****************	***00*000***0***********	22	18
26	************************	***0***0****************	24	22

5.1   Attack on 26-Round Simeck48

Our attack on 26-round Simeck48 uses four 20-round differentials in a similar way as in [5]. Let D_i denote the differentials

$$D_1 : (400000, \text{ } e00000) \xrightarrow{f^{20}} (400000, \text{ } 200000)$$

$$D_2 : (800000, \text{ } c00001) \xrightarrow{f^{20}} (800000, \text{ } 400000)$$

$$D_3 : (000004, \text{ } 00000e) \xrightarrow{f^{20}} (000004, \text{ } 000002)$$

$$D_4 : (000008, \text{ } 00001c) \xrightarrow{f^{20}} (000008, \text{ } 000004)$$

each having probability $\approx 2^{-44}$. We add 4 rounds at the end and 2 rounds on top and obtain the truncated difference (see Table 5). The truncated difference at round 0 for each differential is given by

$$***000000000000000000***01, ***0000000000***0****1*$$
$$**0000000000000000***01*, **00000000000***0****1**$$
$$00000000000000***01***0, 000000000***0****1****0$$
$$00000000000000***01***00, 000000000***0****1****00 \text{ .}$$

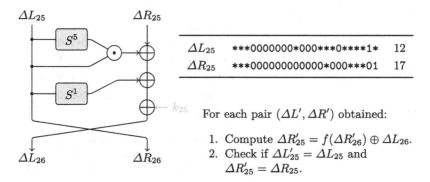

For each pair $(\Delta L', \Delta R')$ obtained:

1. Compute $\Delta R'_{25} = f(\Delta R'_{26}) \oplus \Delta L_{26}$.
2. Check if $\Delta L'_{25} = \Delta L_{25}$ and $\Delta R'_{25} = \Delta R_{25}$.

Fig. 6. Filtering for the correct pairs which we use in the key guessing part. (The key has no influence on the input to the non-linear function in the last round.)

By identifying the unknown and known bit positions in these differentials we can construct a set of 2^{30} plaintext pairs where the bit positions corresponding to the aligned 0s in the truncated differentials are fixed to an arbitrary value for all plain-texts. By guessing 6 round key bits we can also identify the 2^{31} pairs satisfying the difference $(\Delta L^2, \Delta R^2)$ after the first two round encryption. Hence we can get 4 sets of 2^{31} pairs of plain-texts where the difference is satisfied after the first two rounds of encryption. By varying the fixed bit positions we can get 4 sets of 2^{46} pairs of plain-texts, each satisfying the difference after two rounds for each key guess.

Filtering the Pairs. First we encrypt the 2^{46} plaintext pairs. Then we unroll the last round and use the truncated differential to verify if a pair is valid. This is possible due to the last key addition not having any influence on the difference $(\Delta L^{25}, \Delta R^{25})$. As there are $12 + 17$ bits known in this round we will have $2^{46-29} = 2^{17}$ plaintext pairs left (Fig. 6).

Key Guessing. In the key guessing phase we guess the necessary round key bits (or linear combination of round key bits) to verify the difference at the beginning of round 22, i.e. Δ^{22}. For each differential we counted that a total of 30 round key bits and linear combinations of round key bits are necessary to be guessed during this process. The required key bits D_1^K for D_1 are

$$K^{23} = \{2, 17\}$$
$$K^{24} = \{2, 3, 4, 8, 12, 16, 17, 18, 22\}$$
$$K^{25} = \{1, 2, 3, 4, 5, 7, 8, 9, 11, 12, 13, 15, 16, 17, 18, 19, 21, 22, 23\}$$

We describe this process for one round in Fig. 7. An interesting difference to Simon in the key guessing part is that the required number of key guesses is much lower, as many bits required to guess coincide when partially recovering

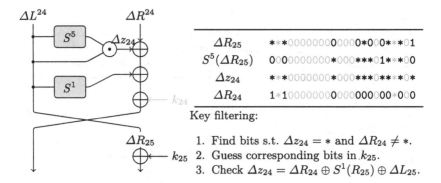

ΔR_{25}	$**{*}000000000000{*}000{**}01$
$S^5(\Delta R_{25})$	$000000000{*}000{***}01{**}00$
Δz_{24}	$**{*}0000000{*}000{***}0{***}0{*}$
ΔR_{24}	$1{*}10000000000000000{*}000$

Key filtering:

1. Find bits s.t. $\Delta z_{24} = *$ and $\Delta R_{24} \neq *$.
2. Guess corresponding bits in k_{25}.
3. Check $\Delta z_{24} = \Delta R_{24} \oplus S^1(R_{25}) \oplus \Delta L_{25}$.

Fig. 7. Outline of the process of key guessing and filtering for a single round.

the state which can reduce the overall complexity. This is always the case if one of the rotation constants is zero, but similar effects can occur with other choices as well.

For the key guessing part, we keep an array of 2^{30} counters and increment a counter when it is correctly verified with the difference after partial decryption of the cipher-text pairs. For each differential we can verify the remaining $19(= 48 - 29)$ bits with the key guessing process. For the 2^{30} counters we expect to have $(2^{17} \times 2^{30})/2^{19} = 2^{28}$ increments. The probability of a counter being incremented is $2^{28}/2^{30} = 2^{-2}$. Since 4 correct pairs are expected to be among the filtered pairs, the expected number of counters having at least 4 increments is

$$2^{30} \cdot (1 - \Pr(X < 4)) \approx 2^{17.13}. \tag{6}$$

We observe that there are 18 common key guesses required for the differentials D_1 and D_2. Hence combining the corresponding array of counters T_1 and T_2 we can get $2^{17.13} \times 2^{17.13}/2^{18} = 2^{16.26}$ candidates for 42 bits. Continuing in the same way we observe that $|D_3^K \cap (D_1^K \cup D_2^K)| = 24$, hence we get $2^{16.26} \times 2^{17.13}/2^{24} = 2^{9.39}$ candidates for 48 bits. Using D_4 this can be further reduced, as $|D_4^K \cap (D_1^K \cup D_2^K \cup D_3^K)| = 28$ we expect $2^{9.39} \times 2^{17.13}/2^{28} \approx 2^{-1.5}$ candidates for 50 bits. For the remaining 46 bits we perform an exhaustive search.

Complexity. The complexity of the attack is dominated by the key recovery process. For the partial decryption process we need $2^{17} \times 2^{30} \times \frac{4}{26} \approx 2^{45}$ encryptions, hence the complexity of one key recovery attack is 2^{54}. This key recovery is performed for each differential and each 2^6 round key guesses of the initial rounds. Hence the overall complexity of the attack is $2^{54} \times 2^6 \times 4 = 2^{62}$.

We expect in our attack that at least 4 out of 2^{46} pairs follow our differential, which has probability $\geq 2^{-43.65}$, for the correct key. Therefore we get a success rate of

$$1 - \Pr(X < 4) \approx 0.75 \tag{7}$$

However, in practice this will be much higher as we only use a lower bound on the probability of the differential.

5.2 Key Recovery for 19-Round SIMECK32

For SIMECK32 we also use 4 differentials

$$D_1 : (8000, \ 4011) \xrightarrow{f^{13}} (4000, \ 0000)$$

$$D_2 : (0001, \ 8022) \xrightarrow{f^{13}} (8000, \ 0000)$$

$$D_3 : (0008, \ 0114) \xrightarrow{f^{13}} (0004, \ 0000)$$

$$D_4 : (0010, \ 0228) \xrightarrow{f^{13}} (0008, \ 0000)$$

each having probability $\approx 2^{-28}$ (for the truncated differences see Table 10). We add two rounds at the top of the 13-round differential and identify a set of 2^{30} pairs of plain-texts each satisfying the specific difference $(\Delta L^2, \Delta R^2)$ after the first two round encryption. Identifying a set of plaintext pairs requires to guess 6 key bits.

Filtering. We can filter some wrong pairs by unrolling the last round and verifying the truncated difference (with 18 known bits) at the beginning of the last round. This will leave us with $2^{30-18} = 2^{12}$ pairs.

Key Guessing. We counted that 22 round key bits are necessary to guess for verifying the difference at the end of round 14. The required key bits D_1^K for D_1 are

$$K^{16} = \{3, 9\}$$
$$K^{17} = \{2, 3, 4, 8, 9, 10, 14\}$$
$$K^{18} = \{1, 2, 3, 4, 5, 7, 8, 9, 10, 11, 13, 14, 15\}$$

We use the same method as described for SIMECK48 during this phase. Out of the filtered pairs we expect to get at least 4 correct pairs (those follow the 13-round differential). Hence the number of candidates for 22 key bits are $\approx 2^{9.1}$. The number of common key bits amongst the differentials is given by

$$D_1^K \cap D_2^K = 14$$
$$D_3^K \cap (D_1^K \cup D_2^K) = 16$$
$$D_4^K \cap (D_1^K \cup D_2^K \cup D_3^K) = 20$$

and we expect to 1 key candidate for 38 bits. For the remaining 26 bits of the last four round keys we perform exhaustive search.

Complexity. The complexity of the partial decryption (for the last 4 rounds) is $2^{12} \times 2^{22} \times \frac{4}{19} \approx 2^{32}$ which is the dominating part of the complexity. Since we perform the key recovery for each differential and for each 6-bit round key guesses of the first two rounds the overall complexity of the attack is $2^{32+8} = 2^{40}$.

5.3 Key Recovery for 33-Round SIMECK64

We use the following 4 differentials for SIMECK64

$$D_1 : (0,\ 04400000) \xrightarrow{f^{26}} (08800000,\ 00400000)$$

$$D_2 : (0,\ 44000000) \xrightarrow{f^{26}} (88000000,\ 04000000)$$

$$D_3 : (0,\ 40000004) \xrightarrow{f^{26}} (80000008,\ 40000000)$$

$$D_4 : (0,\ 00000044) \xrightarrow{f^{26}} (00000088,\ 00000004)$$

each having probability $\approx 2^{-60}$ (for the truncated differences see Table 11). We add two rounds at the top of the 26 round differential and identify a set of 2^{62} pairs of plain-texts by guessing 4 round key bits from the first two rounds.

Filtering Wrong Pairs. We add 5 round truncated difference at the end of the 26 round differential. The last round may be unrolled to verify the difference at the beginning of the last round. This helps to filter some wrong pairs using the known bits of the truncated difference and after filtering we are left with $2^{62-30} = 2^{32}$ pairs of plaintext out of which we expect 2^2 correct pairs (those followed 26 round differential).

Key Guessing. In this phase we guess the necessary key bits from the last four rounds to verify the difference at the beginning of round 28. We counted that 76 key bits are necessary to guess for verifying $(\Delta L^{28}, \Delta R^{28})$. The required key bits D_1^K for D_1 are

$$K^{29} = \{0, 18, 22, 28\}$$
$$K^{30} = \{0, 1, 5, 13, 17, 18, 19, 21, 22, 23, 27, 28, 29, 31\}$$
$$K^{31} = \{0, 1, 2, 4 - 6, 8, 10, 12 - 14, 16 - 24, 26 - 31\}$$
$$K^{32} = \{0 - 31\}$$

Out of the filtered pairs we expect to get at least 4 correct pairs (those that follow the 26-round differential). Hence the number of candidates for 76 key bits are $\approx 2^{63.12}$. The number of common key bits amongst the differentials is given by

$$D_1^K \cap D_2^K = 66$$
$$D_3^K \cap (D_1^K \cup D_2^K) = 70$$
$$D_4^K \cap (D_1^K \cup D_2^K \cup D_3^K) = 64$$

By combining all the four differentials we expect to get 2^{52} key candidates for 104 bits. For the remaining 24 bits of the last four round keys we perform exhaustive search.

Complexity. The complexity of the partial decryption (for last 4 rounds) is $2^{32} \times 2^{76} \times \frac{5}{33} \approx 2^{105}$ which is the dominating part of the complexity. Since we perform the key recovery for each differential and for each 6-bit round key guesses of the first two rounds the overall complexity of the attack is $2^{105+10} = 2^{115}$ (Fig. 8).

6   Conclusion and Future Work

We gave a brief overview of the SIMECK and SIMON block cipher and their resistance against differential and linear cryptanalysis. From our comparison we can see that statistical attacks can cover a significant larger number of rounds for SIMECK48 and SIMECK64. Our key recovery attacks still have a significant margin compared to generic attacks (see Table 6) in regard to time complexity, therefore additional rounds can be covered using the dynamic key-guessing approach at the costs of a higher complexity (Table 9).

This also shows that the impact of small design changes in SIMON-like block ciphers can be hard to estimate and requires a dedicated analysis, as the underlying design strategy is still not well understood. Especially for variants with a larger block size it is difficult to find lower bounds or estimate the effect of

Table 6. Comparison of the attacks on SIMECK.

Cipher	Rounds	Time	Data	Memory	Type
SIMECK32/64	20/32	$2^{62.6}$	2^{32}	2^{56}	Imp. Differential [13]
SIMECK32/64	22/32	$2^{57.9}$	2^{32}	–	Diff.(dynamic key-guessing) [8]
SIMECK32/64	18/32	$2^{63.5}$	2^{31}	–	Linear [3]
SIMECK32/64	19/32	$\mathbf{2^{40}}$	$\mathbf{2^{31}}$	$\mathbf{2^{31}}$	Differential (Sect. 5.2)
SIMECK48/96	24/36	$2^{94.7}$	2^{48}	2^{74}	Imp. Differential [13]
SIMECK48/96	28/36	$2^{68.3}$	2^{46}	–	Diff.(dynamic key-guessing) [8]
SIMECK48/96	24/36	2^{94}	2^{45}	–	Linear [3]
SIMECK48/96	26/36	$\mathbf{2^{62}}$	$\mathbf{2^{47}}$	$\mathbf{2^{47}}$	Differential (Sect. 5.1)
SIMECK64/128	25/44	$2^{126.6}$	2^{64}	2^{79}	Imp. Differential [13]
SIMECK64/128	34/44	$2^{116.3}$	2^{63}	–	Diff.(dynamic key-guessing) [8]
SIMECK64/128	35/44	$2^{116.3}$	2^{63}	–	Diff.(dynamic key-guessing) [8]
SIMECK64/128	27/44	$2^{120.5}$	2^{61}	–	Linear [3]
SIMECK64/128	$\mathbf{33/44}$	$\mathbf{2^{115}}$	$\mathbf{2^{63}}$	$\mathbf{2^{63}}$	Differential (Sect. 5.3)

differentials. An open question is whether better differentials exist for both SIMON and SIMECK which give a surprisingly higher probability as in the case of our differential for SIMECK32. This effect could be more significant for larger word sizes and lead to improved attacks.

In this sense SIMECK also has an unexpected advantage over SIMON and SPECK, as the analysis is simpler and requires less computational effort with our approach. This is a property that is especially important in the light of not having cryptanalytic design documentation, nor design rationales for the constants regarding security available by the designers of SIMON and SPECK.

For both SIMON32 and SIMECK32 reduced to 13 rounds we observed that for some keys a surprisingly large number of valid pairs can be found. This gives an interesting open problem in classifying the keys which give a significant higher probability for a given differential.

A   Bounds for Linear Trails

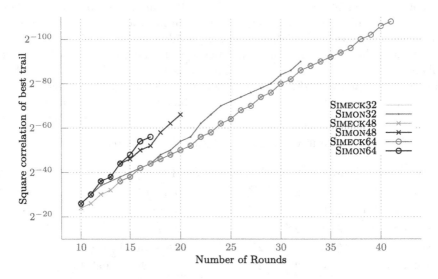

Fig. 8. Bounds for the best linear trails for variants of SIMON and SIMECK. For the different variants of SIMECK the bounds are the same.

Table 7. Classification of all the 40 rotation invariant 13-round differentials for SIMECK32.

Type 1			
$(0,22) \xrightarrow{f^{13}} (2a,1)$	$(4,8a8) \xrightarrow{f^{13}} (88,0)$	$(4,8e8) \xrightarrow{f^{13}} (88,)$	$(0,11) \xrightarrow{f^{13}} (1d,8)$
$(0,11) \xrightarrow{f^{13}} (115,8)$	$(0,88) \xrightarrow{f^{13}} (8e8,4)$	$(4,a8) \xrightarrow{f^{13}} (88,0)$	$(1,3a) \xrightarrow{f^{13}} (22,0)$

Type 2			
$(4,8a) \xrightarrow{f^{13}} (aa,4)$	$(4,8a) \xrightarrow{f^{13}} (ae,4)$	$(1,a8) \xrightarrow{f^{13}} (228,1)$	$(4,aa) \xrightarrow{f^{13}} (a,4)$
$(4,8e) \xrightarrow{f^{13}} (aa,4)$	$(4,2e) \xrightarrow{f^{13}} (a,4)$	$(4,2e) \xrightarrow{f^{13}} (e,4)$	$(2,57) \xrightarrow{f^{13}} (5,2)$
$(2,5) \xrightarrow{f^{13}} (55,2)$	$(4,8e) \xrightarrow{f^{13}} (2a,4)$	$(1,2a8) \xrightarrow{f^{13}} (228,1)$	$(2,7) \xrightarrow{f^{13}} (55,2)$
$(4,aa) \xrightarrow{f^{13}} (8e,4)$	$(4,ae) \xrightarrow{f^{13}} (e,4)$	$(4,8a) \xrightarrow{f^{13}} (2e,4)$	$(2,15) \xrightarrow{f^{13}} (5,2)$
$(2,7) \xrightarrow{f^{13}} (17,2)$	$(4,e) \xrightarrow{f^{13}} (ae,4)$	$(4,ae) \xrightarrow{f^{13}} (8e,4)$	$(4,8a) \xrightarrow{f^{13}} (2a,4)$
$(4,e) \xrightarrow{f^{13}} (2a,4)$	$(4,a) \xrightarrow{f^{13}} (2a,4)$	$(4,2e) \xrightarrow{f^{13}} (8a,4)$	$(4,2a) \xrightarrow{f^{13}} (8e,4)$
$(4,a) \xrightarrow{f^{13}} (ae,4)$	$(4,8e) \xrightarrow{f^{13}} (ae,4)$	$(1,28) \xrightarrow{f^{13}} (b8,1)$	$(4,8e) \xrightarrow{f^{13}} (2e,4)$
$(1,b8) \xrightarrow{f^{13}} (238,1)$	$(4,ae) \xrightarrow{f^{13}} (8a,4)$	$(2,15) \xrightarrow{f^{13}} (7,2)$	$(1,2a8) \xrightarrow{f^{13}} (38,1)$

Table 8. Distribution of the trails for the different type of differentials in 13-round SIMECK32.

$\log_2 \Pr(Q)$	Type 1	Type 2	Type 3
-32	1	1	0
-33	0	0	0
-34	9	7	0
-35	6	5	0
-36	38	24	8
-37	44	28	2
-38	124	71	87
-39	166	96	79
-40	367	210	560
-41	521	308	868
-42	1014	625	2911
-43	1566	1002	5170
-44	2629	1752	12485
-45	4232	2975	22007
-46	6448	5101	43969
-47	9620	8234	75212
-48	13952	14439	133341
-49	19425	24653	220359
$\sum$	$2^{-27.88}$	$2^{-28.43}$	$2^{-27.29}$

Table 9. Number of trails and time to find them for the SIMECK48 differential $(400000, e00000) \xrightarrow{f^{20}} (400000, 200000)$.

$\log_2 \Pr(Q)$	#Trails	Pr(Differential)	T
-50	1	-50.0	3.72s
-51	0	-50.0	6.9s
-52	12	-48.0	19.78s
-53	6	-47.7520724866	31.77 s
-54	80	-46.7145977811	42.62 s
-55	68	-46.4301443917	55.68 s
-56	413	-45.804012702	77.58 s
-57	484	-45.5334136623	104.69 s
-58	1791	-45.1367816524	180.02 s
-59	2702	-44.8963843436	265.5 s
-60	7225	-44.6271009401	528.39 s
-61	12496	-44.4289288164	1068.95 s
-62	28597	-44.2312406041	2603.59 s
-63	52104	-44.0720542548	6146.77 s
-64	111379	-43.9193398907	19276.9 s
-65	207544	-43.7902765446	41938.08 s
-66	238939	-43.7209043818	70720.98 s
-67	228530	-43.6888725691	96657.81 s
-68	229018	-43.6730860168	123706.38 s
-69	276314	-43.6636455186	160688.8 s
-70	271192	-43.6590352669	197354.41 s
-71	269239	-43.6567522016	232641.34 s
-72	267563	-43.6556191172	271083.28 s
-73	266716	-43.6550547005	308072.68 s
-74	227971	-43.6548135551	336027.17 s

Table 10. Truncated differential for SIMECK32 obtained by extending $(8000, 4011) \xrightarrow{f^{13}} (4000, 0)$ in both directions until all bits are unknown.

Round	ΔL	ΔR	*	*
-4	***0************	****************	15	16
-3	**000***0****1**	***0************	11	15
-2	0*0000*000***01*	**000***0****1**	6	11
-1	0100000000010001	0*0000*000***01*	0	6
0	1000000000000000	0100000000010001	0	0
13 rounds				
13	0100000000000000	0000000000000000	0	0
14	1*0000000000*000	0100000000000000	2	0
15	**00000*000**001	1*0000000000*000	5	2
16	***000**00***01*	**00000*000**001	9	5
17	***00***0*******	***000**00***01*	13	9
18	***0************	***00***0*******	15	13
19	****************	***0************	16	15

Table 11. Truncated differential for SIMECK64 obtained by extending $(0, 4400000) \xrightarrow{f^{26}}$ $(8800000, 400000)$ in both directions until all bits are unknown.

Round	ΔL	ΔR	*	*
−8	***************0******************	********************************	31	32
−7	***********0**00***0*************	**************0*****************	28	31
−6	***********00*000**00***0********	***********0**00***0*************	24	28
−5	**********0000000*000**00***0****	***********00*000**00***0********	19	24
−4	*0****1***000000000000*000**00**	**********0000000*000**00***0***	13	19
−3	*00***01**0000000000000000*000*	*0****1***000000000000*000**00**	8	13
−2	*000**001*0000000000000000000000	*00***01**0000000000000000*000*	4	8
−1	00001000100000000000000000000000	*000**001*000000000000000000000	0	4
0	00000000000000000000000000000000	00001000100000000000000000000000	0	0
26 rounds				
26	00001000100000000000000000000000	00000000010000000000000000000000	0	0
27	000**001*10000000000000000000000*	00001000100000000000000000000000	4	0
28	00***01***0000000000000*000**	000**001*10000000000000000000000*	9	4
29	0****1****00000000000*000**00***	00***01***0000000000000*000**	14	9
30	**********000000*000**00***0****	0****1****00000000000*000**00***	20	14
31	***********0*000**00***0*********	**********000000*000**00***0****	25	20
32	*************00***0**************	***********0*000**00***0*********	29	25
33	**************0*****************	*************00***0**************	31	29
34	********************************	**************0*****************	32	31

References

1. Abed, F., List, E., Lucks, S., Wenzel, J.: Differential cryptanalysis of round-reduced SIMON and SPECK. In: Cid, C., Rechberger, C. (eds.) FSE 2014. LNCS, vol. 8540, pp. 525–545. Springer, Heidelberg (2015). doi:10.1007/978-3-662-46706-0_27
2. Alizadeh, J., Alkhzaimi, H.A., Aref, M.R., Bagheri, N., Gauravaram, P., Kumar, A., Lauridsen, M.M., Sanadhya, S.K.: Cryptanalysis of SIMON variants with connections. In: Saxena, N., Sadeghi, A.-R. (eds.) RFIDSec 2014. LNCS, vol. 8651, pp. 90–107. Springer, Cham (2014). doi:10.1007/978-3-319-13066-8_6
3. Bagheri, N.: Linear cryptanalysis of reduced-round SIMECK variants. In: Biryukov, A., Goyal, V. (eds.) INDOCRYPT 2015. LNCS, vol. 9462, pp. 140–152. Springer, Cham (2015). doi:10.1007/978-3-319-26617-6_8
4. Beaulieu, R., Shors, D., Smith, J., Treatman-Clark, S., Weeks, B., Wingers, L.: The SIMON and SPECK families of lightweight block ciphers. Cryptology ePrint Archive, Report 2013/404 (2013). http://eprint.iacr.org/
5. Biryukov, A., Roy, A., Velichkov, V.: Differential analysis of block ciphers SIMON and SPECK. In: Cid, C., Rechberger, C. (eds.) FSE 2014. LNCS, vol. 8540, pp. 546–570. Springer, Heidelberg (2015). doi:10.1007/978-3-662-46706-0_28
6. Kölbl, S.: CryptoSMT: an easy to use tool for cryptanalysis of symmetric primitives (2015). https://github.com/kste/cryptosmt

7. Kölbl, S., Leander, G., Tiessen, T.: Observations on the SIMON block cipher family. In: Gennaro, R., Robshaw, M. (eds.) CRYPTO 2015. LNCS, vol. 9215, pp. 161–185. Springer, Heidelberg (2015). doi:10.1007/978-3-662-47989-6_8

8. Qiao, K., Hu, L., Sun, S.: Differential security evaluation of simeck with dynamic key-guessing techniques. Cryptology ePrint Archive, Report 2015/902 (2015). http://eprint.iacr.org/

9. Sun, S., Hu, L., Wang, M., Wang, P., Qiao, K., Ma, X., Shi, D., Song, L., Fu, K.: Constructing mixed-integer programming models whose feasible region is exactly the set of all valid differential characteristics of SIMON. Cryptology ePrint Archive, Report 2015/122 (2015). http://eprint.iacr.org/

10. Sun, S., Hu, L., Wang, P., Qiao, K., Ma, X., Song, L.: Automatic security evaluation and (related-key) differential characteristic search: application to SIMON, PRESENT, LBlock, DES(L) and other bit-oriented block ciphers. In: Sarkar, P., Iwata, T. (eds.) ASIACRYPT 2014. LNCS, vol. 8873, pp. 158–178. Springer, Heidelberg (2014). doi:10.1007/978-3-662-45611-8_9

11. Wang, N., Wang, X., Jia, K., Zhao, J.: Differential attacks on reduced simon versions with dynamic key-guessing techniques. Cryptology ePrint Archive, Report 2014/448 (2014). http://eprint.iacr.org/

12. Wang, Q., Liu, Z., Varıcı, K., Sasaki, Y., Rijmen, V., Todo, Y.: Cryptanalysis of reduced-round SIMON32 and SIMON48. In: Meier, W., Mukhopadhyay, D. (eds.) INDOCRYPT 2014. LNCS, vol. 8885, pp. 143–160. Springer, Cham (2014). doi:10.1007/978-3-319-13039-2_9

13. Yang, G., Zhu, B., Suder, V., Aagaard, M.D., Gong, G.: The Simeck family of lightweight block ciphers. In: Güneysu, T., Handschuh, H. (eds.) CHES 2015. LNCS, vol. 9293, pp. 307–329. Springer, Heidelberg (2015). doi:10.1007/978-3-662-48324-4_16

Lightweight Designs and Implementations

Bitsliced Masking and ARM: Friends or Foes?

Wouter de Groot[2], Kostas Papagiannopoulos[1]($\boxtimes$), Antonio de La Piedra[1],
Erik Schneider[2], and Lejla Batina[1]

[1] Radboud University Nijmegen, Nijmegen, The Netherlands
kostaspap88@gmail.com
[2] Eindhoven University of Technology, Eindhoven, The Netherlands

Abstract. Software-based cryptographic implementations can be vulnerable to side-channel analysis. Masking countermeasures rank among the most prevalent techniques against it, ensuring formally the protection vs. value-based leakages. However, its applicability is halted by two factors. First, a masking countermeasure involves a *computational overhead* that can render implementations inefficient. Second, physical effects such as glitches and distance-based leakages can cause the *reduction of the security order* in practice, rendering the masking protection less effective. This paper, attempts to address both factors. In order to reduce the computational cost, we implement a high-throughput, bitsliced, 2nd-order masked implementation of the PRESENT cipher, using assembly in ARM Cortex-M4. The implementation outperforms the current state of the art and is capable of encrypting a 64-bit block of plaintext in 6,532 cycles (excluding RNG), using 1,644 bytes of data RAM and 1,552 bytes of code memory. Second, we analyze experimentally the effectiveness of masking in ARM devices, i.e. we examine the effects of distance-based leakages on the security order of our implementation. We confirm the theoretical model behind distance leakages for the first time in ARM-based architectures.

Keywords: PRESENT · ARM Cortex-M · Bitslicing · Masking · SCA

1 Introduction

Nowadays, everyday devices, sensors, vehicles and other items are embedded with electronics, allowing network connectivity and information exchange. Often, these fairly simple devices need to maintain a high level of security against powerful adversaries with passive monitoring, as well as active tampering capabilities.

For instance, side-channel attacks (SCA) allow attackers to learn sensitive data by observing physical characteristics of a cryptographic implementation. Their discovery in 1999 by Kocher et al. [32] exposed a blind spot in theoretical, proof-driven cryptography and has motivated researchers to find efficient

The work described in this paper has been supported by the Netherlands Organization for Scientific Research NWO under project ProFIL (628.001.007).

© Springer International Publishing AG 2017
A. Bogdanov (Ed.): LightSec 2016, LNCS 10098, pp. 91–109, 2017.
DOI: 10.1007/978-3-319-55714-4_7

countermeasures. A very common option for provably secure software counter-measures is masking [18], which uses secret-sharing techniques to hinder key recovery.

However, the masking countermeasure can imply a severe *performance over-head* in terms of processing speed due to the quadratic computational complexity required [30]. Moreover, masking can formally ensure protection against a theo-retical leakage model, namely the value-based model. As a result, device-specific divergence from the assumed model can lead to security order reduction. For instance, software devices often exhibit *distance-based leakages*, which have been theorized to reduce the order of a masked scheme by 50% [2].

This paper attempts to answer whether masking countermeasures and ARM devices are *friends or foes*. The contribution is twofold and extends to both the performance factor as well as the security order factor.

First, we improve the current state of the art by creating an efficient, bit-sliced, 2nd-order implementation of PRESENT. The PRESENT cipher was selected due to its widespread applicability in the Internet of Things context. Our implementation requires 1,644 bytes of RAM, 1,552 bytes of code memory and encrypts 32 blocks of data in 209,023 clock cycles, achieving a throughput of 6,532 clock cycles per block, excluding the cost of random number generation. Thus, we demonstrate that ARM-based architectures can host masked imple-mentations efficiently, given that the implementors opt for full-scale assembly programs and use efficient state representations.

Second, we examine potential distance-based leakages in ARM architectures. That is, we perform side-channel experiments in order to test whether our ARM Cortex-M4 device is prone to causing order reduction in our 2nd-order imple-mentation. In addition, we confirm that the observed order reduction follows the theorized reduction established by Balasch et al. [2]. That is, we confirm the *order-reduction theorem* (Sect. 5) in ARM-based architectures for the first time.

In the next section, we describe the work of other practitioners who imple-mented PRESENT and relate their performance figures with our work. In Sect. 3 we offer a brief description of the PRESENT cipher. Section 4 discusses the design options and optimizations w.r.t. the masked ARM implementation, as well as the performance results. Section 5 links the order reduction model sug-gested by Balasch et al. [2] to our ARM-based device. Finally, Sect. 6 concludes and discusses future work.

2   Related Work

In this section, we describe the work of those implementors that addressed the implementation of PRESENT in software. We do this in ascending order of word size according to the architecture.

4-Bit Architectures. Poschmann implemented PRESENT in different soft-ware platforms [39]. In a 4-bit μC, particularly an Atmel ATAM893-D at 2 MHz he obtained a performance figure of 55,734 cycles per block. He also implemented PRESENT in an 8-bit ATmega μC clocked at 4 MHz, obtaining a performance of 10,089 cycles.

8-Bit Architectures. Papagiannopoulos presented a bitsliced implementation of PRESENT on the 8-bit ATtiny85 μC. He applied bitslicing to the permutation and substitution layers using a bitslice factor of 8 [38]. That work relied on the PRESENT Sboxes resulting from the application of 2-stage Boyar-Peralta heuristic in tandem with SAT solvers [12]. He obtained a throughput (cycles per block) of 2,967 using 3,816 bytes of Flash and 256 bytes of SRAM. In this work, we use the same Sbox. Dinu et al. also analyzed the suitability of a wide range of lightweight block ciphers in sensor-based applications in three different architectures: an 8-bit ATmega, 16-bit MSP430 and 32-bit ARM processor. They do not apply bitslicing and implemented the Cipher Block Chaining (CBC) and counter (CTR) modes of operation [23]. The CBC implementation requires 121,906 cycles on the ATmega processor whereas the CTR implementation can obtain one block of ciphertext in 15,239 cycles. Furthermore, the authors from [25] implement PRESENT in an ATiny 8-bit μC, using 80 bits keys the required 11,343 cycles, 1,000 bytes of code and 18 bytes of RAM. Using the same platform Papagiannopoulos decreased the amount of cycles to 8,712 cycles in [37] by using a merged SP layer, squared and compact representations of the Sbox and minimal key register rotations. Finally Rauzy et al. presented a design methodology for inserting Dual-rail with Precharge Logic (DPL) in a software implementation of PRESENT in an automatic way [41]. They relied on an 8-bit AVR ATmega 163 implementation (bitsliced). They require 235,427 cycles for obtaining a single block of ciphertext.

16-Bit Architectures. Poschmann also implemented PRESENT on an 16-bit Infineon C167CR processor, obtaining a performance figure 19,460 cycles per block [39]. On the other hand, Dinu et al. relied on the MSP430 of 16-bit for implementing both the CBC and CTR modes of PRESENT, obtaining a performance of 100,786 and 12,226 cycles respectively. In [17], Cazorla et al. evaluated a variety of lightweight primitives on the 16-bit MSP430 μC that sensor nodes usually equip due to its low-power and cost. Clocked at 8 MHz, their performance figures are 364,587 cycles and 45,573 cycles/byte (they do not employ bitslicing).

32-Bit Architectures. Dinu et al. implemented PRESENT on the ARM Cortex architecture [23]. Their CBC implementation requires 138,947 cycles on the ARM processor whereas their CTR implementation can obtain one block of ciphertext in 16,919 cycles.

64-Bit Architectures. Benadjila et al. explored the software implementation of the LED, Piccolo and PRESENT block ciphers [5,29,43]. They relied on table-based implementations, vector permutations and bitslice approaches. The best results for bitsliced PRESENT-80 are 18.7 cycles/byte for 16 plaintexts in 2,221 cycles in an Intel Core i3 2367M clocked at 1.4 GHz. Matsuda et al. proposed in [34] the utilization of PRESENT in sensor-related applications for processing a high-amount of data gathered by nodes. They relied on 3 Intel architectures, particularly on the Core 45 nm and Nehalem (equipped with the Streaming SIMD extensions (SSE) 4.1 and 128-bit XMM registers) and on the Sandy Bridge, equipped with the Advanced Vector Extension (AVX). Executing 32 plaintexts simultaneously via a bitsliced implementation, the require 4.73 cycles/byte on the Sandy Bridge architecture.

Contribution. In this manuscript we present a very fast and 2nd-order protected implementation of the PRESENT block cipher by combining bitslicing and 2nd-order masking. We rely on the 32-bit ARM Cortex-M4 CPU[1]. The analytical results can be seen in Sect. 4.3. Our implementation can encrypt one PRESENT plain text in 6,532 cycles using 1,644 bytes of RAM and 1,552 bytes of ROM. To our knowledge, this is the first high-order protected implementation of PRESENT that includes side-channel evaluation. We have evaluated our implementation against first, second and third-order security using state-of-the art techniques (Sect. 5). None of the works described in this section performed such exhaustive evaluation on their implementation while protecting it against second-order attacks [5, 17, 23, 25, 34, 37–39, 41]. Our performance figures suggest that our implementation is between 2.5 and 21.2 times faster than prior art relying on the same architecture (Sect. 4.4). Further, we have made our implementation available under the General Public License (GPL)[2].

Finally, since the constructions found in PRESENT are also used on the hash functions SPONGENT and H-PRESENT [8,10], the same approaches we present in this manuscript can be applied to their implementation.

3   PRESENT

Given the need of alternative cryptographic primitives aimed at low-power and compact applications such as RFID and sensor networks, a variety of lightweight primitives such as PRESENT has been proposed in the last few years [9]. Standardized in ISO/IEC 29192-2:2012[3], it consists of a substitution-permutation (SP) network, 80/128-bit key sizes and 64-bit data blocks. PRESENT applies the following layers during 31 rounds to a 64-bit state b:

1. **addRoundKey:** During the execution of PRESENT, 32 round keys (K_i w.r.t. $1 \leq i \leq 32$) are generated via a key schedule using the encryption key K as an input. The last subkey, K_{32} is used for post-whitening.

---

[1] In particular, we used an STM32F417IG SoC by ST clocked at 168 MHz with 1,024 Kbytes of Flash and 196 Kbytes of RAM.

[2] http://tinyurl.com/zw7zlkv (Accessed 24 June 2016).

[3] http://www.iso.org/iso/iso_catalogue/catalogue_tc/catalogue_detail.htm? csnumber=56552 (Accessed 24 June 2016).

Each round key K_i has a size of 64 bits. Thus, each execution of **addRound-Key** is comprised of the XOR operation between the state and the round key, i.e. $b' \leftarrow b \oplus K_i$.

2. **sBoxLayer:** This layer is a non-linear substitution operation that relies on a 4-bit Sbox ($\mathbb{F}_2^4 \rightarrow \mathbb{F}_2^4$), applied 16 times per round to the state. The 64-bit state is divided in 16 groups of 4 bits that feed the PRESENT Sbox (Table 1).

3. **pLayer:** This layer consists of a linear bit-wise permutation where each bit i of the state (b_i) is moved to another position $P(i)$ according to Table 2.

Table 1. 4-bit PRESENT Sbox

x	0	1	2	3	4	5	6	7	8	9	A	B	C	D	E	F
$S[x]$	c	5	6	b	9	0	a	d	3	e	f	8	4	7	1	2

Table 2. Permutation table of PRESENT

i	0	1	2	3	4	5	6	7	8	9	10	11	12	13	14	15
$P(i)$	0	16	32	48	1	17	33	49	2	18	34	50	3	19	35	51
i	16	17	18	19	20	21	22	23	24	25	26	27	28	29	30	31
$P(i)$	4	20	36	52	5	21	37	53	6	22	38	54	7	23	39	55
i	32	33	34	35	36	37	38	39	40	41	42	43	44	45	46	47
$P(i)$	8	24	40	56	9	25	41	57	10	26	42	58	11	27	43	59
i	48	49	50	51	52	53	54	55	56	57	58	59	60	61	62	63
$P(i)$	12	28	44	60	13	29	45	61	14	30	46	62	15	31	47	63

Finally, the round subkeys are generated as follows. Given a key K of 80 bits s.t. $K_{79}, K_{78}, ..., K_0$, a round key i of 64 bits is the 64 left most bits of K updated via the following operations:

1. 61 bits rotations to the left of K.
2. The left most 4 bits are processed in the PRESENT Sbox.
3. The round counter is exclusive-ored with the bits $K_{19}, ..., K_{15}$ of K.

4 Bitsliced Masking of PRESENT for ARM Cortex-M4

The current section describes the design choices investigated in order to develop a protected, high-throughput, assembly-based PRESENT implementation. Sections 4.1 and 4.2 describe the logic-level optimizations performed, while Sect. 4.3 discusses the instruction-level improvements.

4.1 Bitslicing and Efficient Sbox Representation

CPU architectures tend to operate best on their native word size or half-words and they encounter performance issues with bit-level manipulation. To deal with this issue, the Cortex-M4 features bit-banding support[4], as well as a wide selection of bit-field instructions. However, applying them in the context of PRESENT requires extensive use of load and store instructions or numerous bit extractions/insertions, often resulting in poor performance.

Bitslicing is a technique introduced by Biham to tackle this inefficiency for DES [6]. Instead of using registers to store consecutive bits of a state, one uses them to hold one specific bit from several different states, effectively transforming bit-level operations into SIMD equivalents.

In our implementation, we employ a bitsliced representation of factor 32, i.e. we process in parallel 32 cipher blocks, 64 bits each, resulting in 256 bytes per bitsliced encryption. Doing so, allows us to efficiently compute both the substitution and the permutation layer of PRESENT. Analytically, the Sbox can be decomposed into $GF(2)$ operations which can be accelerated by via the SIMD-like instructions and it no longer requires the application of memory lookup tables.[5] Similarly, the bit permutations can be accelerated by directly exchanging the memory contents of the corresponding bitsliced bits according to the permutation pattern, instead of relying on bit extraction, insertion and shifting.

The $GF(2)$ decomposition of the Sbox has sparked interest in the optimization of boolean circuits w.r.t. computational efficiency. In our implementation, we use the optimized boolean circuit suggested for PRESENT by Courtois et al. [21]. The optimized representation was generated by applying the Boyar-Peralta heuristic [12], which reduces the circuit's *gate complexity*, i.e. the number of AND, OR, XOR, NOT operations. The representation is shown below.

```
T1 = X2^X1;   T2 = X1&T1;   T3 = X0^T2;   Y4 = X3^T3;   T2 = T1&T3;
T1 ^= Y4;     T2 ^= X1;     T4 = X3|T2;   Y3 = T1^T4;   X3 =~ X3;
T2^ = X3;     Y1 = Y3^T2;   T2 |= T1;     Y2 = T3^T2;
```

Values X1–X4 represent an Sbox input, T1–T4 hold temporary values and Y1–Y4 are output values. The total cost is 14 operations, 4 non-linear (AND, OR) and 10 linear (XOR,NOT).

4.2 Boolean Masking

Chari et al. [18] were among the first to suggest that splitting intermediate values using a secret sharing scheme would force attackers to analyze joint distribution functions on multiple points. That is, a dth-order masking scheme splits a sensitive value x into $d + 1$ shares $(x_0, x_1, \ldots, x_d)$ as follows:

$$x = x_0 \oplus x_1 \cdots \oplus x_d \tag{1}$$

---

[4] Bit-banding allows individual bits to be addressed as though they were bytes in RAM.

[5] Note that implementations based on lookup tables can be prone to timing side-channel attacks in the presence of memory caches.

Assuming sufficient noise, it has been shown that the number of traces required for a successful attack grows exponentially w.r.t. the order d [18,40].

Masking involves several implementation angles, e.g. Goubin et al. [26], Messerges [35] and recently Coron [19] applied the masking principle in *lookup tables* used in Sbox computation. Adopting a different implementation angle, Trichina [47], Canright [14], Akkar et al. [1] and Blömer et al. [7] applied masking in the context of *GF operations* used in Sbox computation. This operation-based approach was formalized by Ishai, Sahai, and Wagner's shared secret approach (ISW), which introduced the notion of private boolean circuits [30]. ISW provided implementors with a provably secure method to mask operations in $GF(2)$ for any masking order d.

This work employs a bitsliced representation of PRESENT and enhances the implementation using a 2nd-order protection scheme. As demonstrated in Sect. 4.1, the Sbox is decomposed into $GF(2)$ operations. Thus, ISW is our technique of choice in order to apply 2nd-order protection on the boolean operations required for the Sbox computation.

Table 3 shows the ISW equivalent of common boolean operations when applied to bitsliced operands a and b, as well as the computational cost involved for each operation. The values $z_{i,j}$ where $1 \leq i < j \leq (d+1)$ are drawn from a uniform random distribution and the remaining $z_{i,j}$ are computed using $(z_{i,j} \oplus a_i b_j) \oplus a_j b_i$. Note that the cost of the NOT operation is a single negation, the cost of the XOR operation is linear and the cost of the AND,OR operations is quadratic. In our implementation, the OR operation is converted to a single AND and three NOT operations in order to apply the ISW method.

Table 3. ISW equivalents of common boolean operations

Operation	ISW equivalent	Cost
NOT(a)	$\neg a_0$	$\mathcal{O}(1)$
XOR(a,b)	$a_i \oplus b_i$	$\mathcal{O}(d)$
OR(a,b)	**NOT(AND(NOT(a),NOT(b)))**	$\mathcal{O}(d^2)$
AND(a,b)	$a_i b_i \oplus \bigoplus_{i \neq j} z_{i,j}$	$\mathcal{O}(d^2)$

The quadratic computational complexity of non-linear operations can result in a computationally demanding masked Sbox. To avoid this, several techniques [15,16,21,27,45] on reducing the *multiplicative complexity of an Sbox*, i.e. the number of AND,OR operations. The decomposition that we currently use (shown in Sect. 4.1) is optimal w.r.t. multiplicative complexity, since brute-force techniques [28] demonstrate that the minimal complexity in $GF(2)$ of cryptographically relevant, 4-bit Sboxes is 4 non-linear operations.

4.3 ARM-Based Optimizations

Our implementation targets the ARM Cortex-M4 microcontroller architecture using ARM assembly with Thumb2 encoding. Thus, we use a 32-bit architecture with 14 general purpose registers designed for low-cost, low-power applications. The implementation board is the Riscure Pinata[6] which is based on the STM32F417IG SoC by ST and embeds an ARM 32-bit Cortex-M4 CPU clocked at 168 MHz. It features 1,024 Kbytes of Flash and 196 Kbytes of RAM. The device is also equipped with a TRNG on the board in order to generate the random values associated to our masking implementation. In the case of the STM32F417IG, the TRNG generates 32-bit random numbers via an integrated analog circuit. Note that the computational penalty w.r.t. random number generation is particularly steep when implemented on-the-fly, amounting to roughly 25% of the total computation. Still, we note that the random numbers can be precomputed in advance, given that the application context allows for idle intervals between consecutive encryptions. Below, we discuss implementation details and efficiency improvements pertaining to the ARM architecture, memory organization and assembly instructions.

1. **Memory organization:** Our design requires two full bitsliced states in RAM, each comprising of three sub-states corresponding to the three-share masking scheme. The two full bitsliced states are needed because the permutation layer would otherwise overwrite unprocessed data. We optimize for cycles by integrating the permutation into the Sbox and writing words to their permuted destination immediately after the Sbox computation.
   Wherever the code operates on shares we organize our fetch and store data in batches so as to reduce overhead. In most cases we use the LDM and STM instructions to load or store three or four words at a time. This yields improvements in the Sbox computation when reading in the next four words to be substituted, in the key schedule, where three words at a time are read in for processing and also when converting a regular state representation from/to a bitsliced one.

2. **Loop Unrolling:** To improve the efficiency of our Sbox implementation, which encrypts twelve shares (four bit-sliced data blocks of three shares each), we unroll the substitution process to reduce the unnecessary read/write steps required for a looped construction. The unrolling adds considerable size to the code, yet we achieve trading code size for throughput. Note that unrolling is performed with memory access in mind. For example, we mentioned that adding the key schedule is performed in a loop of three words. This optimizes the key schedule operation and maximizes the amount of data we can bring from/to the RAM.

3. **Key Schedule:** The round key is not stored in a bitsliced fashion and the key schedule is computed on the fly. Note that round key precomputation is also a valid implementation option, assuming that the key does not need to be renewed often. Since, key refreshing can act as a side-channel countermeasure,

---

[6] https://www.riscure.com/security-tools/hardware/pinata (Accessed 24 June 2016).

we chose to retain the on-the-fly key updates. Updating the round key requires a push through the Sbox for four bits each round. To that purpose, we use Cortex-M4's UBFX instruction for extracting a contiguous series of bits from a word in an efficient manner. In addition, we used ARM's barrel shifter function, which allows the second operand to be shifted with no additional cost before an instruction is performed.

4.4 Performance Results

The current section summarizes the achieved performance results w.r.t. throughput and size. We depict in Tables 4 and 5 the performance figures of the works described in Sect. 2. As mentioned, we outperform prior art on the same architecture between 2.5 and 21.2 times [23].

Table 4. PRESENT implementations, comparison with prior art (performance)

Work	Implementation	Bitslicing	Bitslicing factor	Protected	Platform	No. cycles per block
This work	PRESENT-80	yes	32	yes	ARM Cortex–M4	6,532
[23]	PRESENT-80, CBC	no	-	no	ATmega	121,906
[23]	PRESENT-80, CBC	no	-	no	MSP430	100,786
[23]	PRESENT-80, CBC	no	-	no	ARM Cortex-M3	138,947
[23]	PRESENT-80, CTR	no	-	no	ATmega	15,239
[23]	PRESENT-80, CTR	no	-	no	MSP430	12,226
[23]	PRESENT-80, CTR	no	-	no	ARM	16,919
[37]	PRESENT-80	no	-	no	ATiny	8,721
[41]	PRESENT-80	yes	8	no	ATMega163	78,403
[41]	PRESENT-80, DPL	yes	8	yes	ATMega163	235,427
[38]	PRESENT-80	yes	8	no	ATiny85	2,967
[5]	PRESENT-80, table	no	-	no	Corei3-2367M	988
[5]	PRESENT-80, vperm	yes	2	no	Corei3-2367M	890
[5]	PRESENT-80	yes	8	no	Corei3-2367M	2,039
[5]	PRESENT-80	yes	16	no	Corei3-2367M	3,138
[34]	PRESENT-80	yes	32	no	Xeon E3-1280	37.84
[34]	PRESENT-80	yes	16	no	Xeon E3-1280	52.16
[34]	PRESENT-80	yes	8	no	Xeon E3-1280	67.68
[17]	PRESENT-80	no	-	no	MSP430	364,587
[39]	PRESENT-80	no	-	no	ATAM893-D	55,734
[39]	PRESENT-80	no	-	no	ATMega163	10,089
[39]	PRESENT-80	no	-	no	C167CR	19,460

As expected, the ISW implementation of the Sbox dominated CPU time, accounting for 95,88% of all clock cycles within the encryption process. A complete breakdown of the memory and time overheads required for different modules is provided in Table 6.

Table 5. PRESENT implementations, comparison with prior art (size)

Work	Implementation	Code (bytes)	RAM (bytes)
This work	PRESENT-80	1,548	1,644
[38]	PRESENT-80	3,816	256
[39]	PRESENT-80, ATMega	1,494	272
[39]	PRESENT-80, C167CR	$45.9 \cdot 10^3$	-
[23]	PRESENT-80, CBC, ATMega	1,388	56
[23]	PRESENT-80, CBC, MSP430	1,108	52
[23]	PRESENT-80, CBC, ARM	1,304	124
[23]	PRESENT-80, CTR, ATMega	1,416	54
[23]	PRESENT-80, CTR, MSP430	1,244	58
[23]	PRESENT-80, CTR, ARM	1,532	140
[37]	PRESENT-80	1,794	-
[41]	PRESENT-80, bitslicing	1,620	288
[41]	PRESENT-80, bitslicing + DPL	3,056	352

Table 6. SW transformations of common logical operations

Operation	Code size (%)	No. cycles (%)
main	208 (13.44)	3,807 (1.82)
sbox	892 (57.62)	200,404 (95.88)
updatekey	146 (9.43)	1,688 (0.81)
addroundkey	176 (11.37)	1,209 (0.58)
split data	60 (3.88)	1,292 (0.62)
unsplit data	66 (4.26)	623 (0.30)

5   Masking Effectiveness in ARM Cortex-M4

In this section, we assess experimentally the security level (masking order) provided by the ISW masking scheme, taking into account the possibility of distance-based leakages in ARM Cortex-M4. In addition, we investigate whether the theoretical repercussions of distance-based leakages can be confirmed experimentally. In other words, we examine whether the cost of "lazy engineering" as introduced by Balasch et al. [2] is applicable to an ARM-based microcontroller.

5.1   Experimental Pitfalls

The *effective* and *efficient* evaluation of the *actual mask order* of cryptographic implementations remains an open problem due to several evaluation pitfalls.

Effectivity-wise, when evaluating a masking scheme via the measured power consumption, we face the pitfall of the *limited attack scope*. That is, a particular attack technique in use may fail to exploit the available leakage due to e.g. an unsuitable choice of intermediate values or an incorrect power model assumption[7]. Moreover, introducing additional countermeasures on top of the masking scheme may render particular exploitation techniques ineffective, while the implementation remains vulnerable to different lines of attack.

In order to tackle this issue, the research community followed several approaches. Prior research established generic side-channel distinguishers such as Mutual Information Analysis (MIA) [4], the Kolmogorov-Smirnov and the Cràmer-von Mises tests [48,49], which require minimal assumptions about the noise and the power model of the device under test. On the other side of the spectrum, Standaert et al. [44] proposed an evaluation framework assuming the strongest possible adversary, equipped with extensive profiling capabilities and Bayesian templates.

While being effective, the aforementioned approaches focus on leakage *exploitation* and perform key recovery, which may require a large number of traces. Thus, they face the *efficiency* pitfall w.r.t. computational and storage requirements. Note that this increased demand for resources is magnified when inserting extra countermeasures in a masked implementation. Thus, it can be difficult to decide with confidence whether the masking order is reduced or not.

In order to evaluate the *effective masking order*, we opt for a more recent approach called *leakage detection methodology* [31]. This approach focuses on leakage *detection* and disregards exploitation. Thus, the acquisition and the computational cost is reduced while the methodology can retain its generic nature.

Despite the gain achieved via decoupling detection and exploitation, the leakage detection methodology still presents challenges w.r.t. efficiency. In the context of software masking, we need to combine multiple time samples in order to evaluate the masked implementation. Thus, we rely on the work by Schneider et al. [42], who extended the leakage detection methodology into higher-order evaluations by providing efficient, incremental formulas that can handle the computation involved with minimal memory requirements. In certain cases, we also resort to traditional evaluation techniques such as correlation-power analysis (CPA) [13], despite their limited attack scope, so as to enhance our discussion.

5.2   Bitsliced Masking and Distance-Based Leakages

In order to perform leakage detection and determine the actual masking order, we opt to use the *fixed vs. random, non-specific* t-test statistic. The process involves two steps: a custom acquisition of two trace sets (populations) and a population comparison based on statistical inference.

In the first step, we perform a *fixed vs. random* acquisition and obtain two distinct trace sets for comparison: S_{fixed} and S_{random}, under the same encryption key. For S_{fixed}, the input plaintext is set to a fixed value, while for S_{random},

---

[7] Knowledge about the device can often be limited in the context of black-box evaluations.

the input is drawn from a uniformly random distribution. Following the sugges-
tion from Shneider et al. [42], the implementation receives the fixed or random
plaintext in a non-deterministic and randomly-interleaved manner. This type
of acquisition is performed in order to randomize the implementation's internal
state and avoid measurement-related variations over time, e.g. due to environ-
mental parameters. The evaluation test to be performed is *non-specific*, i.e. we
target all sensitive values computed during encryption. Thus, we maintain a wide
attack scope, without any prior assumptions on the leakage model or intermediate values.

The acquisition is performed on the ARM-based Pinata device, using a Pico-
scope 5203 oscilloscope and the Riscure current probe[8]. The device clock operates
on 168 MHz and the oscilloscope's sample rate is 1 GSample/sec. We also apply
post-processing in the form of signal resampling.

For the second step, we model the sets S_{fixed} and S_{random} as inde-
pendent random samples $\{S_{fixed}^1 \dots S_{fixed}^n\}$ and $\{S_{random}^1 \dots S_{random}^m\}$ drawn
from normal distributions with means $\mu_{fixed}, \mu_{random}$, standard deviations
$\sigma_{fixed}, \sigma_{random}$ and $\sigma_{fixed} \neq \sigma_{random}$. Subsequently, leakage detection methods will test the equality of means $\mu_{fixed}, \mu_{random}$ (null hypothesis). Finding a
statistic for this test is known as the Behrens-Fisher problem and an approximate
solution is the Welch t-test [33] with v degrees of freedom, as shown below.

$$
\begin{aligned}
H_{null} &: \quad \mu_{fixed} = \mu_{random} \\
H_{alt} &: \quad \mu_{fixed} \neq \mu_{random}
\end{aligned}
\tag{2}
$$

$$
w = \frac{\mu_{fixed} - \mu_{random}}{\sqrt{\frac{\sigma_{fixed}^2}{n} + \frac{\sigma_{random}^2}{m}}}
\tag{3}
$$

$$
v = \frac{\left(\frac{\sigma_{fixed}^2}{n} + \frac{\sigma_{random}^2}{m}\right)^2}{\frac{\sigma_{fixed}^4}{n^2(n-1)} + \frac{\sigma_{random}^4}{m^2(m-1)}}
\tag{4}
$$

The null hypothesis H_{null} is rejected at a given level of significance α, if
$|w| > t_{\alpha/2,v}$, where $t_{\alpha/2,v}$ is the value of the Student t distribution with v degrees
of freedom[9]. In the evaluation context, rejecting H_{null} implies leakage detection,
i.e. potential evidence of an ineffective masking scheme. A common rejection
criterion that we also use in our analysis is $|w| > 4.5$, which corresponds to $v >
1000$ and $\alpha > 0.99999$ [22]. Note that H_{null} rejection shouldn't be interpreted
directly as an applicable vulnerability. Even after detection, the amount of traces
required for exploitation may render an attack infeasible.

In this work, we need to evaluate the masking order provided by our ARM-
based, 2nd-order masked cipher. From a theoretical point of view, a 2nd-order
ISW masking countermeasure is capable of preventing value-based leakages

---

[8] https://www.riscure.com/security-tools/hardware/current-probe (Accessed 24 June
2016).

[9] Note that side-channel analysis usually employs two-tailed tests.

of order 2 or less. However, practice has demonstrated that software implementations, including ARM microcontrollers, may exhibit leakages with large
divergence from the value-based leakage abstraction. An exemplary case is the
distance-based leakage model, observed by Daemen et al. [46], addressed by
Coron et al. [20] and recently formalized by Balasch et al. [42]. This particular
divergence leads in the reduction of the security order. Balasch et al. theorized
that a dth-order scheme can reduce to order $\lfloor \frac{d}{2} \rfloor$ and provided experimental val-
idation using an AVR-based microcontroller. We will refer to this formalization
as the *order-reduction theorem*. To address such leakage divergence issues in our
implementation, we use the Welch t-test in order to verify *experimentally* the
theoretical security claims.

We commence the evaluation by testing the 1st-order security of our masked
cipher. We perform the 1st-order t-test on the first round of bitsliced PRESENT.
The size of both S_{fixed} and S_{random} is 10 k traces with 30 k samples per trace.
The trace waveform and t-test results are visible in Figs. 1 and 2. We observe that
we remain well below the 4.5 threshold, indicating that our 2nd-order masked
PRESENT implementation is able to maintain 1st-order security.

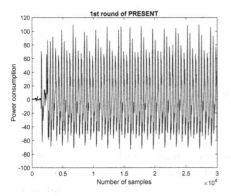

Fig. 1. Trace waveform of 1st round,
masked, bitsliced PRESENT after
resampling.

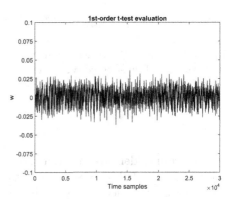

Fig. 2. 1st-order t-test evaluation for
2nd-order masked PRESENT cipher.
The results suggest absence of 1st-order
leakage.

To enhance our confidence, we also perform a 1st-order CPA attack, with
a large amount of traces (800 k) to exploit potential 1st-order leakages. We use
the HW model and a custom-made selection function due to the bitsliced Sbox
computation. Similarly to Balasch et al. [3], the selection function must take into
account that not all Sbox output bits leak at the same time due to the $GF(2)$-
oriented Sbox implementation. Thus, our selection function focuses on key bits
from different registers that once combined through the Sbox, affect a single
bit of the Sbox output. Attacking a section of the 1st round with 10 k traces,

while the RNG is disabled, is successful, confirming the validity of our choice
w.r.t. the leakage model (HW) and selection function. The results are visible in
Fig. 3. We also perform the CPA attack with enabled RNG and the results are
visible in Fig. 4. In order to manage the computation required, we employ the
techniques suggested by Bottinelli et al. [11], i.e. we partition the 800 k traces,
compute correlation coefficient per partition, then recombine in order to reduce
the execution and memory workload.

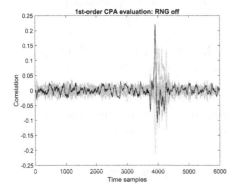 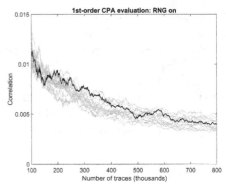

Fig. 3. 1st-order CPA attack results with RNG turned off, in selected section of the 1st round.

Fig. 4. 1st-order CPA attack results with RNG turned on, from 100 k to 800 k traces. The attack does not exploit any leakage.

The results demonstrate that no 1st-order leakage can be exploited in the
presence of our 2nd-order scheme. Both the t-test and the CPA result is in accordance with the order-reduction theorem, since a 2nd-order masked implementation can maintain $\lfloor \frac{2}{2} \rfloor = 1$ order of security in the presence of distance-based
leakages.

Assuming that our device exhibits distance-based leakage, it is of particular
interest to prove experimentally that the order-reduction theorem holds when
we test the 2nd-order security of our ARM-based masked implementation. Performing a 2nd-order evaluation requires pre-processing the acquired trace sets
in order to generate all possible 2-tuples (pairs) of distinct samples via a combination function. Subsequently, the multivariate 2nd-order t-test is performed on
the generated trace sets in order to determine the robustness of the 2nd order.

The main hindrance of this process is the computational complexity pertaining to generating and processing all $\binom{NoSamples}{2}$ sample pairs. Even with a
small number of samples per trace, the evaluation cost can quickly become prohibitive. To address this issue, researchers have relied on intuitive selection of
points of interest in conjunction with naive search [36] or they deployed heuristic
techniques such as projection pursuits [24] to perform point of interest selection

for higher-order attacks. In our evaluation, we follow the intuitive approach by focusing on a reduced version of the 1st round which contains the substitution layer. Inside this reduced round, we enumerate naively all possible pairs. Given the bitsliced nature of the implementation and the considerable RNG overhead, the reduced round has a length of 800 samples. In order to keep the processing cost manageable, we use the incremental formulas suggested by Schneider et al. which enable the efficient computation of the multivariate statistical moments required for 2nd-order t-tests. The memory-less feature of the computation yields significant improvement compared to straightforward computation techniques. In addition, we partition the reduced round into windows of 150 samples each and perform the attack in each window independently. Figure 6 shows the t-test results using 10k fixed input traces and 10 k random input traces for the sample window with the largest detected leakage (Fig. 5).

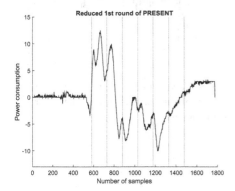 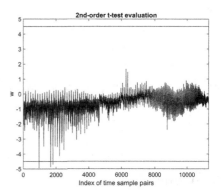

Fig. 5. Trace waveform of reduced 1st round masked, bitsliced PRESENT.

Fig. 6. 2nd-order t-test results. The rejection of H_{null} indicates potential leakage.

The test value slightly exceeds the threshold, indicating potential leakage. Thus, it hints the experimental verification of the order-detection theorem in our ARM-based device for 2nd-order ISW schemes. However, several concerns were raised over the t-test robustness, usually w.r.t. the exact threshold value (Appendix A from [2,22]). As a result, it remains an open question whether 2nd-order leakages are practically exploitable in our context. To investigate this, we perform a 2nd-order CPA-based attack using the centered product combination function and the custom bitsliced selection function on the 1st round of PRESENT. The point selection window has size 100 samples and we use 100 k traces. The results are visible in Fig. 7 and show that the leakage is *exploitable* with roughly 60 k traces.

As a result, we suggest that the order-reduction theorem remains applicable in software-based, masked implementations for the ARM Cortex-M4. However, we recommend that the exploitation is always verified in practice.

Moreover, we need to stress the fact that this type of behavior has been observed in a *specific* ARM-based device. Although it provides indications on the behavior of similar architectures, this experimental result should not be extrapolated as a hard fact w.r.t. all ARM Cortex-M devices. Naturally, a 3rd-order multivariate t-test is able to detect a large amount of leakage, as shown in Fig. 8 and indicates that a 3rd-order attack is also applicable.

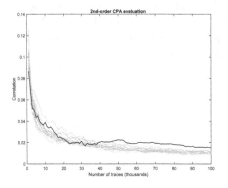

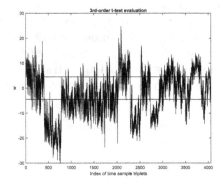

Fig. 7. 2nd-order CPA on section of the 1st round exploiting the available leakage.

Fig. 8. 3rd-order t-test results on a section of the 1st round, indicating strong 3rd-order leakage.

6   Conclusions

This paper investigated the speed and space requirements of a bitsliced implementation of PRESENT on the ARM Cortex-M4 architecture, protected with 2nd-order ISW masking. In addition, we explore and confirm the applicability of the order-reduction theorem in the context of ARM-based devices. From the attacker point of view, future work can involve deciding on the optimal strategy to attack masked implementations, given the amount of leakage available in different security orders. From the defender's point of view, implementors need to also investigate the computational cost of the randomness required for masking, which itself may pose a bigger issue than the quadratic computational complexity of masking.

Acknowledgments. We would like to thank Rafael Boix–Carpi from *Riscure BV* for his advice and help.

References

1. Akkar, M.-L., Bévan, R., Goubin, L.: Two power analysis attacks against one-mask methods. In: Roy, B., Meier, W. (eds.) FSE 2004. LNCS, vol. 3017, pp. 332–347. Springer, Heidelberg (2004). doi:10.1007/978-3-540-25937-4_21

2. Balasch, J., Gierlichs, B., Grosso, V., Reparaz, O., Standaert, F.-X.: On the cost of lazy engineering for masked software implementations. In: Joye, M., Moradi, A. (eds.) CARDIS 2014. LNCS, vol. 8968, pp. 64–81. Springer, Cham (2015). doi:10. 1007/978-3-319-16763-3_5

3. Balasch, J., Gierlichs, B., Reparaz, O., Verbauwhede, I.: DPA, bitslicing and masking at 1 GHz. In: Güneysu, T., Handschuh, H. (eds.) CHES 2015. LNCS, vol. 9293, pp. 599–619. Springer, Heidelberg (2015). doi:10.1007/978-3-662-48324-4_30

4. Batina, L., Gierlichs, B., Prouff, E., Rivain, M., Standaert, F.-X., Veyrat-Charvillon, N.: Mutual information analysis: a comprehensive study. J. Cryptology 24(2), 269–291 (2011)

5. Benadjila, R., Guo, J., Lomné, V., Peyrin, T.: Implementing lightweight block ciphers on x86 architectures. In: Lange, T., Lauter, K., Lisoněk, P. (eds.) SAC 2013. LNCS, vol. 8282, pp. 324–351. Springer, Heidelberg (2014). doi:10.1007/ 978-3-662-43414-7_17

6. Biham, E.: A fast new DES implementation in software. In: Biham, E. (ed.) FSE 1997. LNCS, vol. 1267, pp. 260–272. Springer, Heidelberg (1997). doi:10.1007/ BFb0052352

7. Blömer, J., Guajardo, J., Krummel, V.: Provably secure masking of AES. In: Handschuh, H., Hasan, M.A. (eds.) SAC 2004. LNCS, vol. 3357, pp. 69–83. Springer, Heidelberg (2004). doi:10.1007/978-3-540-30564-4_5

8. Bogdanov, A., Knezevic, M., Leander, G., Toz, D., Varici, K., Verbauwhede, I.: SPONGENT: the design space of lightweight cryptographic hashing. IEEE Trans. Comput. 62(10), 2041–2053 (2013)

9. Bogdanov, A., Knudsen, L.R., Leander, G., Paar, C., Poschmann, A., Robshaw, M.J.B., Seurin, Y., Vikkelsoe, C.: PRESENT: an ultra-lightweight block cipher. In: Paillier, P., Verbauwhede, I. (eds.) CHES 2007. LNCS, vol. 4727, pp. 450–466. Springer, Heidelberg (2007). doi:10.1007/978-3-540-74735-2_31

10. Bogdanov, A., Leander, G., Paar, C., Poschmann, A., Robshaw, M.J.B., Seurin, Y.: Hash functions and RFID tags: mind the gap. In: Oswald, E., Rohatgi, P. (eds.) CHES 2008. LNCS, vol. 5154, pp. 283–299. Springer, Heidelberg (2008). doi:10. 1007/978-3-540-85053-3_18

11. Bottinelli, P., Bos, J.W.: Computational aspects of correlation power analysis. IACR Cryptology ePrint Archive, 2015: 260 (2015)

12. Boyar, J., Peralta, R.: A new combinational logic minimization technique with applications to cryptology. In: Festa, P. (ed.) SEA 2010. LNCS, vol. 6049, pp. 178–189. Springer, Heidelberg (2010). doi:10.1007/978-3-642-13193-6_16

13. Brier, E., Clavier, C., Olivier, F.: Correlation power analysis with a leakage model. In: Joye, M., Quisquater, J.-J. (eds.) CHES 2004. LNCS, vol. 3156, pp. 16–29. Springer, Heidelberg (2004). doi:10.1007/978-3-540-28632-5_2

14. Canright, D., Batina, L.: A very compact "perfectly masked" s-box for AES (corrected). IACR Cryptology ePrint Archive 2009:11 (2009)

15. Carlet, C., Goubin, L., Prouff, E., Quisquater, M., Rivain, M.: Higher-order masking schemes for S-Boxes. In: Canteaut, A. (ed.) FSE 2012. LNCS, vol. 7549, pp. 366–384. Springer, Heidelberg (2012). doi:10.1007/978-3-642-34047-5_21

16. Carlet, C., Prouff, E., Rivain, M., Roche, T.: Algebraic decomposition for probing security. In: Gennaro, R., Robshaw, M. (eds.) CRYPTO 2015. LNCS, vol. 9215, pp. 742–763. Springer, Heidelberg (2015). doi:10.1007/978-3-662-47989-6_36

17. Cazorla, M., Gourgeon, S., Marquet, K., Minier, M.: Survey and benchmark of lightweight block ciphers for MSP430 16-bit microcontroller. Secur. Commun. Netw. 8(18), 3564–3579 (2015)

18. Chari, S., Jutla, C.S., Rao, J.R., Rohatgi, P.: Towards sound approaches to counteract power-analysis attacks. In: Wiener, M. (ed.) CRYPTO 1999. LNCS, vol. 1666, pp. 398–412. Springer, Heidelberg (1999). doi:10.1007/3-540-48405-1_26

19. Coron, J.-S.: Higher order masking of look-up tables. In: Nguyen, P.Q., Oswald, E. (eds.) EUROCRYPT 2014. LNCS, vol. 8441, pp. 441–458. Springer, Heidelberg (2014). doi:10.1007/978-3-642-55220-5_25

20. Coron, J.-S., Giraud, C., Prouff, E., Renner, S., Rivain, M., Vadnala, P.K.: Conversion of security proofs from one leakage model to another: a new issue. In: Schindler, W., Huss, S.A. (eds.) COSADE 2012. LNCS, vol. 7275, pp. 69–81. Springer, Heidelberg (2012). doi:10.1007/978-3-642-29912-4_6

21. Courtois, N., Hulme, D., Mourouzis, T.: Solving circuit optimisation problems in cryptography and cryptanalysis. IACR Cryptology ePrint Archive 2011:475 (2011)

22. Adam Ding, A., Chen, C., Eisenbarth, T.: Simpler, faster, and more robust t-test based leakage detection. IACR Cryptology ePrint Archive, 2015:1215 (2015)

23. Dinu, D., Le Corre, Y., Khovratovich, D., Perrin, L., Großschädl, J., Biryukov, A.: Triathlon of lightweight block ciphers for the internet of things. NIST Lightweight Cryptography Workshop 2015, 2015:209 (2015)

24. Durvaux, F., Standaert, F.-X., Veyrat-Charvillon, N., Mairy, J.-B., Deville, Y.: Efficient selection of time samples for higher-order DPA with projection pursuits. In: Mangard, S., Poschmann, A.Y. (eds.) COSADE 2014. LNCS, vol. 9064, pp. 34–50. Springer, Cham (2015). doi:10.1007/978-3-319-21476-4_3

25. Eisenbarth, T., Gong, Z., Güneysu, T., Heyse, S., Indesteege, S., Kerckhof, S., Koeune, F., Nad, T., Plos, T., Regazzoni, F., Standaert, F.-X., Oldeneel tot Oldenzeel, L.: Compact implementation and performance evaluation of block ciphers in attiny devices. In: Mitrokotsa, A., Vaudenay, S. (eds.) AFRICACRYPT 2012. LNCS, vol. 7374, pp. 172–187. Springer, Heidelberg (2012). doi:10.1007/978-3-642-31410-0_11

26. Goubin, L., Patarin, J.: DES and differential power analysis the "Duplication" method. In: Koç, Ç.K., Paar, C. (eds.) CHES 1999. LNCS, vol. 1717, pp. 158–172. Springer, Heidelberg (1999). doi:10.1007/3-540-48059-5_15

27. Goudarzi, D., Rivain, M.: On the multiplicative complexity of boolean functions and bitsliced higher-order masking. IACR Cryptology ePrint Archive, 2016:557 (2016)

28. Grosso, V., Leurent, G., Standaert, F.-X., Varıcı, K.: LS-designs: bitslice encryption for efficient masked software implementations. In: Cid, C., Rechberger, C. (eds.) FSE 2014. LNCS, vol. 8540, pp. 18–37. Springer, Heidelberg (2015). doi:10.1007/978-3-662-46706-0_2

29. Guo, J., Peyrin, T., Poschmann, A., Robshaw, M.: The LED block cipher. In: Preneel, B., Takagi, T. (eds.) CHES 2011. LNCS, vol. 6917, pp. 326–341. Springer, Heidelberg (2011). doi:10.1007/978-3-642-23951-9_22

30. Ishai, Y., Sahai, A., Wagner, D.: Private circuits: securing hardware against probing attacks. In: Boneh, D. (ed.) CRYPTO 2003. LNCS, vol. 2729, pp. 463–481. Springer, Heidelberg (2003). doi:10.1007/978-3-540-45146-4_27

31. Goodwill, G., Jae, J., Kenworthy, G., Cooper, J., DeMulder, E., Rohatg, P.: Test vector leakage assessment (tvla) methodology in practice

32. Kocher, P., Jaffe, J., Jun, B.: Differential power analysis. In: Wiener, M. (ed.) CRYPTO 1999. LNCS, vol. 1666, pp. 388–397. Springer, Heidelberg (1999). doi:10.1007/3-540-48405-1_25

33. Larsen, R.J., Marx, M.L.: An Introduction to Mathematical Statistics and its Applications, 5th edn. Prentice Hall, Boston, MA (2012)

34. Matsuda, S., Moriai, S.: Lightweight cryptography for the cloud: exploit the power of bitslice implementation. In: Prouff, E., Schaumont, P. (eds.) CHES 2012. LNCS, vol. 7428, pp. 408–425. Springer, Heidelberg (2012). doi:10.1007/978-3-642-33027-8_24

35. Messerges, T.S.: Securing the AES finalists against power analysis attacks. In: Goos, G., Hartmanis, J., Leeuwen, J., Schneier, B. (eds.) FSE 2000. LNCS, vol. 1978, pp. 150–164. Springer, Heidelberg (2001). doi:10.1007/3-540-44706-7_11

36. Oswald, E., Mangard, S., Herbst, C., Tillich, S.: Practical second-order DPA attacks for masked smart card implementations of block ciphers. In: Pointcheval, D. (ed.) CT-RSA 2006. LNCS, vol. 3860, pp. 192–207. Springer, Heidelberg (2006). doi:10.1007/11605805_13

37. Papagiannopoulos, K., Verstegen, A.: Speed and size-optimized implementations of the PRESENT cipher for tiny AVR devices. In: Hutter, M., Schmidt, J.-M. (eds.) RFIDSec 2013. LNCS, vol. 8262, pp. 161–175. Springer, Heidelberg (2013). doi:10.1007/978-3-642-41332-2_11

38. Papapagiannopoulos, K.: High throughput in slices: the case of PRESENT, PRINCE and KATAN64 Ciphers. In: Saxena, N., Sadeghi, A.-R. (eds.) RFID-Sec 2014. LNCS, vol. 8651, pp. 137–155. Springer, Cham (2014). doi:10.1007/978-3-319-13066-8_9

39. Poschmann, A.: Lightweight cryptography - cryptographic engineering for a pervasive world. Cryptology ePrint Archive, Report 2009/516 (2009). http://eprint.iacr.org/

40. Prouff, E., Rivain, M.: Masking against side-channel attacks: a formal security proof. In: Johansson, T., Nguyen, P.Q. (eds.) EUROCRYPT 2013. LNCS, vol. 7881, pp. 142–159. Springer, Heidelberg (2013). doi:10.1007/978-3-642-38348-9_9

41. Rauzy, P., Guilley, S., Najm, Z.: Formally proved security of assembly code against power analysis: A case study on balanced logic. CoRR, abs/1506.05285 (2015)

42. Schneider, T., Moradi, A.: Leakage assessment methodology - a clear roadmap for side-channel evaluations. In: Güneysu, T., Handschuh, H. (eds.) CHES 2015. LNCS, vol. 9293, pp. 495–513. Springer, Heidelberg (2015). doi:10.1007/978-3-662-48324-4_25

43. Shibutani, K., Isobe, T., Hiwatari, H., Mitsuda, A., Akishita, T., Shirai, T.: Piccolo: an ultra-lightweight blockcipher. In: Preneel, B., Takagi, T. (eds.) CHES 2011. LNCS, vol. 6917, pp. 342–357. Springer, Heidelberg (2011). doi:10.1007/978-3-642-23951-9_23

44. Standaert, F.-X., Malkin, T.G., Yung, M.: A unified framework for the analysis of side-channel key recovery attacks. In: Joux, A. (ed.) EUROCRYPT 2009. LNCS, vol. 5479, pp. 443–461. Springer, Heidelberg (2009). doi:10.1007/978-3-642-01001-9_26

45. Stoffelen, K.: Optimizing s-box implementations for several criteria using SAT solvers. IACR Cryptology ePrint Archive, 2016:198 (2016)

46. Keccak team.: Note on side-channel attacks and their countermeasures

47. Trichina, E.: Combinational logic design for AES subbyte transformation on masked data. IACR Cryptology ePrint Archive 2003:236 (2003)

48. Veyrat-Charvillon, N., Standaert, F.-X.: Mutual information analysis: how, when and why? In: Clavier, C., Gaj, K. (eds.) CHES 2009. LNCS, vol. 5747, pp. 429–443. Springer, Heidelberg (2009). doi:10.1007/978-3-642-04138-9_30

49. Whitnall, C., Oswald, E., Mather, L.: An exploration of the kolmogorov-smirnov test as a competitor to mutual information analysis. In: Prouff, E. (ed.) CARDIS 2011. LNCS, vol. 7079, pp. 234–251. Springer, Heidelberg (2011). doi:10.1007/978-3-642-27257-8_15

Classification of 6 × 6 S-boxes Obtained by Concatenation of RSSBs

Selçuk Kavut[1]([⊠]) and Sevdenur Baloğlu[2]

[1] Department of Computer Engineering, Balıkesir University, 10145 Balıkesir, Turkey
skavut@balikesir.edu.tr
[2] Institute of Applied Mathematics, Middle East Technical University,
06800 Ankara, Turkey
sevdenur.baloglu@metu.edu.tr

Abstract. We give an efficient exhaustive search algorithm to enumerate 6×6 bijective S-boxes with the best known nonlinearity 24 in a class of S-boxes that are symmetric under the permutation $\tau(x) = (x_0, x_2, x_3, x_4, x_5, x_1)$, where $x = (x_0, x_1, \ldots, x_5) \in \mathbb{F}_2^6$. Since any S-box $S : \mathbb{F}_2^6 \to \mathbb{F}_2^6$ in this class has the property that $S(\tau(x)) = \tau(S(x))$ for all x, it can be considered as a construction obtained by the concatenation of 5×5 rotation-symmetric S-boxes (RSSBs). The size of the search space, i.e., the number of S-boxes belonging to the class, is $2^{61.28}$. By performing our algorithm, we find that there exist $2^{37.56}$ S-boxes with nonlinearity 24 and among them the number of differentially 4-uniform ones is $2^{33.99}$, which indicates that the concatenation method provides a rich class in terms of high nonlinearity and low differential uniformity. Moreover, we classify those S-boxes achieving the best possible trade-off between nonlinearity and differential uniformity within the class with respect to absolute indicator, algebraic degree, and transparency order.

1 Introduction

The design of vectorial Boolean functions, or so-called S-boxes, is one of the most important subjects in secret-key cryptography since the S-boxes are the only nonlinear parts of iterated block ciphers, providing confusion for the cryptosystem. It is usually crucial for an S-box to be bijective, e.g. in a Substitution-Permutation Network (SPN), which in practice is required to exist in even dimension for implementation efficiency. Constructing such S-boxes with desirable cryptographic properties such as high nonlinearity, low differential uniformity, and high algebraic degree is essential in order to resist against linear [20], differential [1], and higher order differential [17] cryptanalyses, respectively. For instance, the SPN-based block cipher Advanced Encryption Standard (AES) uses the S-box affine equivalent to the inverse function [24] over $\mathbb{F}_{2^8}$, which achieves the best known trade-off (in dimension 8) among these cryptographic properties, i.e., the nonlinearity 112, differential uniformity 4, and maximum possible algebraic degree 7. Yet, in even dimension n, there are very few differentially 4-uniform constructions that are bijective with the nonlinearity $2^{n-1} - 2^{\frac{n}{2}}$ (conjectured [7]

© Springer International Publishing AG 2017
A. Bogdanov (Ed.): LightSec 2016, LNCS 10098, pp. 110–127, 2017.
DOI: 10.1007/978-3-319-55714-4_8

to be the maximum) in the relevant literature (e.g., Gold [10], Kasami [11], the binomial function [3], and the constructions in [2,18,19,31]). In fact, most of these constructions exhibit some potential weaknesses; for instance, the binomial function and the power mappings except the inverse and Kasami functions have low algebraic degrees, which should be greater than 3 to provide robustness against higher order differential cryptanalysis. In addition, there exists only one sporadic example of an Almost Perfect Nonlinear (APN; that is, differentially 2-uniform) permutation in dimension $n=6$, identified [4] in 2009. It is well-known that there is no APN bijections over $\mathbb{F}_{2^2}$ and $\mathbb{F}_{2^4}$, and the construction of more APN bijections over $\mathbb{F}_{2^n}$ for even $n \geq 6$ is an important open problem.

Recall that in [9], a cryptographic criterion, so-called the non-possession of linear redundancy, was proposed as an indicator of randomness for S-boxes. Let m_{lr} denote the number of distinct (extended) affine equivalence classes to which the component Boolean functions of an S-box belong. For any S-box described as a power map over $\mathbb{F}_{2^n}$, it is well-known that $m_{lr} = 1$ (notice that $m_{lr} = 1$ for the AES S-box), and hence such S-boxes are considered [9] as a potential source of a new cryptanalysis. For our case, if we take the symmetric S-boxes into account in terms of linear redundancy, m_{lr} can be at most one less than the number of distinct orbits (which can be deduced from Corollary 5 in [13]). However, we here focuse only on the most important cryptographic properties mentioned previously and do not analyze our results in terms of linear redundancy.

While the aforementioned cryptanalytic attacks are realized independently from the hardware or software implementation of a cryptographic system, the side channel analysis (SCA) can be mounted using the information leaked through its implementation such as the timing of operations [15], power consumption [16], and electromagnetic radiation [28]. Therefore, the resistance of cryptographic primitives against SCA attacks is of great importance as well. In this class of attacks, one of the most powerful is the differential power analysis (DPA) attacks, which have received significant attention from cryptographers for nearly two decades. In 2005, the DPA resistivity of an S-box was quantified [27] introducing the notion of transparency order (TO). A decade later, the definition of TO was modified [6] by taking the cross-correlation terms between the coordinate functions into account. We here use the former definition [27] in our classification, for which its validity has been verified by several implementation results on cryptographic devices such as SASEBO-GII board [21–23] and ATmega163 smartcard [25,26].

In this paper, we aim to classify 6×6 bijective S-boxes with nonlinearity ≥ 24 and differential uniformity ≤ 4 belonging to a rich class in terms of these cryptographic properties, for which the search space is of size $2^{61.28}$, with respect to absolute indicator, algebraic degree, and transparency order. This class corresponds to the S-boxes that are symmetric under the permutation $\tau(x) = (x_0, x_2, x_3, x_4, x_5, x_1)$, where $x = (x_0, x_1, \ldots, x_5) \in \mathbb{F}_2^6$ (an $n \times n$ S-box is called symmetric under a permutation π if it satisfies $S(\pi(x)) = \pi(S(x))\ \forall x \in \mathbb{F}_2^n$). In [13], all 6! permutations are classified up to the linear equivalence of 6×6 S-boxes that are symmetric under them, and 11 different classes are obtained. Among these classes, the one for which the S-boxes are symmetric under the representative permutation $\sigma(x) = (x_0, x_4, x_1, x_2, x_5, x_3)$ seems to be rich in terms of desirable cryptographic properties, since highly nonlinear S-boxes with low differential uniformity could be obtained [13] in this class by heuristic search. In fact one can find that (using Proposition 13 in [13]) the latter class is linearly equivalent to the former one. We here prefer using the former permutation, since in this case the S-boxes can be interpreted as those obtained by the concatenation of two 5 × 5 RSSBs and of two 5-variable rotation-symmetric Boolean functions (RSBFs). Notice that since an RSSB can be represented by a single rotation-symmetric Boolean function (RSBF), all the output bits of an S-box that is symmetric under τ can be described by only four 5-variable RSBFs, which can be utilized to provide implementation advantages in both hardware or software.

Note that the class of 6 × 6 bijective RSSBs with nonlinearity 24 and differential uniformity 4 (which is the best possible trade-off within the class) are classified in [13] in terms of algebraic degree and absolute indicator (later their TOs are computed in [8]). This class corresponds to another one among the aforementioned 11 classes. The search strategy in [13] uses the fact that some of the component functions of an $n \times n$ RSSB are k-rotation-symmetric Boolean functions (k-RSBFs) [12], and thus it is mainly based on first sieving some of these k-RSBFs and then regenerating the RSSBs containing those k-RSBFs. Here, since none of the component functions of an S-box (symmetric under the permutation τ) is a k-RSBFs, it is not possible to apply the search method of [13]. Hence, we give a different search strategy in which the 5 × 5 RSSBs mentioned above are eliminated efficiently.

The remainder of this paper is organized as follows. In the following section, we provide some preliminaries and technical background on the symmetric S-boxes constructed by the concatenation of RSSBs. In Sect. 3, we present our search strategy to enumerate 6 × 6 bijective S-boxes having nonlinearity 24 that are symmetric under the permutation τ. The classification results of those with differential uniformity 4 are presented in Sect. 4, and we draw our conclusions in Sect. 5.

2   Preliminaries

2.1   Cryptographic Properties

For completeness, we briefly review the basic definitions regarding to the cryptographic properties of the S-boxes. Let us consider an $n \times m$ S-box $S : \mathbb{F}_2^n \to \mathbb{F}_2^m$ and represent S as a composition of m Boolean functions $f_0, f_1, \ldots, f_{m-1}$ each of which is a mapping from $\mathbb{F}_2^n$ to $\mathbb{F}_2$, that is, $S(x) = (f_0(x), f_1(x), \ldots, f_{m-1}(x))$ for all $x \in \mathbb{F}_2^n$. The functions $(f_i)_{0 \leq i \leq m-1}$ are called the coordinate functions, and their linear combinations $\bigoplus_{i=0}^{m-1} v_i f_i$ with non all-zero masking (or coefficient) vectors $v = (v_0, v_1, \ldots, v_{m-1}) \in \mathbb{F}_2^m$ are called the component functions.

Algebraic Degree. There are two notions of the algebraic degree relevant to cryptography [5]: The maximum degree of the coordinate functions and the minimum degree of the component functions, which we denote as $d_{\max}$ and $d_{\min}$ respectively. The degree of a component (or coordinate) function can be computed using the algebraic normal form (ANF) of a Boolean function $f(x)$ of n-variable $x = (x_0, x_1, \ldots, x_{n-1}) \in \mathbb{F}_2^n$, which is a unique representation in the form of a multivariate polynomial over $\mathbb{F}_2$,

$$\bigoplus_{u \in \mathbb{F}_2^n} a_u \left(\prod_{i=0}^{n-1} x_i^{u_i} \right),$$

where the coefficients $a_u \in \mathbb{F}_2$. The algebraic degree, or simply the degree of f is defined as the maximum Hamming weight of u such that $a_u \neq 0$. A Boolean function is called affine if its algebraic degree is ≤ 1. An affine function with zero constant term is called a linear function.

Nonlinearity. Nonlinearity of S is defined as the minimum Hamming distance of all $2^m - 1$ component functions from all n-variable affine functions, which can be expressed in terms of its Walsh transformation defined as an even integer-valued function $W_S : \mathbb{F}_2^n \times \mathbb{F}_2^m \to [-2^n, 2^n]$:

$$W_S(\omega, v) = \sum_{x \in \mathbb{F}_2^n} (-1)^{\omega \cdot x \oplus v \cdot S(x)},$$

where the inner product is over $\mathbb{F}_2$, $\omega \in \mathbb{F}_2^n$, and $v \in \mathbb{F}_2^{m*}$. It can be seen that if one of the component functions $v \cdot S(x)$ is affine, then the maximum value in the absolute Walsh spectrum is 2^n, giving rise to zero nonlinearity. Nonlinearity of S is then given by

$$NL_S = 2^{n-1} - \frac{1}{2} \max_{\substack{\omega \in \mathbb{F}_2^n, \\ v \in \mathbb{F}_2^{m*}}} |W_F(\omega, v)|.$$

Differential Uniformity. The differential uniformity δ [24] of S is defined as the maximum number of solutions of the equation $S(x) \oplus S(x \oplus \gamma) = \beta$, where $\gamma \neq (0, 0, \ldots, 0)$, i.e.,

$$\delta = \max_{\substack{\gamma \in \mathbb{F}_2^{n*}, \\ \beta \in \mathbb{F}_2^m}} |\{x \in \mathbb{F}_2^n | S(x) \oplus S(x \oplus \gamma) = \beta\}|,$$

Accordingly, S is called differentially-δ uniform.

Absolute Indicator. The absolute indicator is an important cryptographic criterion related to the autocorrelation spectrum, which is used to have good diffusion properties. The autocorrelation function of S is defined as

$$r_S(a, v) = \sum_{x \in \mathbb{F}_2^n} (-1)^{v \cdot (S(x) \oplus S(x \oplus a))},$$

where $a \in \mathbb{F}_2^n$. The maximum absolute value in the autocorrelation spectrum, except those values for all-zero input difference and masking vectors, is referred to as the absolute indicator, denoted as

$$\Delta_S = \max_{\substack{a \in \mathbb{F}_2^{n*}, \\ v \in \mathbb{F}_2^{m*}}} |r_S(a, v)|.$$

Transparency Order. For an $n \times m$ S-box S, it is given [6] by

$$\tau_S = m - \frac{1}{2^{2n} - 2^n} \sum_{a \in \mathbb{F}_2^{n*}} \left| \sum_{\substack{v \in \mathbb{F}_2^m, \\ wt(v)=1}} r_S(a, v) \right|.$$

In the following, we first restate some basic definitions related to RSSBs and then explain our method to construct a bijective S-box that is symmetric under the permutation $\tau(x) = (x_0, \ x_2, x_3, x_4, x_5, x_1)$ as a concatenation of two 5×5 RSSBs. After that, the search space of size $2^{61.28}$ (mentioned in Introduction) is partitioned into four subspaces, each of which is traversed efficiently as explained in Sect. 3.

2.2   (Concatenation of) RSSBs

Rotation-symmetric S-boxes (RSSBs) were defined in [29]. Let

$$\rho^k(x_0, x_1, \ldots, x_{n-1}) = (x_{0+k \ (\text{mod } n)}, x_{1+k \ (\text{mod } n)}, \ldots, x_{n-1+k \ (\text{mod } n)})$$

be the k-cyclic shift operator. An S-box $S : \mathbb{F}_2^n \to \mathbb{F}_2^m$ is called rotation-symmetric if $\rho^k(S(x)) = S(\rho^k(x)) \ \forall \ x = (x_0, x_1, \ldots, x_{n-1}) \in \mathbb{F}_2^n$ and $1 \leq k \leq n$. If $m = 1$, then it is called rotation-symmetric Boolean function (RSBF). Let S be generated from $s : \mathbb{F}_{2^n} \to \mathbb{F}_{2^n}$ using a normal basis for $\mathbb{F}_{2^n}$. Then, as indicated in [29], the S-boxes satisfying $(s(\alpha))^2 = s(\alpha^2), \ \forall \ \alpha \in \mathbb{F}_{2^n}$, can be regarded as rotation-symmetric. In the rest of this paper, we consider the S-boxes for which $m = n$.

The orbit of $x \in \mathbb{F}_2^n$ under the cyclic rotation is given by the set $G_n(x) = \{\rho^k(x) \mid 1 \leq k \leq n\}$. Let g_n be the number of distinct orbits. Using Burnside's Lemma, it can be shown [30] that $g_n = \frac{1}{n} \sum_{t|n} \phi(t) 2^{\frac{n}{t}} (\approx \frac{2^n}{n})$, where $\phi(t)$ is the Euler's *phi*-function. The lexicographically first element within the ith orbit is called the orbit representative and denoted by Λ_i, where $1 \leq i \leq g_n$.

Since an $n \times n$ RSSB S is uniquely defined by its outputs for the orbit representatives Λ_i's, the concatenation $F : \mathbb{F}_2^{n+1} \to \mathbb{F}_2^n$ of two $n \times n$ RSSBs S_1 and S_2, described by $F(x) = (x_0 \oplus 1)S_1(x_1, ..., x_n) + x_0 S_2(x_1, ..., x_n)$, is denoted as

$$(S_1(\Lambda_1), ..., S_1(\Lambda_{g_n})) \| (S_2(\Lambda_1), ..., S_2(\Lambda_{g_n})),$$

or simply as $S_1 \| S_2$, where $x = (x_0, x_1, ..., x_n) \in \mathbb{F}_2^{n+1}$. Let $f : \mathbb{F}_2^{n+1} \to \mathbb{F}_2$ be a Boolean function such that the S-box $\mathcal{S} : \mathbb{F}_2^{n+1} \to \mathbb{F}_2^{n+1}$, given by $\mathcal{S}(x) = (f(x), F(x))$, is bijective and symmetric under the permutation $\tau(x) = (x_0, x_2, x_3, \ldots, x_n, x_1)$. Then, notice that as f is invariant under τ, $f(x)$ is either equal to 1 or 0 for all cyclic rotations of $(x_1, ..., x_n)$. In addition, since $\mathcal{S}$ is bijective, the outputs of F contain all the orbit representatives Λ_i's, $i = 1, 2, \ldots, g_n$, and these orbit representatives are pairwise the same with one another. Accordingly, for such a pair $f(x) = 1$ for one orbit and $f(x) = 0$ for the other one.

More specifically, let $H_n(x)$ and $H_n(x')$ be two distinct sets with the same cardinality, where $H_n(x) = \{\tau^k(x) | 1 \leq k \leq n\}$. Then, for all Λ_i there exist $\nu, \mu \in G_n(\Lambda_i)$ such that $F(\tau^l(x)) = \rho^l(\nu)$ and $F(\tau^l(x')) = \rho^l(\mu)$ for which $f(\tau^l(x)) = e$ and $f(\tau^l(x')) = e \oplus 1 \; \forall \; l = 1, \ldots, n$, where $e \in \mathbb{F}_2$. As a consequence, f is a balanced function such that it is a concatenation of two n-variable RSBFs f_1 and f_2, i.e., $f(x) = (x_0 \oplus 1) f_1(x_1, \ldots, x_n) + x_0 f_2(x_1, \ldots, x_n)$, and the number of f's to construct a bijective $\mathcal{S}$ given the concatenation F is equal to 2^{g_n}.

2.3 Partitioning Search Space

As already mentioned, the concatenation $F = S_1 \| S_2$ contains each orbit representative Λ_i pairwisely in its outputs, from which one can see that both the S-boxes S_1 and S_2 follow a certain structure. For instance, if one of the RSSBs has a pair of the same orbit representatives in its outputs, then the other one cannot have these outputs. Following this argument, the output orbit representatives of S_1 can be completely determined given those of S_2, and vice versa. For our case $n = 5$, the number of orbits $g_5 = 8$ such that six of them are of size 5 and the rest two are of size 1. Therefore, F contains four orbits of size 1, that is,

$$(F(0, \Lambda_1), F(0, \Lambda_8), F(1, \Lambda_1), F(1, \Lambda_8)) = (S_1(\Lambda_1), S_1(\Lambda_8), S_2(\Lambda_1), S_2(\Lambda_8))$$
$$\in \mathcal{P}(\Lambda_1, \Lambda_1, \Lambda_8, \Lambda_8),$$

where Λ_1 and Λ_8 are the all-zero and all-one vectors, respectively, and $\mathcal{P}(\Lambda_1, \Lambda_1, \Lambda_8, \Lambda_8)$ is the set of permutations of $\{\Lambda_1, \Lambda_1, \Lambda_8, \Lambda_8\}$. Similarly, the outputs $(f(0, \Lambda_1), f(0, \Lambda_8), f(1, \Lambda_1), f(1, \Lambda_8)) \in \mathcal{P}(0, 0, 1, 1)$.

Now, let us consider the output orbits of size 5. In this case, since the S-box $\mathcal{S} = (f, F)$ is bijective, any choice of the output orbit representatives for both S_1 and S_2 belong to one of the following four sets:

1. $\mathbb{S}_0 = \{(\Lambda_2, \ldots, \Lambda_7)\}$,
2. $\mathbb{S}_1 = \{(\Lambda_{i_1}, \ldots, \Lambda_{i_6}) \mid i_1 = i_2, i_1 \neq i_3 \neq i_4 \neq i_5 \neq i_6\}$,
3. $\mathbb{S}_2 = \{(\Lambda_{i_1}, \ldots, \Lambda_{i_6}) \mid i_1 = i_2, i_3 = i_4, i_1 \neq i_3 \neq i_5 \neq i_6\}$,
4. $\mathbb{S}_3 = \{(\Lambda_{i_1}, \ldots, \Lambda_{i_6}) \mid i_1 = i_2, i_3 = i_4, i_5 = i_6, i_1 \neq i_3 \neq i_5\}$,

where $i_1, \ldots, i_6 \in \{2, \ldots, 7\}$ and $(\Lambda_{i_1}, \ldots, \Lambda_{i_6})$'s are different up to permutation. As can be seen, the set $\mathbb{S}_0$ consists of only one choice $(\Lambda_2, \ldots, \Lambda_7)$ for the output orbit representatives, which implies that all the output orbits (of size 5) are different from each other for both S_1 and S_2. The other sets are interpreted similarly, e.g., if the representatives of the output orbits of S_1 belong to $\mathbb{S}_1$, then those of S_2 should also belong to $\mathbb{S}_1$, and each of S_1 and S_2 have one pair of the same orbit representatives in their outputs. Notice that the numbers of the choices for the sets $\mathbb{S}_1$, $\mathbb{S}_2$, and $\mathbb{S}_3$ are $\binom{6}{1}\binom{5}{4} = 30$, $\binom{6}{2}\binom{4}{2} = 90$, and $\binom{6}{3} = 20$, respectively.

Here, we give an example which shows that given the output orbit representatives of S_1, those of S_2 and all possible choices of the Boolean function f can be completely found.

Example 1. Let

$$(S_1(\Lambda_1), \ldots, S_1(\Lambda_8)) = (F(0, \Lambda_1), \ldots, F(0, \Lambda_8))$$
$$= (\mathbf{1}, \pi_1(\rho^{k_1}(\Lambda_4), \rho^{k_2}(\Lambda_4), \rho^{k_3}(\Lambda_7), \rho^{k_4}(\Lambda_7), \rho^{k_5}(\Lambda_2), \rho^{k_6}(\Lambda_3)), \mathbf{0}),$$

where $(k_1, \ldots, k_6) \in \{1, \ldots, 5\}^6$, π_1 is any permutation of the six outputs, $\mathbf{0}$ and $\mathbf{1}$ are the all-zero and all-one vectors, respectively. It can be seen that the output orbit representatives (of size 5) of S_1 belong to the set $\mathbb{S}_2$. Hence, those of S_2 should also belong to the same set as given below:

$$(S_2(\Lambda_1), \ldots, S_2(\Lambda_8)) = (F(1, \Lambda_1), \ldots, F(1, \Lambda_8))$$
$$= (u, \pi_2(\rho^{l_1}(\Lambda_5), \rho^{l_2}(\Lambda_5), \rho^{l_3}(\Lambda_6), \rho^{l_4}(\Lambda_6), \rho^{l_5}(\Lambda_2), \rho^{l_6}(\Lambda_3)), u \oplus \mathbf{1}),$$

where $u \in \{\mathbf{0}, \mathbf{1}\}$, $(l_1, \ldots, l_6) \in \{1, \ldots, 5\}^6$, and π_2 is also a permutation. Further, if $F(x) = F(x')$ for two distinct $x, x' \in \mathbb{F}_2^6$, then $f(\tau^l(x')) = f(\tau^l(x)) \oplus 1 \,\forall\, 1 \le l \le 5$. For instance, considering the orbits Λ_1 and Λ_8, if $(F(0, \Lambda_1), F(0, \Lambda_8), F(1, \Lambda_1), F(1, \Lambda_8)) = (\mathbf{1}, \mathbf{0}, \mathbf{0}, \mathbf{1})$ (i.e. $u = \mathbf{0}$), then

$$(f(0, \Lambda_1), f(0, \Lambda_8), f(1, \Lambda_1), f(1, \Lambda_8)) \in$$
$$\{(0, 0, 1, 1), (0, 1, 0, 1), (1, 0, 1, 0), (1, 1, 0, 0)\}.$$

Otherwise, if $(F(0, \Lambda_1), F(0, \Lambda_8), F(1, \Lambda_1), F(1, \Lambda_8)) = (\mathbf{1}, \mathbf{0}, \mathbf{1}, \mathbf{0})$ (i.e., $u = \mathbf{1}$), then

$$(f(0, \Lambda_1), f(0, \Lambda_8), f(1, \Lambda_1), f(1, \Lambda_8)) \in$$
$$\{(0, 0, 1, 1), (0, 1, 1, 0), (1, 0, 0, 1), (1, 1, 0, 0)\}.$$

Let us refer to the set of S-boxes $\mathcal{S} = (f, F)$ for which the output orbit representatives (other than Λ_1 and Λ_8) of both S_1 and S_2 belong to $\mathbb{S}_k$ as 'Set-k', $k = 0, 1, 2, 3$. Then, each Set-k is generated by the algorithm given below.

Algorithm 1. Forming Set-k from the orbit representatives in $\mathbb{S}_k$.

Input: $\mathbb{S}_k$
Output: Set-k

1 Set-k is empty;
2 **for** each $(S_1(\Lambda_1), S_1(\Lambda_8), S_2(\Lambda_1), S_2(\Lambda_8)) \in \mathcal{P}(\Lambda_1, \Lambda_1, \Lambda_8, \Lambda_8)$ **do**
3 $\quad$ **for** each $(S_1(\Lambda_2), ..., S_1(\Lambda_7)) \in \mathbb{S}_k$ **do**
4 $\quad\quad$ **for** each $(S_1(\Lambda_2), ..., S_1(\Lambda_7)) \in \mathcal{P}(S_1(\Lambda_2), ..., S_1(\Lambda_7))$ **do**
5 $\quad\quad\quad$ Determine the output orbits of S_2 from S_1;
6 $\quad\quad\quad$ **for** each $(S_2(\Lambda_2), ..., S_2(\Lambda_7)) \in \mathcal{P}(S_2(\Lambda_2), ..., S_2(\Lambda_7))$ **do**
7 $\quad\quad\quad\quad$ **for** each $(k_1, ..., k_6) \in \{1, ..., 5\}^6$ **do**
8 $\quad\quad\quad\quad\quad$ $S_1 = (S_1(\Lambda_1), \rho^{k_1}(S_1(\Lambda_2)), ..., \rho^{k_6}(S_1(\Lambda_7)), S_1(\Lambda_8))$;
9 $\quad\quad\quad\quad\quad$ **for** each $(l_1, ..., l_6) \in \{1, ..., 5\}^6$ **do**
10 $\quad\quad\quad\quad\quad\quad$ $S_2 = (S_2(\Lambda_1), \rho^{l_1}(S_2(\Lambda_2)), ..., \rho^{l_6}(S_2(\Lambda_7)), S_2(\Lambda_8))$;
11 $\quad\quad\quad\quad\quad\quad$ $F = S_1 \| S_2$;
12 $\quad\quad\quad\quad\quad\quad$ $\mathcal{F} = \{f : \mathbb{F}_2^6 \to \mathbb{F}_2 | f(\tau^l(x)) = f(\tau^l(x')) \oplus 1,$
$\quad\quad\quad\quad\quad\quad$ for all two distinct $x, x' \in \mathbb{F}_2^5$ s.t. $F(x) = F(x')\}$;
13 $\quad\quad\quad\quad\quad\quad$ **for** each $f \in \mathcal{F}$ **do**
14 $\quad\quad\quad\quad\quad\quad\quad$ Add $\mathcal{S} = (f, F)$ to the Set-k;
15 $\quad\quad\quad\quad\quad\quad$ **end**
16 $\quad\quad\quad\quad\quad$ **end**
17 $\quad\quad\quad\quad$ **end**
18 $\quad\quad\quad$ **end**
19 $\quad\quad$ **end**
20 $\quad$ **end**
21 **end**

In the algorithm, we see that $|\mathcal{P}(\Lambda_1, \Lambda_1, \Lambda_8, \Lambda_8)| = 6$, $|\mathcal{F}| = 2^8$, and the number of all rotations is equal to 5^{12} (as can be seen from the fifth and sixth loops of the algorithm) for each Set-k. Hence, the number of S-boxes, e.g., in Set-1 is computed as $6 \times 30 \times 360^2 \times 5^{12} \times 2^8 \approx 2^{60.34}$, since $|\mathbb{S}_1| = 30$ and $|\mathcal{P}(S_1(\Lambda_2), ..., S_1(\Lambda_7))| = |\mathcal{P}(S_2(\Lambda_2), ..., S_2(\Lambda_7))| = 360$ for all $(S_1(\Lambda_2), ..., S_1(\Lambda_7)), (S_2(\Lambda_2), ..., S_2(\Lambda_7)) \in \mathbb{S}_1$. Similarly, the numbers of S-boxes in Set-0, Set-2, and Set-3 are found to be $2^{57.43}$, $2^{59.92}$, and $2^{55.75}$, respectively.

3 Search Strategy

In this section, we present our search strategy, which can be considered as a three step process, to enumerate the S-boxes with nonlinearity 24 in each of the subsets Set-k, $k = 0, 1, 2, 3$, formed by Algorithm 1.

3.1 Sieving Affine Equivalent Concatenations

Recall that the number of pairwise the same orbit representatives in the outputs of S_1 should be the same as the number of those in the outputs of S_2. Let

$S_j^{(k)}$ denote the RSSB S_j ($j = 1, 2$) for which this number is represented by $k \in \{0, 1, 2, 3\}$. Then, taking all possible permutations of $(S_1^{(k)}(\Lambda_1), S_1^{(k)}(\Lambda_8),$ $S_2^{(k)}(\Lambda_1), S_2^{(k)}(\Lambda_8))$ into account, the number of choices in $\mathbb{S}_k$ is multiplied by 6. More specifically, it can be computed as $\binom{6}{k} \times \binom{6-k}{6-2k} \times 6$ for each $\mathbb{S}_k$. Here, we sieve some of these choices leading to affine equivalent S-boxes, due to the fact that the nonlinearity is invariant under affine transformations.

Let us define the circulant matrix $C^i(a)$, used in the following proposition, which is formed by taking $a = (a_0, a_1 \ldots, a_{n-1}) \in \mathbb{F}_2^n$ as the first row and rotating each row i-bit to the left relative to the preceding row, where $1 \leq i \leq n$:

$$C^i(a) = \begin{bmatrix} a \\ \rho^i(a) \\ \vdots \\ \rho^{(n-1)i \ (\mathrm{mod}\ n)}(a) \end{bmatrix}.$$

The proposition given below defines some affine transformations (which can be obtained using those among the RSSBs given by Proposition 8 in [13]) among the concatenations.

Proposition 1. *Let $F = (S_1 \| S_2)$ be a concatenation of two $n \times n$ RSSBs S_1 and S_2. Then each of the following functions, denoted by F', is also a concatenation of two $n \times n$ RSSBs and affine equivalent to F:*

1. *(complement) $F'(x) = F(x) \oplus \mathbf{1}$,*
2. *(reverse) $F'(x) = F(x \oplus \mathbf{1})$,*
3. *(transposition) $F' = (S_2 \| S_1)$,*
4. *(circulant matrix multiplication) $F'(x) = F(x D^q(a)) C^p(b)$,*

where p, q are co-prime to n such that $pq \equiv 1 \ (\mathrm{mod}\ n)$,

$$D^q(a) = \begin{bmatrix} 1 & 0 \cdots 0 \\ 0 & \\ \vdots & C^q(a) \\ 0 & \end{bmatrix},$$

$a, b \in \mathbb{F}_2^n$, $x \in \mathbb{F}_2^{n+1}$, *and $C^q(a)$, $C^p(b)$ are nonsingular circulant matrices over $\mathbb{F}_2$.*

Using these transformations (or their compositions) we sieve the aforementioned choices for the output orbit representatives, which generate affine equivalent S-boxes as shown by the next proposition.

Proposition 2. *Let $\mathcal{S}(x) = (f(x), F(x))$ be an $(n+1) \times (n+1)$ symmetric S-box under the permutation $\tau(x) = (x_0, x_2, x_3, \ldots, x_n, x_1)$, where $x = (x_0, x_1, \ldots, x_n)$ $\in \mathbb{F}_2^{n+1}$, f is an $(n+1)$-variable Boolean function, and F is a concatenation of two $n \times n$ RSSBs. Assume that F', also a concatenation of two $n \times n$ RSSBs, is obtained by the affine transformations given by Proposition 1. Then, there exists an $(n+1)$-variable Boolean function f' such that $\mathcal{S}' = (f', F')$ is symmetric under τ and affine equivalent to $\mathcal{S}$.*

Proof. It is easy to prove for the first three affine transformations in Proposition 1. Let us consider the last one, i.e., circulant matrix multiplication. Then, we have

$$
\begin{aligned}
S'(x) &= (f'(x), F'(x)) \\
&= (f(xD^q(a)), F(xD^q(a))C^p(b)) \\
&= (f(xD^q(a)), F(xD^q(a)))D^p(b) \\
&= S(xD^q(a))D^p(a),
\end{aligned}
$$

where $f'(x) = f(xD^q(a)) \ \forall \ x \in \mathbb{F}_2^{n+1}$, which shows that S and S' are affine equivalent. Next, we get the following:

$$
\begin{aligned}
S'(\tau(x)) &= S(\tau(x)D^q(a))D^p(b) \\
&= (f(\tau(x)D^q(a)), F(\tau(x)D^q(a))C^p(b)) \\
&= (f(x_0, \rho(x_1, \ldots, x_n)C^q(a)), F(x_0, \rho(x_1, \ldots, x_n)C^q(a))C^p(b)) \\
&= (f(x_0, \rho^{n-q}((x_1, \ldots, x_n)C^q(a))), F(x_0, \rho^{n-q}((x_1, \ldots, x_n)C^q(a)))C^p(b)) \\
&= (f(\tau^{n-q}(x_0, (x_1, \ldots, x_n)C^q(a))), \rho^{n-q}(F(x_0, (x_1, \ldots, x_n)C^q(a)))C^p(b)) \\
&= (f(x_0, (x_1, \ldots, x_n)C^q(a)), \rho^{(n-q)(n-p)}(F(x_0, (x_1, \ldots, x_n)C^q(a))C^p(b))) \\
&= (f(x_0, (x_1, \ldots, x_n)C^q(a)), \rho(F(x_0, (x_1, \ldots, x_n)C^q(a))C^p(b))) \\
&= (f(xD^q(a)), \rho(F(xD^q(a))C^p(b))) \\
&= \tau(S(xD^q(a))D^p(b)) \\
&= \tau(S'(x)),
\end{aligned}
$$

which follows from the fact that $\rho(x_1, \ldots, x_n)C^q(a) = \rho^{n-q}((x_1, \ldots, x_n)C^q(a))$, where ρ is the cyclic shift operator. Hence, S' is also symmetric under τ. $\square$

As mentioned previously, for $k = 0, 1, 2, 3$ the number of choices (obtained by considering the 6 combinations of the orbits of size 1) for $\mathbb{S}_k$ can be found as 6, 180, 540, 120, respectively. After sieving those yielding affine equivalent concatenations these numbers are reduced to 2, 8, 21, and 9, respectively. In Table 1, we give these representative choices for each $\mathbb{S}_k$ along with the number of those generating affine equivalent S-boxes.

In addition, it is clear that any S-box obtained by rotating all of the outputs of an RSSB by the same number of positions is also an RSSB and this operation is an affine transformation (for which a more general form is given by the last item of Proposition 1). Hence, we set $F(0,0,0,0,0,1) = \Lambda_i$, for any $i \in \{2, 3, \ldots, 7\}$, where Λ_i is an orbit representative with orbit size 5, in order to remove affine equivalent concatenations. This provides a reduction of the search space by a factor of $\frac{1}{5}$.

At the end of this step, the number of S-boxes in Set-k reduces from $2^{57.43}$, $2^{60.34}$, $2^{59.92}$, and $2^{55.75}$ to $2^{53.52}$, $2^{53.52}$, $2^{52.92}$, and $2^{49.69}$, respectively. Hence, the total search space reduces from $2^{61.28}$ to $2^{54.97}$.

Table 1. The representative choices and the number (N_i) of those for which the concatenations $(S_1||S_2)$ are affine equivalent for $\mathbb{S}_k$, $k = 0, 1, 2, 3$.

	i	S_1	S_2	N_i
$\mathbb{S}_0$	1	$(\Lambda_1, \Lambda_2, \Lambda_3, \Lambda_4, \Lambda_5, \Lambda_6, \Lambda_7, \Lambda_1)$	$(\Lambda_8, \Lambda_2, \Lambda_3, \Lambda_4, \Lambda_5, \Lambda_6, \Lambda_7, \Lambda_8)$	**2**
	2	$(\Lambda_1, \Lambda_2, \Lambda_3, \Lambda_4, \Lambda_5, \Lambda_6, \Lambda_7, \Lambda_8)$	$(\Lambda_8, \Lambda_2, \Lambda_3, \Lambda_4, \Lambda_5, \Lambda_6, \Lambda_7, \Lambda_1)$	4
$\mathbb{S}_1$	1	$(\Lambda_1, \Lambda_2, \Lambda_2, \Lambda_3, \Lambda_4, \Lambda_5, \Lambda_6, \Lambda_1)$	$(\Lambda_8, \Lambda_3, \Lambda_4, \Lambda_5, \Lambda_6, \Lambda_7, \Lambda_7, \Lambda_8)$	**6**
	2	$(\Lambda_1, \Lambda_2, \Lambda_2, \Lambda_3, \Lambda_4, \Lambda_5, \Lambda_7, \Lambda_1)$	$(\Lambda_8, \Lambda_3, \Lambda_4, \Lambda_5, \Lambda_6, \Lambda_6, \Lambda_7, \Lambda_8)$	24
	3	$(\Lambda_1, \Lambda_2, \Lambda_2, \Lambda_3, \Lambda_5, \Lambda_6, \Lambda_7, \Lambda_1)$	$(\Lambda_8, \Lambda_3, \Lambda_4, \Lambda_4, \Lambda_5, \Lambda_6, \Lambda_7, \Lambda_8)$	**12**
	4	$(\Lambda_8, \Lambda_2, \Lambda_2, \Lambda_3, \Lambda_4, \Lambda_5, \Lambda_6, \Lambda_8)$	$(\Lambda_1, \Lambda_3, \Lambda_4, \Lambda_5, \Lambda_6, \Lambda_7, \Lambda_7, \Lambda_1)$	6
	5	$(\Lambda_8, \Lambda_2, \Lambda_2, \Lambda_3, \Lambda_5, \Lambda_6, \Lambda_7, \Lambda_8)$	$(\Lambda_1, \Lambda_3, \Lambda_4, \Lambda_4, \Lambda_5, \Lambda_6, \Lambda_7, \Lambda_1)$	12
	6	$(\Lambda_1, \Lambda_2, \Lambda_2, \Lambda_3, \Lambda_4, \Lambda_5, \Lambda_6, \Lambda_8)$	$(\Lambda_8, \Lambda_3, \Lambda_4, \Lambda_5, \Lambda_6, \Lambda_7, \Lambda_7, \Lambda_1)$	24
	7	$(\Lambda_1, \Lambda_2, \Lambda_2, \Lambda_3, \Lambda_4, \Lambda_5, \Lambda_7, \Lambda_8)$	$(\Lambda_8, \Lambda_3, \Lambda_4, \Lambda_5, \Lambda_6, \Lambda_6, \Lambda_7, \Lambda_1)$	**48**
	8	$(\Lambda_1, \Lambda_2, \Lambda_2, \Lambda_3, \Lambda_5, \Lambda_6, \Lambda_7, \Lambda_8)$	$(\Lambda_8, \Lambda_3, \Lambda_4, \Lambda_4, \Lambda_5, \Lambda_6, \Lambda_7, \Lambda_1)$	48
*$\mathbb{S}_2$	1	$(\Lambda_1, \Lambda_2, \Lambda_2, \Lambda_3, \Lambda_3, \Lambda_4, \Lambda_5, \Lambda_1)$	$(\Lambda_8, \Lambda_4, \Lambda_5, \Lambda_6, \Lambda_6, \Lambda_7, \Lambda_7, \Lambda_8)$	12
	2	$(\Lambda_1, \Lambda_2, \Lambda_2, \Lambda_3, \Lambda_3, \Lambda_4, \Lambda_6, \Lambda_1)$	$(\Lambda_8, \Lambda_4, \Lambda_5, \Lambda_5, \Lambda_6, \Lambda_7, \Lambda_7, \Lambda_8)$	12
	3	$(\Lambda_1, \Lambda_2, \Lambda_2, \Lambda_3, \Lambda_3, \Lambda_4, \Lambda_7, \Lambda_1)$	$(\Lambda_8, \Lambda_4, \Lambda_5, \Lambda_5, \Lambda_6, \Lambda_6, \Lambda_7, \Lambda_8)$	24
	4	$(\Lambda_1, \Lambda_2, \Lambda_2, \Lambda_3, \Lambda_3, \Lambda_5, \Lambda_7, \Lambda_1)$	$(\Lambda_8, \Lambda_4, \Lambda_4, \Lambda_5, \Lambda_6, \Lambda_6, \Lambda_7, \Lambda_8)$	24
	5	$(\Lambda_1, \Lambda_2, \Lambda_2, \Lambda_3, \Lambda_5, \Lambda_5, \Lambda_6, \Lambda_1)$	$(\Lambda_8, \Lambda_3, \Lambda_4, \Lambda_4, \Lambda_6, \Lambda_7, \Lambda_7, \Lambda_8)$	12
	6	$(\Lambda_1, \Lambda_2, \Lambda_2, \Lambda_3, \Lambda_5, \Lambda_5, \Lambda_7, \Lambda_1)$	$(\Lambda_8, \Lambda_3, \Lambda_4, \Lambda_4, \Lambda_6, \Lambda_6, \Lambda_7, \Lambda_8)$	**12**
	7	$(\Lambda_1, \Lambda_2, \Lambda_2, \Lambda_4, \Lambda_5, \Lambda_5, \Lambda_6, \Lambda_1)$	$(\Lambda_8, \Lambda_3, \Lambda_3, \Lambda_4, \Lambda_6, \Lambda_7, \Lambda_7, \Lambda_8)$	6
	8	$(\Lambda_1, \Lambda_2, \Lambda_2, \Lambda_3, \Lambda_5, \Lambda_7, \Lambda_7, \Lambda_1)$	$(\Lambda_8, \Lambda_3, \Lambda_4, \Lambda_4, \Lambda_5, \Lambda_6, \Lambda_6, \Lambda_8)$	12
	9	$(\Lambda_8, \Lambda_2, \Lambda_2, \Lambda_3, \Lambda_3, \Lambda_4, \Lambda_5, \Lambda_8)$	$(\Lambda_1, \Lambda_4, \Lambda_5, \Lambda_6, \Lambda_6, \Lambda_7, \Lambda_7, \Lambda_1)$	12
	10	$(\Lambda_8, \Lambda_2, \Lambda_2, \Lambda_3, \Lambda_3, \Lambda_4, \Lambda_7, \Lambda_8)$	$(\Lambda_1, \Lambda_4, \Lambda_5, \Lambda_5, \Lambda_6, \Lambda_6, \Lambda_7, \Lambda_1)$	**24**
	11	$(\Lambda_8, \Lambda_2, \Lambda_2, \Lambda_3, \Lambda_5, \Lambda_5, \Lambda_6, \Lambda_8)$	$(\Lambda_1, \Lambda_3, \Lambda_4, \Lambda_4, \Lambda_6, \Lambda_7, \Lambda_7, \Lambda_1)$	12
	12	$(\Lambda_8, \Lambda_2, \Lambda_2, \Lambda_3, \Lambda_5, \Lambda_5, \Lambda_7, \Lambda_8)$	$(\Lambda_1, \Lambda_3, \Lambda_4, \Lambda_4, \Lambda_6, \Lambda_6, \Lambda_7, \Lambda_1)$	12
	13	$(\Lambda_8, \Lambda_2, \Lambda_2, \Lambda_4, \Lambda_5, \Lambda_5, \Lambda_6, \Lambda_8)$	$(\Lambda_1, \Lambda_3, \Lambda_3, \Lambda_4, \Lambda_6, \Lambda_7, \Lambda_7, \Lambda_1)$	6
	14	$(\Lambda_1, \Lambda_2, \Lambda_2, \Lambda_3, \Lambda_3, \Lambda_4, \Lambda_5, \Lambda_8)$	$(\Lambda_8, \Lambda_4, \Lambda_5, \Lambda_6, \Lambda_6, \Lambda_7, \Lambda_7, \Lambda_1)$	**48**
	15	$(\Lambda_1, \Lambda_2, \Lambda_2, \Lambda_3, \Lambda_3, \Lambda_4, \Lambda_6, \Lambda_8)$	$(\Lambda_8, \Lambda_4, \Lambda_5, \Lambda_5, \Lambda_6, \Lambda_7, \Lambda_7, \Lambda_1)$	**24**
	16	$(\Lambda_1, \Lambda_2, \Lambda_2, \Lambda_3, \Lambda_3, \Lambda_4, \Lambda_7, \Lambda_8)$	$(\Lambda_8, \Lambda_4, \Lambda_5, \Lambda_5, \Lambda_6, \Lambda_6, \Lambda_7, \Lambda_1)$	96
	17	$(\Lambda_1, \Lambda_2, \Lambda_2, \Lambda_3, \Lambda_3, \Lambda_5, \Lambda_7, \Lambda_8)$	$(\Lambda_8, \Lambda_4, \Lambda_4, \Lambda_5, \Lambda_6, \Lambda_6, \Lambda_7, \Lambda_1)$	**48**
	18	$(\Lambda_1, \Lambda_2, \Lambda_2, \Lambda_3, \Lambda_5, \Lambda_5, \Lambda_6, \Lambda_8)$	$(\Lambda_8, \Lambda_3, \Lambda_4, \Lambda_4, \Lambda_6, \Lambda_7, \Lambda_7, \Lambda_1)$	48
	19	$(\Lambda_1, \Lambda_2, \Lambda_2, \Lambda_3, \Lambda_5, \Lambda_5, \Lambda_7, \Lambda_8)$	$(\Lambda_8, \Lambda_3, \Lambda_4, \Lambda_4, \Lambda_6, \Lambda_6, \Lambda_7, \Lambda_1)$	48
	20	$(\Lambda_1, \Lambda_2, \Lambda_2, \Lambda_4, \Lambda_5, \Lambda_5, \Lambda_6, \Lambda_8)$	$(\Lambda_8, \Lambda_3, \Lambda_3, \Lambda_4, \Lambda_6, \Lambda_7, \Lambda_7, \Lambda_1)$	24
	21	$(\Lambda_1, \Lambda_2, \Lambda_2, \Lambda_3, \Lambda_5, \Lambda_7, \Lambda_7, \Lambda_8)$	$(\Lambda_8, \Lambda_3, \Lambda_4, \Lambda_4, \Lambda_5, \Lambda_6, \Lambda_6, \Lambda_1)$	**24**
$\mathbb{S}_3$	1	$(\Lambda_1, \Lambda_2, \Lambda_2, \Lambda_3, \Lambda_3, \Lambda_4, \Lambda_4, \Lambda_1)$	$(\Lambda_8, \Lambda_5, \Lambda_5, \Lambda_6, \Lambda_6, \Lambda_7, \Lambda_7, \Lambda_8)$	6
	2	$(\Lambda_1, \Lambda_2, \Lambda_2, \Lambda_3, \Lambda_3, \Lambda_5, \Lambda_5, \Lambda_1)$	$(\Lambda_8, \Lambda_4, \Lambda_4, \Lambda_6, \Lambda_6, \Lambda_7, \Lambda_7, \Lambda_8)$	**12**
	3	$(\Lambda_1, \Lambda_2, \Lambda_2, \Lambda_5, \Lambda_5, \Lambda_6, \Lambda_6, \Lambda_1)$	$(\Lambda_8, \Lambda_3, \Lambda_3, \Lambda_4, \Lambda_4, \Lambda_7, \Lambda_7, \Lambda_8)$	2
	4	$(\Lambda_8, \Lambda_2, \Lambda_2, \Lambda_3, \Lambda_3, \Lambda_4, \Lambda_4, \Lambda_8)$	$(\Lambda_1, \Lambda_5, \Lambda_5, \Lambda_6, \Lambda_6, \Lambda_7, \Lambda_7, \Lambda_1)$	**6**
	5	$(\Lambda_8, \Lambda_2, \Lambda_2, \Lambda_3, \Lambda_3, \Lambda_5, \Lambda_5, \Lambda_8)$	$(\Lambda_1, \Lambda_4, \Lambda_4, \Lambda_6, \Lambda_6, \Lambda_7, \Lambda_7, \Lambda_1)$	12
	6	$(\Lambda_8, \Lambda_2, \Lambda_2, \Lambda_5, \Lambda_5, \Lambda_6, \Lambda_6, \Lambda_8)$	$(\Lambda_1, \Lambda_3, \Lambda_3, \Lambda_4, \Lambda_4, \Lambda_7, \Lambda_7, \Lambda_1)$	2
	7	$(\Lambda_1, \Lambda_2, \Lambda_2, \Lambda_3, \Lambda_3, \Lambda_4, \Lambda_4, \Lambda_8)$	$(\Lambda_8, \Lambda_5, \Lambda_5, \Lambda_6, \Lambda_6, \Lambda_7, \Lambda_7, \Lambda_1)$	24
	8	$(\Lambda_1, \Lambda_2, \Lambda_2, \Lambda_3, \Lambda_3, \Lambda_5, \Lambda_5, \Lambda_8)$	$(\Lambda_8, \Lambda_4, \Lambda_4, \Lambda_6, \Lambda_6, \Lambda_7, \Lambda_7, \Lambda_1)$	48
	9	$(\Lambda_1, \Lambda_2, \Lambda_2, \Lambda_5, \Lambda_5, \Lambda_6, \Lambda_6, \Lambda_8)$	$(\Lambda_8, \Lambda_3, \Lambda_3, \Lambda_4, \Lambda_4, \Lambda_7, \Lambda_7, \Lambda_1)$	8

3.2   Sieving RSSBs S_1 and S_2

In this step, we generate all the RSSBs S_1's and S_2's used to form the concatenation $F = (S_1||S_2)$. One can see that to construct an S-box $\mathcal{S} = (f, F)$ with nonlinearity ≥ 24, the nonlinearities of S_1 and S_2 have to be ≥ 8. We find that for some choices given in Table 1 there are no RSSBs (S_1 and S_2) with nonlinearity ≥ 8. More specifically, 6 out of the 21 choices (for $\mathbb{S}_2$) and 3 out of the 9 choices (for $\mathbb{S}_3$) in Table 1 generate neither S_1 nor S_2 with nonlinearity ≥ 8, and hence they are removed from the search space. These eliminated choices are N_5, N_7, N_{11}, N_{13}, N_{18}, N_{20} for $\mathbb{S}_2$ and N_3, N_6, N_9 for $\mathbb{S}_3$. Thus, after this preprocessing, the search space slightly reduces from $2^{54.97}$ to $2^{54.86}$.

Next, we apply a more efficient sieving method to reduce the number of choices for the output orbit representatives of S_1 and S_2. Let the sets Ω_1 and Ω_2 contain all the S_1's and S_2's generated from one of the remaining choices after the above elimination, respectively. Let the subset $\Omega_1^{[t,(\omega,v)]}$ of Ω_1 denote the S_1's for which the absolute Walsh spectrum value of a component function $v \cdot S_1$ at a position $\omega \in \mathbb{F}_2^5$ is equal to t (i.e., $|W_{S_1}(\omega, v)| = t$), where $v \neq \mathbf{0} \in \mathbb{F}_2^5$ and $t \in \{0, 2, ..., 16\}$. Similarly, given the triplet $[t, (\omega, v)]$, we constitute the subsets $\Omega_2^{[0,(\omega,v)]}$, $\Omega_2^{[2,(\omega,v)]}$, ..., $\Omega_2^{[16-t,(\omega,v)]}$ of Ω_2. As can be seen, the S_1's in $\Omega_1^{[t,(\omega,v)]}$ can be concatenated only with the S_2's in $\cup_{i\in\{0,2,...,16-t\}}\Omega_2^{[i,(\omega,v)]}$, since otherwise the nonlinearity of the concatenation F cannot reach to or exceed 24, leading to the fact that the nonlinearity of $\mathcal{S}$ is less than 24. Hence, if there is no S_2 in $\cup_{i\in\{0,2,...,16-t\}}\Omega_2^{[i,(\omega,v)]}$, then we update Ω_1 by $\Omega_1 \setminus \Omega_1^{[t,(\omega,v)]}$. Note that the set Ω_2 can also be updated similarly considering the concatenations formed by the S_2's in $\Omega_2^{[t,(\omega,v)]}$ and S_1's in $\cup_{i\in\{0,2,...,16-t\}}\Omega_1^{[i,(\omega,v)]}$. In addition, since for an RSSB S the component functions ($v \cdot S$) for which the corresponding masking vectors (v) belong to the same orbit are affine equivalent (Proposition 4 in [13]), it suffices to apply this procedure only for the masking vectors that are orbit representatives.

Hence, we have performed the above method for all the triplets $[t, (\omega, v)]$, where the v's are orbit representatives, and found that the updated sets Ω_1 and Ω_2 are empty for some of the remaining choices in Table 1. More specifically, we find that these choices are N_1 for $\mathbb{S}_0$, N_2, N_4, N_5, N_6, N_8 for $\mathbb{S}_1$, N_1, N_2, N_3, N_4, N_8, N_9, N_{12}, N_{16}, N_{19} for $\mathbb{S}_2$, and N_1, N_5, N_7, N_8 for $\mathbb{S}_3$. Thus, the search space reduces from $2^{54.86}$ to $2^{53.63}$. In Table 1, the choices left after the first two steps of our search strategy are shown by bold font.

3.3   Sieving Concatenations with Nonlinearity < 24

Let the updated sets of Ω_1 and Ω_2 after the previous step be $\overline{\Omega_1}$ and $\overline{\Omega_2}$, respectively. In this last step, we add the coordinate functions f's to the concatenations $F = (S_1||S_2)$ obtained from the S_1's in $\overline{\Omega_1}$ and S_2's in $\overline{\Omega_2}$. Here, as we enumerate the S-boxes in the form of $\mathcal{S} = (f, F)$ with nonlinearity ≥ 24, we select only those f's that achieve nonlinearity ≥ 24 among all possible f's (recall that given F, there can be only $2^{g_5} = 2^8$ f's making $\mathcal{S}$ bijective and symmetric under τ).

In addition, since the nonlinearities of $\mathcal{S} = (f, F)$ and $\mathcal{S}' = (f^c, F)$ are the same, where f^c is the complement of f, we fix $f(\mathbf{0}) = 0$, which reduces the search space by half.

To make this step more efficient, we apply a method similar to the one used in the previous step. Consider the subsets $\overline{\Omega_1}^{[t,(\omega,v)]}$ and $\cup_{i \in \{0,2,\ldots,16-t\}} \overline{\Omega_2}^{[i,(\omega,v)]}$ of $\overline{\Omega_1}$ and $\overline{\Omega_2}$, respectively. We choose each of the S_1's in the former subset and each of the S_2's in the latter one. If for some S_1 and S_2, the nonlinearity of $F \geq 24$, then we add each possible coordinate function f to form the S-box $\mathcal{S}$. If the nonlinearity of $\mathcal{S} \geq 24$, then we save $\mathcal{S}$ in a file. After that, as in the preceding step, since the S_1's in $\overline{\Omega_1}^{[t,(\omega,v)]}$ cannot be concatenated with any S_2's in $\overline{\Omega_2}$ except those in $\cup_{i \in \{0,2,\ldots,16-t\}} \overline{\Omega_2}^{[i,(\omega,v)]}$, we update $\overline{\Omega_1}$ by $\overline{\Omega_1} \setminus \overline{\Omega_1}^{[t,(\omega,v)]}$. Note that when we eliminate the S_1's in $\overline{\Omega_1}^{[t,(\omega,v)]}$, we also eliminate these S_1's belonging to the other subsets of Ω_1. Finally, by performing this procedure for all the triplets $[t, (\omega, v)]$, we reduce the search space to $2^{48.47}$.

4   Results

We find that in the class of 6×6 bijective S-boxes that are symmetric under the permutation τ, there are $2^{37.56}$ S-boxes with nonlinearity 24 and there is no S-box exceeding this nonlinearity. Further, among these S-boxes, the best differential uniformity is 4 and the number of differentially 4-uniform S-boxes is $2^{33.99}$. In [13], the S-boxes with the same cryptographic properties are enumerated in the class of bijective RSSBs for which the search space is of size $2^{47.90}$. In this class, it has been found that there are $2^{28.25}$ S-boxes with nonlinearity 24 and among them the number of those that are differentially 4-uniform is $2^{24.74}$. Compared to these results, our search identifies a much larger set of S-boxes achieving the same cryptographic properties than those found in [13].

Since the TO of an S-box is not in general invariant under the affine transformations, in our classification we generate (after completing the search) the S-boxes using those under which the TO is not invariant and compute the corresponding TOs. More specifically, let us consider an $n \times n$ S-box $T(x) = S(xA \oplus d)B \oplus e$, where A, B are nonsingular binary matrices and $d, e \in \mathbb{F}_2^n$. In [8], it was shown that the TO of $T(x)$ is the same as that of $S(xA \oplus d) \oplus e$, and later in [14] it has been shown that the TO of $T(x)$ is also invariant under the column permutation of B. Hence, we note that only the affine equivalent S-boxes obtained by the circulant matrix multiplication in Proposition 1 can have different the TOs.

In Table 2, we present the classification of the $2^{33.99}$ differentially 4-uniform S-boxes in terms of their absolute indicator (AI), algebraic degrees ($d_{\min}$ and $d_{\max}$, i.e., the minimum and maximum algebraic degrees among the component functions of a given S-box, resp.), and transparency order (TO). For each Set-k, $k = 0, 1, 2, 3$, the classification results are also given in Tables 3, 4, 5 and 6, from which it is seen that the numbers of differentially 4-uniform S-boxes with nonlinearity 24 are $2^{29.91}$, $2^{32.87}$, $2^{32.82}$, and $2^{29.09}$, respectively. It is seen

Table 2. The classification of the 6 × 6 bijective S-boxes, constructed by the concatenation of RSSBs, with nonlinearity 24 and differential uniformity 4.

AI	d_{min}	d_{max}	TO	Number of S-boxes
24	3	4	$\geq 5.619, \leq 5.786$	10368×10
24	4	4	$\geq 5.413, \leq 5.889$	42695424×10
32	3	4	$\geq 5.548, \leq 5.849$	165888×10
32	4	4	$\geq 5.349, \leq 5.905$	629213184×10
32	4	5	$\geq 5.607, \leq 5.813$	10368×10
40	4	4	$\geq 5.421, \leq 5.905$	97096320×10
48	4	4	$\geq 5.480, \leq 5.889$	3400704×10
64	2	2	$\geq 5.714, \leq 5.714$	5184×10
64	2	3	$\geq 5.381, \leq 5.873$	730944×10
64	2	4	$\geq \mathbf{5.270}, \leq 5.905$	176613696×10
64	3	3	$\geq 5.500, \leq 5.905$	383616×10
64	3	4	$\geq 5.341, \leq 5.905$	753769152×10
64	3	5	$\geq 5.655, \leq 5.817$	10368×10
64	4	4	$\geq 5.607, \leq 5.770$	10368×10

Table 3. The classification of the S-boxes in Set-0 with nonlinearity 24 and differential uniformity 4.

AI	d_{min}	d_{max}	TO	Number of S-boxes
24	3	4	$\geq 5.619, \leq 5.730$	288×40
24	4	4	$\geq 5.440, \leq 5.889$	438336×40
32	3	4	$\geq 5.655, \leq 5.734$	288×40
32	4	4	$\geq 5.421, \leq 5.905$	9214560×40
32	4	5	$\geq 5.675, \leq 5.738$	288×40
40	4	4	$\geq 5.448, \leq 5.905$	1978848×40
48	4	4	$\geq 5.500, \leq 5.845$	126144×40
64	2	2	$\geq 5.714, \leq 5.714$	288×40
64	2	3	$\geq 5.381, \leq 5.873$	26496×40
64	2	4	$\geq 5.302, \leq 5.885$	2320704×40
64	3	3	$\geq 5.540, \leq 5.905$	25632×40
64	3	4	$\geq 5.341, \leq 5.905$	11161440×40
64	4	4	$\geq 5.607, \leq 5.770$	288×40

from Table 2 that the minimum transparency order the S-boxes have in this classification is 5.270. This value is attained from Set-2 and Set-3 as can be seen from Tables 5 and 6 (shown by bold font).

Table 4. The classification of the S-boxes in Set-1 with nonlinearity 24 and differential uniformity 4.

AI	d_{min}	d_{max}	TO	Number of S-boxes
24	3	4	$\geq 5.619, \leq 5.778$	3456×10
24	4	4	$\geq 5.417, \leq 5.889$	20560896×10
32	3	4	$\geq 5.556, \leq 5.849$	91008×10
32	4	4	$\geq 5.349, \leq 5.905$	290878848×10
32	4	5	$\geq 5.667, \leq 5.813$	3456×10
40	4	4	$\geq 5.429, \leq 5.905$	43205760×10
48	4	4	$\geq 5.480, \leq 5.889$	1359360×10
64	2	2	$\geq 5.714, \leq 5.714$	1152×10
64	2	3	$\geq 5.381, \leq 5.873$	271872×10
64	2	4	$\geq 5.341, \leq 5.905$	80786304×10
64	3	3	$\geq 5.500, \leq 5.905$	118656×10
64	3	4	$\geq 5.361, \leq 5.905$	350350848×10
64	3	5	$\geq 5.655, \leq 5.817$	4608×10
64	4	4	$\geq 5.607, \leq 5.770$	3456×10

Table 5. The classification of the S-boxes in Set-2 with nonlinearity 24 and differential uniformity 4.

AI	d_{min}	d_{max}	TO	Number of S-boxes
24	3	4	$\geq 5.619, \leq 5.786$	5760×10
24	4	4	$\geq 5.413, \leq 5.889$	19401984×10
32	3	4	$\geq 5.548, \leq 5.849$	71424×10
32	4	4	$\geq 5.349, \leq 5.905$	280242432×10
32	4	5	$\geq 5.607, \leq 5.813$	5760×10
40	4	4	$\geq 5.421, \leq 5.905$	41551488×10
48	4	4	$\geq 5.480, \leq 5.889$	1299456×10
64	2	2	$\geq 5.714, \leq 5.714$	2304×10
64	2	3	$\geq 5.381, \leq 5.873$	313344×10
64	2	4	$\geq \mathbf{5.270}, \leq 5.905$	81669888×10
64	3	3	$\geq 5.500, \leq 5.905$	110592×10
64	3	4	$\geq 5.361, \leq 5.905$	333317376×10
64	3	5	$\geq 5.655, \leq 5.817$	5760×10
64	4	4	$\geq 5.607, \leq 5.770$	5760×10

Table 6. The classification of the S-boxes in Set-3 with nonlinearity 24 and differential uniformity 4.

AI	d_{min}	d_{max}	TO	Number of S-boxes
24	4	4	$\geq 5.468, \leq 5.873$	979200×10
32	3	4	$\geq 5.599, \leq 5.746$	2304×10
32	4	4	$\geq 5.417, \leq 5.873$	21233664×10
40	4	4	$\geq 5.460, \leq 5.865$	4423680×10
48	4	4	$\geq 5.516, \leq 5.837$	237312×10
64	2	2	$\geq 5.714, \leq 5.714$	576×10
64	2	3	$\geq 5.500, \leq 5.794$	39744×10
64	2	4	$\geq \mathbf{5.270}, \leq 5.873$	4874688×10
64	3	3	$\geq 5.540, \leq 5.778$	51840×10
64	3	4	$\geq 5.341, \leq 5.873$	25455168×10

As mentioned in the previous section, we do not take the concatenations obtained by rotating all of the outputs by a fixed number of positions into account reducing the search space by a factor of $\frac{1}{5}$. Recall that, in addition, we fix $f(\mathbf{0}) = 0$, which further reduces the search space by a factor of $\frac{1}{2}$. Hence, the numbers of the S-boxes in Tables 2, 3, 4, 5 and 6 are the multiples of 10.

The search algorithm is performed on a workstation with 2 CPUs of Intel Xeon Processor E5-2620v3 (15M Cache, 2.40 GHz, 6 cores) and 16 GB RAM under Windows 8.1 Professional 64-bit operating system. It takes around 10 days (236 h) exploiting all the cores.

5   Conclusions

We have presented an efficient exhaustive search algorithm to enumerate the 6×6 bijective S-boxes with the best known nonlinearity 24 within the class of symmetric S-boxes under the permutation $\tau(x) = (x_0, x_2, x_3, x_4, x_5, x_1)$, where $x = (x_0, x_1 \ldots, x_5) \in \mathbb{F}_2^6$. Carrying out the search algorithm, which reduces the space from $2^{61.28}$ to $2^{48.47}$, we have classified differentially 4-uniform S-boxes among them in terms of absolute indicator, algebraic degree, and transparency order. Our results provide a large pool of choices for small-size S-boxes with desirable cryptographic properties such as low differential uniformity and high nonlinearity, especially suitable for lightweight cryptography.

Acknowledgement. This work is a part of a project supported financially by The Scientific and Technological Research Council of Turkey (TÜBİTAK) under grant 114E486.

References

1. Biham, E., Shamir, A.: Differential cryptanalysis of DES-like cryptosystems. J. Cryptol. **4**(1), 3–72 (1991)
2. Bracken, C., Leander, G.: A highly nonlinear differentially 4 uniform power mapping that permutes fields of even degree. Finite Fields Appl. **16**(4), 231–242 (2010)
3. Bracken, C., Tan, C.H., Tan, Y.: Binomial differentially 4 uniform permutations with high nonlinearity. Finite Fields Appl. **18**(3), 537–546 (2012)
4. Browning, K.A., Dillon, J.F., McQuistan, M.T., Wolfe, A.J.: An APN permutation in dimension six. In: The 9th Conference on Finite Fields and Applications - Fq9, Contemporary Mathematics, vol. 518, pp. 33–42, AMS USA (2010)
5. Carlet, C.: Vectorial Boolean functions for cryptography. Chapter of the Monography In: Crama, Y., Hammer, P.L. (eds.) Boolean Models and Methods in Mathematics, Computer Science, and Engineering, pp. 398–469. Cambridge University Press (2010)
6. Chakraborty, K., Sarkar, S., Maitra, S., Mazumdar, B., Mukhopadhyay, D., Prouff, E.: Redefining the transparency order. In: Workshop on Coding and Cryptography (WCC), Paris, France (2015). http://eprint.iacr.org/2014/367.pdf
7. Dobbertin, H.: Almost perfect nonlinear power functions on $GF(2^n)$: the Welch case. IEEE Trans. Inf. Theory **45**(4), 1271–1275 (1999)
8. Evci, M.A., Kavut, S.: DPA resilience of rotation-symmetric S-boxes. In: Yoshida, M., Mouri, K. (eds.) IWSEC 2014. LNCS, vol. 8639, pp. 146–157. Springer, Cham (2014). doi:10.1007/978-3-319-09843-2_12
9. Fuller, J., Millan, W.: Linear redundancy in S-Boxes. In: Johansson, T. (ed.) FSE 2003. LNCS, vol. 2887, pp. 74–86. Springer, Heidelberg (2003). doi:10.1007/978-3-540-39887-5_7
10. Gold, R.: Maximal recursive sequences with 3-valued recursive crosscorrelation functions. IEEE Trans. Inform. Theory **14**, 154–156 (1968)
11. Kasami, T.: The weight enumerators for several classes of subcodes of the second order binary Reed-Muller codes. Inform. Control **18**, 369–394 (1971)
12. Kavut, S., Yücel, M.D.: 9-variable Boolean functions with nonlinearity 242 in the generalized rotation symmetric class. Inf. Comput. **208**(4), 341–350 (2010). Elsevier
13. Kavut, S.: Results on rotation-symmetric S-boxes. Inf. Sci. **201**, 93–113 (2012)
14. Kavut, S.: DPA resistivity of small size S-boxes. In: Proceedings of the 3rd International Symposium on Digital Forensics and Security, ISDFS 2015, pp. 64–69 (2015)
15. Kocher, P.C.: Timing attacks on implementations of Diffie-Hellman, RSA, DSS, and other systems. In: Koblitz, N. (ed.) CRYPTO 1996. LNCS, vol. 1109, pp. 104–113. Springer, Heidelberg (1996). doi:10.1007/3-540-68697-5_9
16. Kocher, P., Jaffe, J., Jun, B.: Differential power analysis. In: Wiener, M. (ed.) CRYPTO 1999. LNCS, vol. 1666, pp. 388–397. Springer, Heidelberg (1999). doi:10.1007/3-540-48405-1_25
17. Lai, X.: Higher order derivatives and differential cryptanalysis. In: Blahut, R.E., Costello, D.J., Maurer, U., Mittelholzer, T. (eds.) Symposium on Communication Coding and Cryptography, in Honor of J.L. Massey on the Occasion of his 60'th Birthday. The Springer International Series in Engineering and Computer Science, vol. 276, pp. 27–233. Springer, Heidelberg (1994)
18. Li, Y., Wang, M., Yu, Y.: Constructing differentially 4-uniform permutations over $GF(2^{2k})$ from the inverse function revisited (2013). http://eprint.iacr.org/2013/731

19. Li, Y., Wang, M.: Constructing differentially 4-uniform permutations over $GF(2^{2m})$ from quadratic APN permutations over $GF(2^{2m+1})$. Des. Codes Cryptogr. **72**(2), 249–264 (2014)

20. Matsui, M.: Linear cryptanalysis method for DES cipher. In: Helleseth, T. (ed.) EUROCRYPT 1993. LNCS, vol. 765, pp. 386–397. Springer, Heidelberg (1994). doi:10.1007/3-540-48285-7_33

21. Mazumdar, B., Mukhopadhyay, D., Sengupta, I.: Constrained search for a class of good bijective S-boxes with improved DPA resistivity. IEEE Trans. Inf. Forensics Secur. **8**(12), 2154–2163 (2013)

22. Mazumdar, B., Mukhopadhyay, D., Sengupta, I.: Design and implementation of rotation symmetric S-boxes with high nonlinearity and high DPA resiliency. In: IEEE International Symposium on Hardware-Oriented Security and Trust - HOST, pp. 87–92 (2013)

23. Mazumdar, B., Mukhopadhyay, D.: Construction of RSSBs with high nonlinearity and improved DPA resistivity from balanced RSBFs. IEEE Trans. Comput. (2016). doi:10.1109/TC.2016.2569410

24. Nyberg, K.: Differentially uniform mappings for cryptography. In: Helleseth, T. (ed.) EUROCRYPT 1993. LNCS, vol. 765, pp. 55–64. Springer, Heidelberg (1994). doi:10.1007/3-540-48285-7_6

25. Picek, S., Ege, B., Batina, L., Jakobovic, D., Chmielewski, Ł., Golub, M.: On using genetic algorithms for intrinsic side-channel resistance: the case of AES S-box. In: The First Workshop on Cryptography and Security in Computing Systems, CS2 2014, pp. 13–18. ACM, New York (2014)

26. Picek, S., Ege, B., Papagiannopoulos, K., Batina, L., Jakobović, D.: Optimality and beyond: the case of 4 × 4 S-boxes. In: IEEE International Symposium on Hardware-Oriented Security and Trust - HOST, pp. 80–83 (2014)

27. Prouff, E.: DPA attacks and S-Boxes. In: Gilbert, H., Handschuh, H. (eds.) FSE 2005. LNCS, vol. 3557, pp. 424–441. Springer, Heidelberg (2005). doi:10.1007/11502760_29

28. Quisquater, J.-J., Samyde, D.: ElectroMagnetic analysis (EMA): measures and counter-measures for smart cards. In: Attali, I., Jensen, T. (eds.) E-smart 2001. LNCS, vol. 2140, pp. 200–210. Springer, Heidelberg (2001). doi:10.1007/3-540-45418-7_17

29. Rijmen, V., Barreto, P.S.L.M., Filho, D.L.G.: Rotation symmetry in algebraically generated cryptographic substitution tables. Inf. Process. Lett. **106**(6), 246–250 (2008)

30. Stănică, P., Maitra, S.: Rotation symmetric boolean functions – count and cryptographic properties. Discrete Appl. Math. **156**(10), 1567–1580 (2008)

31. Yu, Y., Wang, M., Li, Y.: Constructing differential 4-uniform permutations from know ones (2011). http://eprint.iacr.org/2011/047

Concealing KETJE: A Lightweight PUF-Based Privacy Preserving Authentication Protocol

Gerben Geltink[(✉)]

Institute for Computing and Information Sciences,
Radboud University, Nijmegen, The Netherlands
g.geltink@gmail.com

Abstract. In this paper, we focus on the design of a novel authentication protocol that preserves the privacy of embedded devices. A Physically Unclonable Function (PUF) generates challenge-response pairs that form the source of authenticity between a server and multiple devices. We rely on Authenticated Encryption (AE) for confidentiality, integrity and authenticity of the messages. A challenge updating mechanism combined with an authenticate-before-identify strategy is used to provide privacy. The major advantage of the proposed method is that no shared secrets need to be stored into the device's non-volatile memory. We design a protocol that supports server authenticity, device authenticity, device privacy, and memory disclosure. Following, we prove that the protocol is secure, and forward and backward privacy-preserving via game transformations. Moreover, a proof of concept is presented that uses a 3-1 Double Arbiter PUF, a concatenation of repetition and BCH error-correcting codes, and the AE-scheme KETJE. We show that our device implementation utilizes 8,305 LUTs on a 28 nm Xilinx Zynq XC7Z020 System on Chip (SoC) and takes only 0.63 ms to perform an authentication operation.

Keywords: Privacy-preserving authentication protocol · Physically Unclonable Function · Authenticated Encryption · SoC · FPGA

1 Introduction

Nowadays, RFID-technology and the Internet of Things (IoT) are hot topics due to the increasing desire to simplify our everyday lives via the use of pervasive devices. Hence, we see a shift from simple identification of devices towards complex authentication protocols, in which a challenging feature to implement is the protection of the entity's privacy. Because these entities belong to individuals who may want to preserve their privacy, we notice a shift on focusing more on privacy-preserving authentication protocols [6]. With the use of state-of-the-art cryptographic techniques, device-to-server authentication can be implemented while protecting the privacy with respect to outsiders.

One solution is to use symmetric key cryptography, with a pre-shared key and a key-updating mechanism in order to randomize device credentials at each

© Springer International Publishing AG 2017
A. Bogdanov (Ed.): LightSec 2016, LNCS 10098, pp. 128–148, 2017.
DOI: 10.1007/978-3-319-55714-4_9

successful authentication. However, storing these keys requires non-volatile memory which is easily compromised by an attacker. Another option is to use PUFs, physical entities that are similar to algorithmic one-way functions. PUFs act on challenges, returning noisy PUF responses that are close enough between equal challenges on the same PUF instance, but far enough between different instances. As a result, one only needs to store a challenge which, similar to the aforementioned construction, is updated on a successful authentication. The strength of this construction is that these challenges are not secret and can safely be stored in non-volatile memory. By using a PUF, one needs to implement a Fuzzy Extractor (FE) [7] that can produce an unpredictable key from the noisy PUF responses. On top of that, a FE provides for the recovery of old PUF responses from fresh PUF responses using error-correcting codes.

This research focusses on integrating a single, compact mode, namely Authenticated Encryption, into a PUF-based privacy-preserving authentication protocol. In contrast to [2], we construct a secure FE and abstain from using a pre-shared key between server and devices. With this, we hope to improve overall efficiency of the protocol.

The remainder of this paper is structured as follows. Section 2 describes the related work and our contributions. In Sect. 3 we introduce the protocol, describing the security considerations and overall design. Following, in Sect. 4 we theoretically support the protocol by proving the security and privacy of the protocol. In Sect. 5 we give a proof of concept of the proposed protocol, showing that a concrete software/hardware realization is possible. Then, in Sect. 6 we present the results, giving an analysis of the implemented PUF as well as giving the performance and a comparison to relevant previous works, i.e. [2,15]. Finally, in Sect. 7 we conclude the paper.

2   Related Work

Many PUF based protocols have been proposed [2,9,15]. Herrewegge et al. propose using a reverse Fuzzy Extractor, putting the computationally less complex generation procedure in the device, and the more complex reproduction procedure on the server [9]. However, the proof of concept is subjected to a PRNG exploitation [6]. Moriyama et al. propose a provably secure privacy-preserving authentication protocol that uses a different PUF response at every authentication, and thus changing the device credential after every successful authentication [15]. Aysu et al. [2] propose a provably secure protocol based on [9,15]. While the authors present the first effort to describe an end-to-end design and evaluation of a provable secure privacy-preserving PUF-based authentication protocol, the interleaved FE construction is vulnerable to linear equation analysis [2, p. 12]. Moreover, the authors use an additional pre-shared key that does not increase the entropy of the communication messages.

We summarize the contributions of this research as follows: (i) We introduce a novel PUF-based privacy-preserving authentication protocol using AE. (ii) Further, we prove that the protocol is mathematically secure, and forward and backward privacy-preserving. (iii) Finally, we present a proof of concept of the device on a development board and the server on a PC.

3   Protocol Design

In this section, we present the novel protocol design. Before doing that, we describe the notation that is used throughout this paper and we describe the security considerations for the protocol.

3.1   Notation

We denote the security level as k (in bits). $A, A', A^1 \in \mathcal{A} \subseteq \{0,1\}^*$ denote three distinct binary strings. B_i denotes the i'th bit of B. $\langle C, D \rangle$ denotes a tuple of strings C and D. $\mathbf{HD}(Y, Y')$ denotes the Hamming distance between two vectors $Y, Y' \leftarrow \mathcal{Y}$ of the same length. $\mathbf{HW}(Y)$ denotes the Hamming weight of vector $Y \leftarrow \mathcal{Y}$. $\mathbf{H}(Y)$ denotes the Shannon entropy of a discrete random variable $Y \leftarrow \mathcal{Y}$. $\tilde{\mathbf{H}}_\infty(Y)$ denotes the min-entropy of a random variable $Y \in \mathcal{Y}$. The entropy of a binary variable $Y \leftarrow \{0,1\}^l$ with probabilities $\mathbf{Pr}(Y_i = 1) = p$ and $\mathbf{Pr}(Y_i = 0) = 1 - p$ $(0 \leq i < l)$ is defined in the binary entropy function:

$$\mathbf{h}(p) = -p \log_2(p) - (1-p) \log_2(1-p). \tag{1}$$

Besides, $Y \leftarrow \mathbf{puf}_i(X) \in \mathcal{P}$ denotes a PUF instance $\mathbf{puf}_i \in \mathcal{P}$ which takes challenge X and produces response Y. Here, the $\mathcal{P}$ denotes the PUF class that contains all PUF instances of a PUF construction. A Fuzzy Extractor (FE) consists of two algorithms: a key generation algorithm **Gen** and a reconstruction algorithm **Rec**. **Gen** takes as input variable Z and outputs key R and helper data H, **Rec** recovers the key R from input variable Z' and helper data H. An AE-scheme with associated data (AEAD-scheme) is a three-tuple $\Pi = (\mathcal{K}, \mathcal{E}, \mathcal{D})$ [16]. Associated to Π are sets of strings $\mathcal{N} \subseteq \{0,1\}^*$ indicating the nonce, $\mathcal{M} \subseteq \{0,1\}^*$ indicating the message and $\mathcal{A}^{\mathcal{D}} \subseteq \{0,1\}^*$ indicating the associated data. The key space $\mathcal{K}$ is a finite nonempty set of strings. The encryption algorithm $\mathcal{E}$ is a deterministic algorithm that takes strings $K \in \mathcal{K}$, $N \in \mathcal{N}$, $M \in \mathcal{M}$ and $A \in \mathcal{A}^{\mathcal{D}}$ and returns string $\langle C, T \rangle = \mathcal{E}_K^{N,A}(M)$. The decryption algorithm $\mathcal{D}$ is a deterministic algorithm that takes strings $K \in \mathcal{K}$, $N \in \mathcal{N}$, $A \in \mathcal{A}^{\mathcal{D}}$, $C \in \{0,1\}^*$ and $T \in \{0,1\}^*$ and returns $\mathcal{D}_K^{N,A}(\langle C, T \rangle)$, which is either a string in $\mathcal{M}$ or the distinguished symbol INVALID. We require that $\mathcal{D}_K^{N,A}(\mathcal{E}_K^{N,A}(M)) = M$ for all $K \in \mathcal{K}$, $N \in \mathcal{N}$, $M \in \mathcal{M}$ and $A \in \mathcal{A}^{\mathcal{D}}$.

3.2   Security Considerations

The security considerations we take are based on assumptions made in earlier work on lightweight authentication protocols [2,9,15].

Devices are enrolled in a secure environment using a one-time interface. Following, a trusted server and a number of devices will authenticate each other while devices need to remain anonymous. For the communication, we consider that our channel is ideal, i.e. no errors will occur in the channel. After enrollment, the server remains trusted but devices are subjected to an attacker. The attacker may not know the identity of a device such that the device cannot be tracked.

We identified that the attacker may have two goals, i.e. the attacker may want to: (i) impersonate a device which will result in a violation of the security; (ii) trace devices in between authentications which will result in a violation of the privacy. The power of the attacker is that he can change all communication between the server and devices. Moreover, he may know the result of the authentication and can access the non-volatile memory of the devices, which he cannot modify (which is needed for the privacy-preserving proof)[1]. He can also not perform implementation attacks on the device and the server or reverse engineer the PUF such that he can predict PUF responses. Also, he does not have access to the intermediate registers on the device and cannot physically trace every device in between authentications. Furthermore, the attacker is not able to use other (non-cryptographic) mechanisms to identify a device [11].

3.3 Protocol

The setup phase of the proposed protocol is illustrated in Protocol 1, the authentication phase is illustrated in Protocol 2. The protocol is based on a PUF that produces noisy, but recoverable, responses on equal challenges due to the unique physical characteristics of the IC [13]. Because of this behavior, the PUF is identifiable from other PUFs. A FE can extract a key from this noisy data produced by the PUF using helper data generated from a previous key-extraction [7]. However, the recovery procedure is of a higher complexity than the generation of the helper data that is used for this reconstruction. A reverse FE reverses this behavior by placing the helper data generation in the device and the more complex reconstruction in the server [9]. In order to preserve privacy, the device credential is updated every successful authentication, which results in fresh PUF responses, and thus fresh keys.

The setup phase (Protocol 1) works as follows. In a trusted environment, the server produces a random challenge X^1. The device uses this challenge to produce a PUF response Y^1 which is being sent to the server. The challenge is being stored in the device non-volatile memory. The server stores the response in a database on index n, indicating the number of the device. Notice that the response is stored at Y and Y^{old} in order to prevent desynchronization, which occurs when there is a loss of communication in the transmission of T^2 in the authentication phase and only Y is stored.

The authentication phase (Protocol 2) works as follows. First, the server generates an unpredictable challenge A and sends this to the device. The device uses

---

[1] A modification of challenge X in non-volatile memory does not break the security of the protocol, only the theoretical privacy preservation because an attacker can distinguish a device with modified challenge X (cannot successfully authenticate) from a device with unmodified challenge X (can successfully authenticate).

Server $\mathcal{S}(\{\langle Y, Y^{old}\rangle\}_n)$ **Device** $\mathbf{Dev}_i(\mathbf{puf}_i(\,\cdot\,), X)$

$X^1 \leftarrow \mathbf{TRNG}$

$$\xrightarrow{\quad X^1 \quad}$$

$Y^1 \leftarrow \mathbf{puf}_i(X^1)$
$X := X^1$

$$\xleftarrow{\quad Y^1 \quad}$$

$\langle Y, Y^{old}\rangle_n := \langle Y^1, Y^1\rangle$
$n := n + 1$

Protocol 1. Setup phase.

Server $\mathcal{S}(\{\langle Y, Y^{old}\rangle\}_n)$ **Device** $\mathbf{Dev}_i(\mathbf{puf}_i(\,\cdot\,), X)$

$A \leftarrow \mathbf{TRNG}$

$$\xrightarrow{\quad A \quad}$$

$Y^{1'} \leftarrow \mathbf{puf}_i(X)$
$\langle R, H\rangle \leftarrow \mathbf{FE.Gen}(Y^{1'})$
$X^2 \leftarrow \mathbf{TRNG}$
$Y^2 \leftarrow \mathbf{puf}_i(X^2)$
$N \leftarrow \mathbf{TRNG}$
$\langle C^1, T^1\rangle \leftarrow \mathcal{E}_R^{N\|0,A}(Y^2)$

$$\xleftarrow{\quad \langle H, N, C^1, T^1\rangle \quad}$$

$T^2 \leftarrow \mathbf{TRNG}$
for $0 \le i < n$:
$\quad R = \mathbf{FE.Rec}(Y, H)$
$\quad$ if $Y^2 \leftarrow \mathcal{D}_R^{N\|0,A}(\langle C^1, T^1\rangle)$:
$\qquad \langle\,\cdot\,, T^2\rangle \leftarrow \mathcal{E}_R^{N\|1,A}(\,\cdot\,)$
$\qquad \langle Y, Y^{old}\rangle_{num} := \langle Y^2, Y\rangle$
"if no device was authenticated" :
"repeat search with old values"

$$\xrightarrow{\quad T^2 \quad}$$

$\langle\,\cdot\,, T^{2'}\rangle \leftarrow \mathcal{E}_R^{N\|1,A}(\,\cdot\,)$
if $T^{2'} == T^2$:
$\quad X := X^2$

Protocol 2. Authentication phase. $|A|, |H|, |N|, |C^1|, |T^1|, |T^2| \ge k$ and PUF responses Y should contain enough entropy w.r.t. H s.t. $|R| \ge k$.

the challenge X stored in its non-volatile memory to produce a PUF response $Y^{1'}$. From this PUF response, helper data H and an unpredictable key R is generated using the FE's generation procedure **FE.Gen**. Consecutively, a new challenge X^2 is randomly generated by the device such that it can be updated on a successful authentication. This challenge is fed to the device's PUF in order to receive a new PUF response Y^2. Following, a nonce N is randomly generated such that the PUF response can be encrypted using the AEAD-scheme. The resulting cipher-text C^1, its tag T^1 and the nonce N will be sent to the server. The server performs an exhaustive search over the database, recovering a key for each index. These keys are used to try to decrypt the cipher-text C^1 using the tag T^1, challenge A and nonce N. If there is a successful authentication, the server produces another tag T^2 using $\mathcal{E}$, but with nonce $N^2 \parallel 1$ instead of $N^2 \parallel 0$ in order to create another instance of $\mathcal{E}$. This tag is sent to the device. Moreover, the server updates the old PUF-response Y with the new PUF response Y^2. If there were no successful authentications, the server repeats the procedure over the previous PUF responses in the database. If after this there were still no successful authentications, the server responds with a random value for T^2. Finally, the device checks the tag T^2 with its own produced tag in order to reveal whether the authentication succeeded. If the authentication succeeded, the device updates the old challenge X with the new challenge X^2.

4 Security Analysis

In this section, we describe the security analysis of the proposed protocol. We first present the security model and the formal security definitions before proving the security, and forward and backward privacy.

4.1 Security Model

The security model is composed of the communication model, the security experiment and the privacy experiment.

Communication Model. We take one trusted server $\mathcal{S}(\{\langle Y, Y^{old} \rangle\}_n)$ with n devices $\mathbf{Dev}_i(\mathbf{puf}_i(\cdot), X)$. Here, the set of n devices is denoted as $\Delta := \{\mathbf{Dev}_0, \mathbf{Dev}_1, \ldots, \mathbf{Dev}_{n-1}\}$. We denote the security parameter as k.

Following [2,15], devices will be enrolled in a trusted environment using a one-time interface, this happens in a setup phase using a setup algorithm $\mathbf{Setup}(1^k)$ which generates public parameter P and shared-secret Y. Here P denotes all the public parameters available to the environment and Y denotes the secret PUF response. During the authentication phase, the server $\mathcal{S}$ remains trusted, however, the devices Δ and the communication channel will be subjected to the actions of an attacker. At the end of the authentication phase, both the server and the device will output acceptance ($B_0 = 1$) or rejection ($B_0 = 0$) as result of the authentication.

We call the sequence of communication between the server and the device a session, which is distinguished by a session identifier I, the transcript of the authentication phase. Whenever the communication messages generated by the server and the device are honestly transferred until they authenticate each other, we call that a session has a matching session. The correctness of the proposed authentication protocol is that the server and the device always accept the session if the session has the matching session.

Security. Following [2,15], we consider the canonical security level for authentication protocols, namely the resilience to the man-in-the-middle attack. This means that power of an attacker is modeled by letting the attacker control all communication between server and devices. Supplementary to the security requirement of resilience to man-in-the-middle attacks, we permit the attacker to access the information stored in the non-volatile memory of the device in between sessions.

Experiment 1 illustrates the security evaluation on a theoretical level. In this experiment, $\mathbf{Exp}_{\Psi,\mathcal{A}}^{\mathbf{Sec}}(k)$ denotes the security experiment between the proposed protocol Ψ and an attacker $\mathcal{A}$ with security parameter k.

$\mathbf{Exp}_{\Psi,\mathcal{A}}^{\mathbf{Sec}}(k)$

$\langle P, Y \rangle \leftarrow \mathbf{Setup}(1^k)$
$\langle \mathbf{Dev}_i, I' \rangle \leftarrow \mathcal{A}^{\langle \mathbf{Launch},\mathbf{SendServer},\mathbf{SendDev},\mathbf{Result},\mathbf{Reveal}\rangle}(P, \mathcal{S}, \Delta)$
$B_0 := \mathbf{Result}(\mathbf{Dev}_i, I')$
Output B_0

Experiment 1. Security experiment.

After the setup phase, and thus after receiving $\langle P, \mathcal{S}, \Delta \rangle$, the attacker $\mathcal{A}$ can query the server $\mathcal{S}$ and the device $\mathbf{Dev}_i$ with the oracle queries $\mathcal{O} := \langle \mathbf{Launch}, \mathbf{SendServer}, \mathbf{SendDev}, \mathbf{Result}, \mathbf{Reveal} \rangle$, where

- **Launch**(1^k): launch the server $\mathcal{S}$ to start a new session with security parameter k;
- **SendServer**(M): send an arbitrary message M to the server $\mathcal{S}$;
- **SendDev**$(\mathbf{Dev}_i, M)$: send an arbitrary message M to device $\mathbf{Dev}_i \in \Delta$;
- **Result**(G, I): output whether the session I of G is accepted or not where $G \in \{\mathcal{S}, \Delta\}$;
- **Reveal**$(\mathbf{Dev}_i)$: output all the information stored in the non-volatile memory of $\mathbf{Dev}_i$.

The advantage of attacker $\mathcal{A}$ against Ψ is defined as:

$$\mathbf{Adv}_{\Psi,\mathcal{A}}^{\mathbf{Sec}}(k) := \mathbf{Pr}(\mathbf{Exp}_{\Psi,\mathcal{A}}^{\mathbf{Sec}}(k) \rightarrow 1 \mid \text{``I of G has no matching session''}) \quad (2)$$

We define security of an authentication protocol as follows:

Definition 1 (Security). *An authentication protocol Ψ holds the security against man-in-the-middle attacks with memory compromise if for any probabilistic polynomial time attacker $\mathcal{A}$, $\mathbf{Adv}_{\Psi,\mathcal{A}}^{\mathbf{Sec}}(k)$ is negligible in k (for large enough k).*

Privacy. Following [2,15], we define the privacy using indistinguishability between two devices. Here, an attacker selects two devices and tries to distinguish the communication, and thus the identification, between the two devices.

We use the privacy experiment between an attacker $\mathcal{A} := \langle \mathcal{A}_1, \mathcal{A}_2, \mathcal{A}_3 \rangle$ as illustrated in Experiment 2.

$$
\begin{array}{l}
\mathbf{Exp}_{\Psi,\mathcal{A}}^{\mathrm{IND}^*-b}(k) \\
\hline
\langle P, Y \rangle \leftarrow \mathbf{Setup}(1^k) \\
\langle \mathbf{Dev}_0^*, I^{0'}, \mathbf{Dev}_1^*, I^{1'} \rangle \leftarrow \mathcal{A}_1^{\mathcal{O}}(P, \mathcal{S}, \Delta) \\
b \leftarrow \{0, 1\} \\
\Delta' := \Delta \setminus \langle \mathbf{Dev}_0^*, \mathbf{Dev}_1^* \rangle \\
\psi_0 \leftarrow \mathbf{Execute}(\mathcal{S}, \mathbf{Dev}_0^*) \\
\psi_1 \leftarrow \mathbf{Execute}(\mathcal{S}, \mathbf{Dev}_1^*) \\
\langle I^{0''}, I^{1''} \rangle \leftarrow \mathcal{A}_2^{\mathcal{O}}(\mathcal{S}, \Delta', \mathcal{I}(\mathbf{Dev}_b^*), \psi_0, I^{0'}, \psi_1, I^{1'}) \\
\psi_0' \leftarrow \mathbf{Execute}(\mathcal{S}, \mathbf{Dev}_0^*) \\
\psi_1' \leftarrow \mathbf{Execute}(\mathcal{S}, \mathbf{Dev}_1^*) \\
B_0 \leftarrow \mathcal{A}_3^{\mathcal{O}}(\mathcal{S}, \Delta', \psi_0', I^{0''}, \psi_1', I^{1''}) \\
\mathrm{Output} \quad B_0
\end{array}
$$

Experiment 2. Privacy experiment in which it is allowed to communicate with two devices.

After the setup-phase, and similar to the security experiment, the attacker interacts with the server and two randomly chosen devices through the oracle queries $\mathcal{O}$. These two devices $\mathbf{Dev}_0^*, \mathbf{Dev}_1^*$ are being sent to the challenger who flips a coin to choose with which device the attacker will communicate anonymously. This anonymous communication is accomplished by adding a special identity $\mathcal{I}$ which honestly transfers the communication messages between $\mathcal{A}$ and $\mathbf{Dev}_b^*$.

It is trivial that the attacker can trace devices in case the **Reveal** query is issued when there are no successful authentications. Hence, we provide re-synchronization before and after the anonymous access by adding the **Execute** query. This query does a normal protocol execution between the server $\mathcal{S}$ and the device $\mathbf{Dev}_i^*$. During this execution, the attacker cannot modify the communication, however the transcript ψ_i is delivered to the attacker. Once an honest protocol execution is finished, no one can trace the device even if the information from the non-volatile memory before and after the session is continuously leaked to the attacker. The advantage of the attacker is defined as:

$$
\mathbf{Adv}_{\Psi,\mathcal{A}}^{\mathrm{IND}^*}(k) := |\mathbf{Pr}(\mathbf{Exp}_{\Psi,\mathcal{A}}^{\mathrm{IND}^*-0}(k) \to 1) - \mathbf{Pr}(\mathbf{Exp}_{\Psi,\mathcal{A}}^{\mathrm{IND}^*-1}(k) \to 1)| \quad (3)
$$

We define privacy of an authentication protocol as follows:

Definition 2 (Privacy). *An authentication protocol Ψ holds forward and backward privacy if for any probabilistic polynomial time attacker $\mathcal{A}$, $\mathbf{Adv}_{\Psi,\mathcal{A}}^{\mathrm{IND}^*}(k)$ is negligible in k (for large enough k).*

4.2   Formal Security Definitions

We define Physically Unclonable Functions, the Fuzzy Extractor and the AEAD-scheme.

Physical Unclonable Functions. We define PUFs using the definition described in [2, p. 24].

We denote the set of all possible challenges X which can be applied to an instance of $\mathcal{P}$ as $\mathcal{X}_\mathcal{P}$. We say that the PUF class $\mathcal{P}$ is a $\langle n, l, d, h, \epsilon \rangle$-secure PUF class $\mathcal{P}$ if the following conditions hold:

1. For any PUF instance $\mathbf{puf}_i(\,\cdot\,) \leftarrow \mathcal{P}$ and for any input $X \leftarrow \mathcal{X}_\mathcal{P}$,

$$\mathbf{Pr}(\mathbf{HW}(Y \leftarrow \mathbf{puf}_i(X), Y' \leftarrow \mathbf{puf}'_i(X)) < d) = 1 - \epsilon$$

2. For any two PUF instances $\mathbf{puf}_i(\,\cdot\,), \mathbf{puf}_j(\,\cdot\,) \leftarrow \mathcal{P}$, where $i \neq j$ and for any input $X \leftarrow \mathcal{X}_\mathcal{P}$,

$$\mathbf{Pr}(\mathbf{HW}(Y \leftarrow \mathbf{puf}_i(X), Y' \leftarrow \mathbf{puf}_j(X)) > d) = 1 - \epsilon$$

3. For any PUF instance $\mathbf{puf}_i(\,\cdot\,) \leftarrow \mathcal{P}$ and for any two inputs $X^a, X^b \leftarrow \mathcal{X}_\mathcal{P}$, where $a \neq b$,

$$\mathbf{Pr}(\mathbf{HW}(Y \leftarrow \mathbf{puf}_i(X^a), Y' \leftarrow \mathbf{puf}_i(X^b)) > d) = 1 - \epsilon$$

4. For any PUF instance $\mathbf{puf}_i(\,\cdot\,) \leftarrow \mathcal{P}$ and for any input $X^a \leftarrow \mathcal{X}_\mathcal{P}$,

$$\mathbf{Pr}(\tilde{\mathbf{H}}_\infty(Y \leftarrow \mathbf{puf}_i(X^a) \mid \{Y^j \leftarrow \mathbf{puf}_j(X^b)\}_{0 \leq j < n,\, 0 \leq b < l,\, i \neq j,\, a \neq b}) > h) = 1 - \epsilon$$

These conditions provide that the intra-distance $\mathcal{D}_\mathcal{P}^{\mathrm{intra}}$ is smaller than d, the inter-distance $\mathcal{D}_\mathcal{P}^{\mathrm{inter}}$ (from two metrics) is larger than d and the min-entropy of the PUF class $\mathcal{P}$ is always larger than h.

Definition 3 ($\langle n, l, d, h, \epsilon \rangle$-secure PUF class $\mathcal{P}$). *A PUF class $\mathcal{P}$ satisfies $\langle n, l, d, h, \epsilon \rangle$-secure PUF class $\mathcal{P}$ if all the above conditions hold.*

Fuzzy Extractor. We define a Fuzzy Extractor using the definition described in [2, p. 24].

A $\langle d, h, \epsilon \rangle$-FE consists of two algorithms: a key generation algorithm **Gen** and a reconstruction algorithm **Rec**. **Gen** takes as input variable Z and outputs key R and helper data H. For correctness, **Rec** recovers the key R from input variable Z' and helper data H if the **HD** between Z and Z' is at most d. The FE provides unpredictable outputs if the min-entropy of input Z is at least h. In that case, R is statistically ϵ-close to a uniformly random variable in $\{0, 1\}^k$, even if the helper data H is disclosed.

Definition 4 ($\langle d, h, \epsilon \rangle$-secure FE). *A FE satisfies $\langle d, h, \epsilon \rangle$-secure FE if the following conditions hold:*

1. $\mathbf{Pr}(R := \mathbf{Rec}(Z', H) \mid \langle R, H \rangle = \mathbf{Gen}(Z), \mathbf{HD}(Z, Z') \leq d) = 1$
2. *If $\tilde{\mathbf{H}}_\infty(Z) \geq h$, $\langle R, H \rangle = \mathbf{Gen}(Z)$ is statistically ϵ-close to $\langle R', H \rangle$ where $R' \leftarrow \{0, 1\}^k$ is chosen uniformly at random.*

AEAD-Scheme. The security of the AEAD-scheme Π is defined by the following experiment (chosen-plaintext attack) between a challenger and an attacker $\mathcal{A}$: First, the challenger randomly selects coin $b \leftarrow \{0,1\}$ and secret key $K \leftarrow \{0,1\}^k$. The challenger then prepares a truly random function **RF**. Following, the attacker $\mathcal{A}$ can adaptively issue an oracle query to the challenger to obtain a response of a function. If $b = 1$ and the attacker $\mathcal{A}$ sends message $M \leftarrow \{0,1\}^*$, challenge $N \leftarrow \{0,1\}^k$ and associated data $A \leftarrow \{0,1\}^*$, the challenger responds with $\langle C, T \rangle = \mathcal{E}_K^{N,A}(M)$. On the other hand, if $b = 0$, the challenger inputs the message $M \leftarrow \{0,1\}^*$, challenge $N \leftarrow \{0,1\}^k$ and associated data $A \leftarrow \{0,1\}^*$ to **RF** and responds with its result $\langle C', T' \rangle$. Finally, the attacker outputs a guess b'. If $b' = b$, the attacker wins the experiment. Similarly, this construction can be applied to test the security of the decryption algorithm $\mathcal{D}_K^{N,A}(\langle C, T \rangle)$.

The advantage of the attacker to win the experiment is defined by $\mathbf{Adv}_{\mathcal{A}}^{\Pi}(k) = |2 \cdot \mathbf{Pr}(b' = b) - 1|$.

Definition 5 (ϵ-secure AEAD-scheme). *An AEAD-scheme is an ϵ-secure AEAD-scheme if for any probabilistic polynomial time attacker $\mathcal{A}$, $\mathbf{Adv}_{\mathcal{A}}^{\Pi}(k) \leq \epsilon$.*

4.3 Security Proofs

In this section, we give the security proof and privacy proof for the proposed protocol. We follow the proof by game transformations as described in [2, 15].

Theorem 1 (Security). *Let PUF instance $\mathbf{puf}^* \leftarrow \mathcal{P}$ be a $\langle n, l, d, h, \epsilon_1 \rangle$-secure PUF, FE be a $\langle d, h, \epsilon_2 \rangle$-secure FE and the AEAD-scheme be an ϵ_3-secure AEAD-scheme. Then our protocol Ψ is secure against man-in-the-middle attacks with memory compromise. Especially, we have $\mathbf{Adv}_{\Psi,\mathcal{A}}^{\mathbf{Sec}}(k) \leq l \cdot n \cdot (\epsilon_1 + \epsilon_2 + \epsilon_3)$.*

Proof. The aim of the attacker $\mathcal{A}$ is to violate the security experiment which means that either the server or a device accepts a session without it being the matching session. We call S_i the advantage that the attacker wins the game in **Game** i. We consider the following game transformations:

Game 0: This is the original game between the challenger and the attacker.

Game 1: The challenger randomly guesses the device $\mathbf{Dev}^* \leftarrow \Delta$. If the attacker does not impersonate $\mathbf{Dev}^*$ to the server, the challenger aborts the game. Thus, the attacker needs to participate in session I^* and cannot tamper with the communication.

Game 2: Assume that l is the upper bound of the number of sessions that the attacker can establish in the game. For $0 \leq j < l$, we evaluate or change the variables related to the session between the server and $\mathbf{Dev}^*$ up to the l-th session as the following games:

Game 2-j-1: The challenger evaluates the output from the PUF instance $\mathbf{puf}^*$ implemented in $\mathbf{Dev}^*$ at the j-th session. If the intra-distance is larger than d, the inter-distance is smaller than d or the min-entropy of the output is smaller than h, the challenger aborts the game.

Game 2-j-2: The output from the FE H is changed to a random variable.

Game 2-j-3: The output from the encryption algorithm $\mathcal{E}_R^{N\|0,A}(Y)$ of the AEAD-scheme is derived from a truly random function **RF**.

Game 2-j-4: The output from the encryption algorithm $\mathcal{E}_R^{N\|1,A}(\ \cdot\ )$ of the AEAD-scheme is derived from a truly random function **RF**.

The strategy of the security proof is to change the communication messages corresponding to the target device **Dev*** to random variables. However, we must take care of the PUF construction and challenge-update mechanism in our protocol that updates the PUF response. Hence, we must proceed with the game transformation starting from the first invocation of device **Dev***. The communication messages gradually change from **Game** 2-j-1 to **Game** 2-j-4, and when these are finished, we can move to the next session. This strategy is recursively applied up to the upper bound of l of the sessions that the attacker can establish.

In short, if the implemented PUF instance creates enough entropy, the FE can provide variables that are statistically close to random strings. Then, this output can be applied as a key for the AEAD-scheme which both authenticate the device as well as encrypt the next PUF response. Finally, the server can be authenticated using the AEAD-scheme without encrypting a message.

Lemma 1 (Random Guess). $S_0 = n \cdot S_1$ (where n is the number of devices).

Subproof. The violation of security means that there is a session which the server or device accepts while the communication is modified by the attacker. Since we assume that the number of devices is at most n, the challenger can correctly guess the related session with a probability of at least $1/n$.   ◇

Lemma 2 (PUF Response). $|S_1 - S_{2\text{-}1\text{-}1}| \leq \epsilon_1$ and $|S_{2\text{-}(j-1)\text{-}4} - S_{2\text{-}j\text{-}1}| \leq \epsilon_1$ for any $1 \leq j < l$ if the PUF instance **puf*** is a $\langle n, l, d, h, \epsilon_1 \rangle$-secure PUF.

Subproof. We now assume that the PUF instance **puf*** satisfies a $\langle n, l, d, h, \epsilon_1 \rangle$-secure PUF in advance. This means that the intra-distance $\mathcal{D}_\mathcal{P}^{\text{intra}}$ is smaller than d, the inter-distance $\mathcal{D}_\mathcal{P}^{\text{inter}}$ is larger than d and the min-entropy of the PUF class $\mathcal{P}$ is always larger than h except the negligible probability ϵ_1. Since S_1 and $S_{2\text{-}(j-1)\text{-}4}$ assume these conditions except the negligible probability ϵ_1 and $S_{2\text{-}1\text{-}1}$ and $S_{2\text{-}j\text{-}1}$ require these conditions with probability 1, respectively, the gap between them is bounded by ϵ_1.   ◇

Lemma 3 (FE Output). $\forall\ 0 \leq j < l$, $|S_{2\text{-}j\text{-}1} - S_{2\text{-}j\text{-}2}| \leq \epsilon_2$ if the FE is a $\langle d, h, \epsilon_2 \rangle$-secure FE.

Subproof. From the subproof of Lemma 2, we can assume that the PUF instance **puf*** provides enough min-entropy h. Then the property of the $\langle d, h, \epsilon_2 \rangle$-secure FE guarantees that the output for the FE is statistically close to random and no attacker can distinguish the difference between the two games.   ◇

Lemma 4 (Authenticated Encryption). $\forall\ 0 \leq j < l$, $|S_{2\text{-}j\text{-}2} - S_{2\text{-}j\text{-}3}| \leq \mathbf{Adv}_{\mathcal{A}}^{\Pi}(k)$ for a probabilistic polynomial time algorithm $\mathcal{B}$.

Subproof. We construct the algorithm $\mathcal{B}$ which breaks the security of our AEAD-scheme Π. $\mathcal{B}$ can access the real encryption algorithm $\mathcal{E}_R^{N\|0,A}(Y)$, the real decryption algorithm $\mathcal{D}_R^{N\|0,A}(\langle C^1, T^1 \rangle)$ or the truly random function **RF**. $\mathcal{B}$ sets up all secret keys and simulates our protocol except the n-th session (the current session). When the attacker invokes the n-th session $\mathcal{B}$ sends the uniformly random distributed challenge $A \leftarrow \{0,1\}^k$ as the output of the server. When the attacker $\mathcal{A}$ sends the challenge A^* to a device $\mathbf{Dev}_i$, $\mathcal{B}$ randomly selects a nonce N and issues this to the oracle instead of the real computation of $\mathcal{E}_R^{N\|0,A}(Y)$. Upon receiving $\langle C, T \rangle$, $\mathcal{B}$ continues the computation as the protocol specification and outputs $\langle H, N, C^1, T^1 \rangle$ as the device's response. When the attacker sends $\langle H^*, N^*, C^{1^*}, T^{1^*} \rangle$, $\mathcal{B}$ issues challenge A and nonce N^* to the oracle and obtains either Y or the distinguished symbol INVALID.

If $\mathcal{B}$ accesses the real encryption and decryption algorithms $\langle \mathcal{E}, \mathcal{D} \rangle$, this simulation is equivalent to **Game** 2-j-2. Otherwise, the oracle query issued by $\mathcal{B}$ is completely random and this distribution is equivalent to **Game** 2-j-3. Thus we have $|S_{2\text{-}j\text{-}2} - S_{2\text{-}j\text{-}3}| \leq \mathbf{Adv}_{\mathcal{A}}^{\Pi}(k)$.   ◇

Lemma 5 (Authentication). $\forall\, 0 \leq j < l$, $|S_{2\text{-}j\text{-}3} - S_{2\text{-}j\text{-}4}| \leq 2 \cdot \mathbf{Adv}_{\mathcal{A}}^{\Pi}(k)$ *for a probabilistic polynomial time algorithm* $\mathcal{B}$.

Subproof. Consider an algorithm $\mathcal{B}$ which interacts with the encryption algorithm $\mathcal{E}_R^{N\|1,A}(\,\cdot\,)$ and truly random function **RF**. $\mathcal{B}$ runs the setup procedure and simulates the protocol up to the n-th session. Similarly to the subproof of Lemma 4 when the attacker invokes the n-th session $\mathcal{B}$ sends the uniformly random distributed challenge $A \leftarrow \{0,1\}^k$ as the output of the server. $\mathcal{B}$ continues the computation as the protocol specification and outputs $\langle H, N, C^1, T^1 \rangle$ as the device's response. If the attacker $\mathcal{A}$ has sent the challenge A^* to a device $\mathbf{Dev}_i$, $\mathcal{B}$ randomly selects nonce N and issues this to the oracle instead of the real computation $\mathcal{E}_R^{N\|1,A}(\,\cdot\,)$. When the attacker sends $\langle H^*, N^*, C^{1^*}, T^{1^*} \rangle$, $\mathcal{B}$ issues challenge A and nonce N^* to the oracle and obtains T^2.

If $\mathcal{B}$ accesses the real encryption algorithm $\mathcal{E}$, this simulation is equivalent to **Game** 2-j-3. Otherwise, the oracle query issued by $\mathcal{B}$ is completely random and this distribution is equivalent to **Game** 2-j-4. Thus we have $|S_{2\text{-}j\text{-}3} - S_{2\text{-}j\text{-}4}| \leq \mathbf{Adv}_{\mathcal{A}}^{\Pi}(k)$.   ◇

When we transform **Game** 0 to **Game** 2-l-4, there is no advantage of the attacker to violate the security. Given the fact that the attacker knows the PUF challenge X from the device's non-volatile memory, the attacker cannot produce a corresponding PUF response. This results in the fact that the attacker cannot produce a key R which matches any of the recovered keys from the server's database. This means that the cryptogram produced by an attacker will never be accepted by the decryption algorithm of the AEAD-scheme in the server. Additionally, changing the authenticator T^2 will only prevent the device from updating its PUF challenge, this is why the server also performs an exhaustive search over the old $(j - 1)$ PUF responses.

Therefore, no attacker can successfully mount the man-in-the-middle attack in our proposed protocol.   □

Theorem 2 (Privacy). *Let PUF instance* $\mathbf{puf}^* \leftarrow \mathcal{P}$ *be a* $\langle n, l, d, h, \epsilon_1 \rangle$*-secure PUF, FE be a* $\langle d, h, \epsilon_2 \rangle$*-secure FE and the AEAD-scheme be an* ϵ_3*-secure AEAD-scheme. Then our protocol* Ψ *holds forward and backward privacy.*

Proof This proof is similar to the proof of Theorem 1. However, we remark that it is important to assume that our protocol satisfies security first for privacy to hold. This is because if security does not hold, a malicious attacker might be able to desynchronize the PUF response Y of device $\mathbf{Dev}^*$ to a chosen one. In that case, even if the attacker honestly transfers the communication message between $\mathcal{I}(\mathbf{Dev}^*)$ and the server in the challenging phase the authentication result is always $B_0 = 0$ and the adversary can observe whether device $\mathbf{Dev}^*$ was selected as the challenge device.

Based on the same game transformation that was describes in the proof of Theorem 1, we continuously change the communication messages for the device $\mathbf{Dev}^*$, however, we now call this device $\mathbf{Dev}_1^*$. We do a similar game transformation for a second target device $\mathbf{Dev}_2^*$. In **Game** 1, the attacker can guess which device will be chosen by the challenger in the privacy game with probability of at least $1/n^2$. Upon continuing, the game transformation in **Game** 2 is applied to the sessions related to device $\mathbf{Dev}_1^*$ and device $\mathbf{Dev}_2^*$. Then, all the message transcripts of the **Game** transformations are changed to random variables and no biased information which identifies the challenger's coin is leaked. The information stored in the non-volatile memory of devices $\mathbf{Dev}_1^*$ and $\mathbf{Dev}_2^*$ will not disclose any information because these are updated from random sources.

Therefore, no attacker can distinguish any two devices with probability higher than $1/n^2$, hence, the proposed protocol satisfies the forward and backward privacy. □

5   Proof of Concept

In this section we present a proof of concept with security level $k = 128$ bits.

Figure 1 illustrates the system architecture of the device and server. The device is implemented on a Zedboard [1] which contains a Xilinx Zynq-7000 All Programmable System on Chip (SoC) XC7Z020-CLG484-1 [17]. The server is implemented on a Linux PC. We design the system architecture using Xilinx Vivado and Xilinx Vivado SDK.

The Zynq SoC is composed of 28 nm programmable logic and a processing system, which can both be programmed through the USB JTAG. Apart from other components, the processing system contains two ARM Cortex-A9 cores, of which only one is used to: (i) control the communication between the device and the server by reading and writing AXI-addresses from the device and sending and receiving serial data through the UART; (ii) update the PUF challenge on the device non-volatile memory by re-writing to a SD-card pugged into the Zedboard. The central communication travels through a bus, the Central Interconnect (CI), which is connected with the components on the Zedboard. Communication between the logic and the ARM-core is supported with a 32-bit AXI.

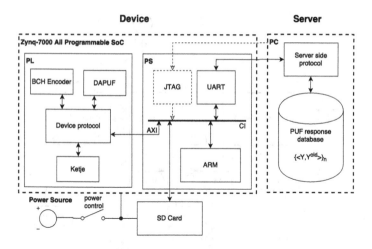

Fig. 1. System architecture of the device and server.

5.1   3-1 Double Arbiter PUF

The type of PUF used in the protocol will motivate most of the other design parameters for the rest of the protocol. For example, depending on the bit-error-probability p_e of a PUF response-bit, the inter- and intra-distances of the PUF responses, the entropy of the PUF responses ρ and the desired maximum for the failure rate of the authentications p_{fail}, both the number of PUF responses as well as the type and size of error-correcting codes is motivated.

Figure 2 illustrates the 3-1 Double Arbiter PUF (DAPUF, $\mathcal{P}_{3\text{-}1}$) as proposed by Machida et al. [12], which we implement because its characteristics are promising for the parameters of our protocol. As an example, the authors state the prediction rate is approximately 57%, which approximates a random guess (i.e. 50%). This is a considerable improvement for arbiter PUF constructions because the prediction rate of conventional arbiter PUFs is 86% [12, p. 8]. In the figure, a selector chain composes of 64 switch blocks that, depending on the input challenge bit, can switch signals from the two paths. The DAPUF is composed of three of these selector chains all acting on the same challenge X. Using an 'enable' signal E (E_L and E_R), the competition is started between the left signals E_L and the right signals E_R. For each of the combination of left- or right signals an arbiter is used to measure which path arrived first at the arbiter. After measuring these race conditions, the results are XORed to collect the 1-bit PUF response Y. By challenging the DAPUF with n different challenges, we obtain a n-bit PUF response.

In order to design a FE that produces a key with sufficient entropy, we analyze the performance parameters of the DAPUF. The authors have based the performance results on a Xilinx Virtex-7 device. Because the architecture of our SoC is similar to the Xilinx 7-series Field Programmable Gate Arrays (FPGAs), we take their performance as a starting point for our design. According to [12],

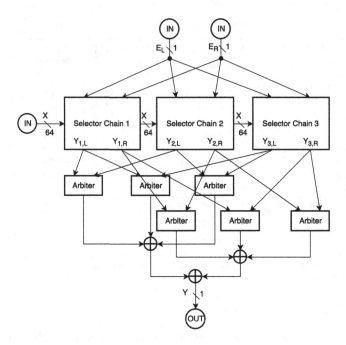

Fig. 2. 3-1 DAPUF as proposed by Machida et al. [12]. $\oplus$ denotes a bitwise XOR, (IN) denotes the input of the DAPUF and (OUT) denotes the output of the DAPUF.

the steadiness is approximately 12%, which means that the bit-error-probability p_e is 0.12 [12]. The average uniqueness of $\mathcal{P}_{3\text{-}1}$ is approximately 50%, which is close to ideal. Finally, the authors achieved a randomness of approximately 54%, meaning that the probability that a response bit is '1' is $\mathbf{Pr}(Y_i = 1) = 0.54$. Using Formula 1 we calculate the entropy of the PUF responses ρ:

$$\rho = -0.54\log_2(0.54) - 0.46\log_2(0.46) = 0.9954 \tag{4}$$

5.2   Reverse Fuzzy Extractor

In order to be able to recover the PUF responses, we use a concatenation of error-correcting codes as introduced by Bosch et al. [5], which is a technique to increase the correction rate while minimizing the computational overhead. Our proposed reverse FE uses a concatenation code of a repetition code and a BCH code. The aim is to construct a 128-bit key from the DAPUF responses with quality $\langle p_e = 0.12, \rho = 0.9954\rangle$. Also, we aim for a fail rate of $p_{\text{fail}} = 10^{-6}$, which is considered an acceptable fail rate for standard performance levels [13].

The probability that a received codeword of n bits has more than t errors is given by [5,8]:

$$\mathbf{Pr}(\text{"}>t\text{ errors"}) = 1 - \sum_{i=0}^{t}\binom{n}{i}p_e^i(1 - p_e)^{n-i}, \tag{5}$$

where p_e is the bit-error-probability. When using a $C_{REP}(5,1,2)$ repetition code, we can decrease the bit-error-probability $p_e = 0.12$ to $p_{e,REP} = 0.01432$ ($t = 2$, $n = 5$). Using a $C_{BCH}(255,139,15)$ BCH code on top of that further decreases the bit-error-probability $p_{e,REP} = 0.01432$ to a fail rate $p_{fail} = 1.176 \cdot 10^{-6}$ ($t = 15$, $n = 255$), which we consider sufficient. As a result, we use 1275 PUF responses on 64-bit PUF challenges, of which 40 bits are used for the challenge that is stored in the device non-volatile memory, 12 bits are used to obtain the 1275 unique PUF responses and 12 bits are used to produce random numbers, including a seed that is updated at the beginning of every authentication. In order to obtain these responses, we diffuse both sets of 12 challenge bits over the challenge space such that one set is updated every clock cycle using a linear-feedback shift register (LFSR) and the other is fixed to a constant value. As a consequence, every unique 40-bit (stored) challenge produces unique 64-bit PUF challenges, and thus produces unpredictable PUF responses. For the 1275 unique PUF responses we start the LFSR with a fixed value each authentication, whereas for the random number responses we start the LFSR with the updated (random) seed.

In order to analyze whether this construction leaves enough entropy in the key, we calculate the entropy losses in the communicated helper data. When using a $C_{REP}(5,1,2)$ repetition code on 5-bit words of the 1275-bit PUF response, 4 bits per word are disclosed as helper data. As a result, the entropy loss of using the repetition code is $\mathbf{H}_{REP\ loss} = 4 \cdot 255 = 1020$ bits. The entropy loss of the $C_{BCH}(255,139,15)$ BCH code is introduced by the random string that is needed to construct the code. As a result, the entropy loss of using this BCH code is $\mathbf{H}_{BCH\ loss} = n - k = 255 - 139 = 116$ bits. Hence, the total entropy loss of the 1275-bit PUF response by disclosing the helper data is $\mathbf{H}_{loss} = 1020 + 116 = 1136$ bits. This leaves $(1275 - 1136) \cdot \rho = 139 \cdot 0.9958 = 138$ bits of entropy left in the 255 bits of the BCH codeword.

These 255 bits will be compressed in a 128-bit key. This method is similar to the constructions in [10,14]. An advantage is that the AEAD-scheme can be used for this construction, minimizing the number of primitives that need to be implemented on the device.

5.3   AEAD-Scheme

In our implementation of the protocol we use the AEAD-scheme KETJE [4] with security level $k = 128$, one of the 56 candidates of the CAESAR competition [3]. We use the AEAD-scheme KETJE for the key construction in the reverse FE, the encryption and decryption of the second PUF response Y^2 and the computation of the authenticator T^2. KETJE relies on nonce uniqueness to be secure, which we have taken into account when designing the implementation.

6   Results

In this section we present the results of the proposed protocol. First, we analyze the PUF responses. Second, we present the hardware and software performance of the proof of concept. Following, we give the benchmark results. Finally, we present the comparison of this work to other, similar authentication protocols.

6.1 PUF Response Analysis

Although we assumed that all the PUF response bits are independent, we found out this is not the case. To illustrate this, take two challenges that have a low Hamming distance. The probability that the responses of both challenges differ is only small because the majority of the travelled paths will match in both measurements. A possible reason why this is not reflected in [12] is that the authors challenge the PUF instances with random challenges. Moreover, the machine learning algorithm is trained with only 1, 000 training samples, which means that the probability of having two challenges with low Hamming distance is small. This characteristic means that the 12 bits that are used to retrieve the PUF responses, and the 12 bits that are used to retrieve the random variables, need to be diffused throughout the challenge space such that the highest probability of having different data paths is achieved.

As an experiment we implemented three PUF instances using this construction. These three PUFs were implemented on the same SoC at different locations, which gives us a good approximation of the PUF response quality on distinct SoCs. The metrics are calculated similarly as [12]. However, these results have been achieved by challenging three PUF instances with 40-bit challenges multiple times, obtaining multiple 1275-bit responses. More specifically, steadiness is calculated by challenging the PUF a number of $m = 1275$ times with a set of $n = 128$ equal challenges, averaging the Hamming distances between two arbitrary responses. Uniqueness is calculated by challenging two PUF instances a number of $m = 1275$ times with a set of $n = 500$ randomly chosen challenges, averaging the Hamming distances of each pair. Finally, randomness is calculated by challenging a PUF instance a number of $m = 1275$ times with a set of $n = 500$ randomly chosen challenges, averaging the Hamming weight of the responses. We find an average steadiness of 5.64%, an average uniqueness of 45.19% and an average randomness of 66.41%.

From this experiment, we see that for the DAPUF in our SoC the measure for steadiness is lower (6% versus 12%), which means that the responses in our implementation have a higher reproducibility. However, the randomness of our implementation is higher (66% versus 54%), meaning that the probability of a response bit being '1' is higher. In order to find out whether the output from our FE still provides enough entropy, we recalculate ρ. Using Formula 1 we find $\rho = 0.9208$. Thus, $139 \cdot 0.9248 = 128$ bits of entropy is left to accumulate the 255-bit BCH codeword, which is just enough to construct the 128-bit key. As a result, our implementation can be considered secure and thus privacy-preserving. Next, we recalculate the fail rate using Formula 5. We find $p_{\text{fail}} = 8.438 \cdot 10^{-15}$, which is a considerable improvement.

6.2   Hardware Performance

The results have been generated by Vivado without the use of BRAM or DSPs and without optimization of the DAPUF design. Synthesis settings are set at `Default` and optimization settings at `Area`. Furthermore, we allow race conditions to occur due to the nature of the DAPUF.

Because of the long paths the signals have to travel through the DAPUF, the path delay is high. In the worst case scenario, the data path delay is 76.509 ns which means that the maximum frequency of the SoC is 12 MHz. The authentication phase of the device takes $8,205$ clock cycles, which on the frequency of 12 MHz takes 0.63 ms. As a result, our proof of concept might be applicable to devices in the IoT and in RFID systems.

In total, our proof of concept utilizes $8,305$ LUTs. The controller utilizes $5,464$ LUTs, KETJE $2,630$ LUTs, the DAPUF 195 LUTs and the BCH encoder 16 LUTs. Similar to the timing results, these utilization results are suboptimal. In this case the registers take a lot of area because of the long variables in the protocol.

6.3   Software Performance

The computation time of the server-side protocol increases linear in the number of devices in the database due to the exhaustive search. In our naive software implementation the execution time of the server-side protocol is approximately $0.05 \cdot n$ seconds. In a real world scenario, the server would be implemented in hardware which substantially decreases the execution time.

6.4   Benchmark Analysis

We analyze our protocol using the recently proposed benchmark for PUF-based authentication protocols [6]. Our device uses a PUF, TRNG, FE **Gen** procedure, cryptographic primitive (AEAD-scheme) and a one-time interface. Our PUF is a so-called strong PUF, indicating that the number of challenge-response pairs (CRPs) is at most 2^l, where l is the number of bits in the challenge. The amount of CRPs for n authentications is $n + 1$ because we use a one-time interface for the setup. The protocol supports server authenticity, device authenticity, device privacy, and memory disclosure. The protocol can support d-authentications for a perfect privacy use-case and ∞-authentications without device anonymity. Our PUF is noise-robust because of the error correction and modeling-robust because of the entropy accumulator in the FE. Mutual authentication provides both server and device authenticity. There is no internal synchronization which means that our implementation is not susceptible to DoS attacks. The execution time of the server per authentication is linear in the amount of devices.

6.5   Protocol Comparison

Table 1 summarizes the comparison between the proposed protocol and the protocols by Moriyama et al. [15] and Aysu et al. [2].

Table 1. Comparison with previous work.

Reference	Moriyama [15]	Aysu [2]	This work
Proofs for security and privacy	✓	✓	✓
Implemented parties	✗	device, server	device, server
Security flaws	✗	✓ᵃ	✗
Reconfiguration method	✗	modify SW, update microcode	follow generic approach, modify HW and SW
Demonstrator	✗	FPGA, PC	SoC, PC
Security-level	k	64-bit/128-bit	128-bit
Memory	PUF challenge & key	PUF challenge & key	PUF challenge
Device FE procedure	**Rec**	**Gen**	**Gen**
PUF type	✗	weak PUF	strong PUF
PUF instance	✗	SRAM	DAPUF
Hardware platform	✗	XC5VLX30	XC7Z020
Execution time (clock cycles)	✗	18,597	8,205
Logic cost (w/o PUF)	✗	1,221 LUTs	8,110 LUTs

ᵃ Due to a vulnerability in the implemented FE [2, p. 12].

The characteristic that all these protocols have in common is that they are all provably secure PUF-based privacy-preserving protocols. However, [15] only provides a theoretical basis for the proposed protocol, instead of also giving a proof of concept. As a result, no sensible answer can be given to the question whether the protocol is practical or not. On the other hand, [2] uses [15] as a basis, but is vulnerable to linear equation analysis of the FE output [2, p. 12]. As a consequence, this protocol does not provide a secure and privacy-preserving implementation. The performance results would highly likely be worsened because the FE needs to be redesigned. Correspondingly, most likely they need more PUF response bits to meet the failure rate requirements. Moreover, the implementation stores a key in non-volatile memory that does not increase the unpredictability of the communication messages. This overhead is eliminated in our protocol. Finally, with a different PUF (or a weak PUF) our results can be improved substantially, decreasing the execution time and logic cost.

7   Conclusion

In this paper we have proposed a new PUF-based privacy-preserving authentication protocol. In the process, we have presented proofs for security and privacy preservation, and an implementation serving as a proof of concept. We have seen that in comparison to other similar authentication protocols our protocol does not need a key stored in the non-volatile memory of the devices and is simpler in its design. Although our implementation is slower and consumes more resources in relation to [2], we claim to have an implementation that is both secure and privacy-preserving. On top of that, the performance results of [2] would highly likely be worsened because the FE needs to be redesigned because of the security flaw [2, p. 12].

Although we have presented a functional implementation, a faster and smaller proof of concept is possible. This is mainly due to the implemented PUF which defines the design of the FE and the variable sizes in the protocol. Moreover, the authentication time of the server is linear in the number of devices in the database, which could make the protocol impractical with a substantially large number of devices. A sound design of the server can settle this issue.

The design of our protocol might be optimized further, similar to what this research has achieved in relation to [2]. Mainly, future research has to be carried out towards strong PUF implementations, because these form the basis of our protocol. A strong PUF that has better quality of PUF responses can substantially reduce the consumption of the device. However, although our protocol is based on a strong PUF, a weak PUF can be used decreasing the maximum amount of authentications per device. Also, biometric data and a single PUF fingerprint can be used at the cost of device anonymity.

Acknowledgments. I would like to thank Lejla Batina, Joan Daemen, Gergely Alpár and Antonio de la Piedra of the Digital Security Group at the Radboud University for their guidance and support which lead to the publication of this work.

References

1. Avnet Inc.: ZedBoard (2016). http://zedboard.org/product/zedboard. Accessed 19 August 2016
2. Aysu, A., Gulcan, E., Moriyama, D., Schaumont, P., Yung, M.: End-to-end design of a puf-based privacy preserving authentication protocol. In: Güneysu, T., Handschuh, H. (eds.) CHES 2015. LNCS, vol. 9293, pp. 556–576. Springer, Heidelberg (2015). doi:10.1007/978-3-662-48324-4_28
3. Bernstein, D., et al.: CAESAR: Competition for Authenticated Encryption: Security, Applicability, and Robustness (2016). http://competitions.cr.yp.to/caesar.html
4. Bertoni, G., Daemen, J., Peeters, M., Van Asche, G., Van Keer, R.: CAESAR submission: Ketje v1. http://ketje.noekeon.org/Ketje-1.1.pdf
5. Bösch, C., Guajardo, J., Sadeghi, A.-R., Shokrollahi, J., Tuyls, P.: Efficient helper data key extractor on FPGAs. In: Oswald, E., Rohatgi, P. (eds.) CHES 2008. LNCS, vol. 5154, pp. 181–197. Springer, Heidelberg (2008). doi:10.1007/978-3-540-85053-3_12

6. Delvaux, J., Peeters, R., Gu, D., Verbauwhede, I.: A survey on lightweight entity authentication with strong pufs. ACM Comput. Surv. **48**(2), 26:1–26:42. http://doi.acm.org/10.1145/2818186

7. Dodis, Y., Reyzin, L., Smith, A.: Fuzzy extractors: how to generate strong keys from biometrics and other noisy data. In: Cachin, C., Camenisch, J.L. (eds.) EUROCRYPT 2004. LNCS, vol. 3027, pp. 523–540. Springer, Heidelberg (2004). doi:10.1007/978-3-540-24676-3_31

8. Guajardo, J., Kumar, S.S., Schrijen, G.J., Tuyls, P.: Physical unclonable functions and public-key crypto for FPGA IP protection. In: 2007 International Conference on Field Programmable Logic and Applications, pp. 189–195, August 2007

9. Herrewege, A., Katzenbeisser, S., Maes, R., Peeters, R., Sadeghi, A.-R., Verbauwhede, I., Wachsmann, C.: Reverse fuzzy extractors: enabling lightweight mutual authentication for PUF-enabled RFIDs. In: Keromytis, A.D. (ed.) FC 2012. LNCS, vol. 7397, pp. 374–389. Springer, Heidelberg (2012). doi:10.1007/978-3-642-32946-3_27

10. Kelsey, J., Schneier, B., Ferguson, N.: Yarrow-160: notes on the design and analysis of the yarrow cryptographic pseudorandom number generator. In: Heys, H., Adams, C. (eds.) SAC 1999. LNCS, vol. 1758, pp. 13–33. Springer, Heidelberg (2000). doi:10.1007/3-540-46513-8_2

11. Lee, M.Z., Dunn, A.M., Waters, B., Witchel, E., Katz, J.: Anon-pass: practical anonymous subscriptions. In: 2013 IEEE Symposium on Security and Privacy (SP), pp. 319–333, May 2013

12. Machida, T., Yamamoto, D., Iwamoto, M., Sakiyama, K.: A New Arbiter PUF for Enhancing Unpredictability on FPGA. Sci. World J. http://dx.doi.org/10.1155/2015/864812

13. Maes, R.: Physically unclonable functions: Constructions, properties and applications. Ph.D. thesis, Dissertation, University of KU Leuven (2012)

14. Maes, R., Herrewege, A., Verbauwhede, I.: PUFKY: a fully functional PUF-based cryptographic key generator. In: Prouff, E., Schaumont, P. (eds.) CHES 2012. LNCS, vol. 7428, pp. 302–319. Springer, Heidelberg (2012). doi:10.1007/978-3-642-33027-8_18

15. Moriyama, D., Matsuo, S., Yung, M.: PUF-Based RFID Authentication Secure and Private under Memory Leakage. Cryptology ePrint Archive, Report 2013/712 (2013). http://eprint.iacr.org/2013/712.pdf

16. Rogaway, P.: Authenticated-encryption with associated-data. In: Proceedings of the 9th ACM Conference on Computer and Communications Security, CCS 2002, NY, USA, pp. 98–107 (2002). http://doi.acm.org/10.1145/586110.586125

17. Xilinx Inc.: Zynq-7000 All Programmable SoC Overview, Product Specification DS190 (v1.9). http://www.xilinx.com/support/documentation/data_sheets/ds190-Zynq-7000-Overview.pdf. Accessed 19 August 2016

Author Index

Printed in the United States
By Bookmasters